THE CAMBRIDGE BIBLE COMMENTARY

NEW ENGLISH BIBLE

GENERAL EDITORS

P. R. ACKROYD, A. R. C. LEANEY, J. W. PACKER

JOB

THE BOOK OF JOB

COMMENTARY BY

NORMAN C. HABEL

Director of Religious Studies
Adelaide College of Advanced Education
South Australia

Former Professor of Old Testament
Studies in Concordia Theological
Seminary, St Louis, U.S.A.

CAMBRIDGE UNIVERSITY PRESS

Published by the Syndics of the Cambridge University Press
Bentley House, 200 Euston Road, London NW1 2DB
American Branch: 32 East 57th Street, New York, N.Y.10022

© Cambridge University Press 1975

Library of Congress Catalogue Card Number: 74 82588

ISBNS
0 521 20653 7 hard covers
0 521 09943 9 paperback

First published 1975

Printed in Great Britain
at the University Printing House, Cambridge
(Euan Phillips, University Printer)

GENERAL EDITORS' PREFACE

The aim of this series is to provide the text of the New English Bible closely linked to a commentary in which the results of modern scholarship are made available to the general reader. Teachers and young people have been especially kept in mind. The commentators have been asked to assume no specialized theological knowledge, and no knowledge of Greek and Hebrew. Bare references to other literature and multiple references to other parts of the Bible have been avoided. Actual quotations have been given as often as possible.

The completion of the New Testament part of the series in 1967 provides a basis upon which the production of the much larger Old Testament and Apocrypha series can be undertaken. The welcome accorded to the series has been an encouragement to the editors to follow the same general pattern, and an attempt has been made to take account of criticisms which have been offered. One necessary change is the inclusion of the translators' footnotes since in the Old Testament these are more extensive, and essential for the understanding of the text.

Within the severe limits imposed by the size and scope of the series, each commentator will attempt to set out the main findings of recent biblical scholarship and to describe the historical background to the text. The main theological issues will also be critically discussed.

Much attention has been given to the form of the volumes. The aim is to produce books each of which will be read consecutively from first to last page. The introductory material leads naturally into the text, which itself leads into the alternating sections of the commentary.

The series is accompanied by three volumes of a more general character. *Understanding the Old Testament* sets out to provide the larger historical and archaeological background, to say something about the life and thought of the people of the Old Testament, and to answer the question 'Why should we study the Old Testament?'. *The Making of the Old Testament* is concerned with the formation of the books of the Old Testament and Apocrypha in the context of the ancient near eastern world, and with the ways in which these books have come down to us in the life of the Jewish and Christian communities. *Old Testament Illustrations* contains maps, diagrams and photographs with an explanatory text. These three volumes are designed to provide material helpful to the understanding of the individual books and their commentaries, but they are also prepared so as to be of use quite independently.

P. R. A.
A. R. C. L.
J. W. P.

CONTENTS

THE FOOTNOTES TO THE
N.E.B. TEXT

The footnotes to the N.E.B. text are designed to help the reader either to understand particular points of detail – the meaning of a name, the presence of a play upon words – or to give information about the actual text. Where the Hebrew text appears to be erroneous, or there is doubt about its precise meaning, it may be necessary to turn to manuscripts which offer a different wording, or to ancient translations of the text which may suggest a better reading, or to offer a new explanation based upon conjecture. In such cases, the footnotes supply very briefly an indication of the evidence, and whether the solution proposed is one that is regarded as possible or as probable. Various abbreviations are used in the footnotes.

(1) Some abbreviations are simply of terms used in explaining a point: *ch(s).*, chapter(s); *cp.*, compare; *lit.*, literally; *mng.*, meaning; *MS(S).*, manuscript(s), i.e. Hebrew manuscript(s), unless otherwise stated; *om.*, omit(s); *or*, indicating an alternative interpretation; *poss.*, possible; *prob.*, probable; *rdg.*, reading; *Vs(s).*, Version(s).

(2) Other abbreviations indicate sources of information from which better interpretations or readings may be obtained.

Aq.   Aquila, a Greek translator of the Old Testament (perhaps about A.D. 130) characterized by great literalness.

Aram.   Aramaic – may refer to the text in this language (used in parts of Ezra and Daniel), or to the meaning of an Aramaic word. Aramaic belongs to the same language family as Hebrew, and is known from about 1000 B.C. over a wide area of the Middle East, including Palestine.

Heb.   Hebrew – may refer to the Hebrew text or may indicate the literal meaning of the Hebrew word.

Josephus   Flavius Josephus (A.D. 37/8–about 100), author of the *Jewish Antiquities*, a survey of the whole history of his people, directed partly at least to a non-Jewish audience, and of various other works, notably one on the *Jewish War* (that of A.D. 66–73) and a defence of Judaism (*Against Apion*).

Luc. Sept.   Lucian's recension of the Septuagint, an important edition made in Antioch in Syria about the end of the third century A.D.

Pesh.   Peshitta or Peshitto, the Syriac version of the Old Testament. Syriac is the name given chiefly to a form of Eastern Aramaic used by the Christian community. The translation varies in quality, and is at many points influenced by the Septuagint or the Targums.

Sam.   Samaritan Pentateuch – the form of the first five books of the Old Testament as used by the Samaritan community. It is written in Hebrew in a special form of the Old Hebrew script, and preserves an important form of the text, somewhat influenced by Samaritan ideas.

Scroll(s)   Scroll(s), commonly called the Dead Sea Scrolls, found at or near Qumran from 1947 onwards. These important manuscripts shed light on the state of the Hebrew text as it was developing in the last centuries B.C. and the first century A.D.

Sept.   Septuagint (meaning 'seventy'); often abbreviated as the Roman numeral (LXX), the name given to the main Greek version of the Old Testament. According to tradition, the Pentateuch was translated in Egypt in the third century B.C. by 70 (or 72) translators, six from each tribe, but the precise nature of its origin and development is not fully known. It was intended to provide Greek-speaking Jews with a convenient translation. Subsequently it came to be much revered by the Christian community.

Symm.   Symmachus, another Greek translator of the Old Testament (beginning of the third century A.D.), who tried to combine literalness with good style. Both Lucian and Jerome viewed his version with favour.

Targ.   Targum, a name given to various Aramaic versions of the Old Testament, produced over a long period and eventually standardized, for the use of Aramaic-speaking Jews.

Theod.   Theodotion, the author of a revision of the Septuagint (probably second century A.D.), very dependent on the Hebrew text.

Vulg.   Vulgate, the most important Latin version of the Old Testament, produced by Jerome about A.D. 400, and the text most used throughout the Middle Ages in western Christianity.

[. . .]   In the text itself square brackets are used to indicate probably late additions to the Hebrew text.

(Fuller discussion of a number of these points may be found in *The Making of the Old Testament* in this series.)

THE BOOK OF

JOB

✣ ✣ ✣ ✣ ✣ ✣ ✣ ✣ ✣ ✣ ✣ ✣ ✣

WHAT THE BOOK IS ABOUT

There are two different Jobs in this book, the patient Job and the angry Job. The patient Job is the hero of the opening story whose wisdom and greatness were known throughout the ancient world. This Job is a perfect wise man whose exemplary faith and life become the focus of special attention by the divine beings of the heavenly council. Satan, a member of that council, challenges the faith of Job. Thereupon God grants permission for Job to be tested by permitting every possible disaster to befall this paragon of piety. Despite the efforts of Satan, Job comes through the ordeal with flying colours, praising God from a loathsome ash heap. The Job of the poem which follows, however, has a very different character. It is as though the angry soul deep within Job comes to the surface and he reveals his true nature. But much more is involved. The poem of Job is the intense struggle of a great poet to probe the very meaning of life, especially life where suffering and injustice prevail for no apparent reason. The poet is searching for human integrity in the face of numerous traditional answers to life offered by the religion of his day. His comforters are the representatives of that religion. Ultimately, however, Job's conflict is with God himself. He is the real enemy; the comforters are but spokesmen in his defence. The only resolution of the case is for God to appear in person and face Job's accusations. When God does come in all his majesty, Job is silenced and the case is closed. Or is it? Is Job vindicated? Does he resolve the dilemma of life and discover a new meaning for existence? To those questions we shall return. In any case, the Job of the opening story, who re-appears at the end of the book, is restored to a greatness exceeding his former glory. (For further comments, cp. pp. 232–4 in the Message of Job.)

THE WISDOM BACKGROUND OF JOB

The book of Job belongs to a group of writings known as wisdom literature, of which Proverbs and Ecclesiastes are two notable examples within the Old Testament and Ecclesiasticus and the Wisdom of Solomon are classic illustrations from the Apocrypha. The concept of wisdom expressed in these books involves a distinctive outlook on life and a peculiar way of thinking. Wisdom thinking, the origins of which are lost in the distant past, is as much at home in Babylon and Egypt as it is in Palestine. The context of wisdom may be the local family, the tribal community, the city gate, the court, or international politics. From the time of Solomon the principles of wisdom were fostered and taught in the royal court at Jerusalem. Solomon, whose sagacity was acknowledged as a direct gift from Yahweh, the God of Israel (1 Kings 3: 1–14), was hailed as the father of wisdom theology in Israel.

The disciples of wisdom did not normally claim to receive direct revelations from God comparable to those of the prophets, or to find in the mighty acts of God in Israel's past the basic message for faith and life. Nor did they turn to the law of Moses as the all-sufficient reservoir for moral and ethical guidance. The student of Moses, for example, would consider adultery taboo because it violated a divine commandment of the decalogue. The wisdom student, however, viewed adultery as foolish; it was likely to ruin his life (Prov. 6: 32). Wisdom disciples were realists who attempted to understand the world as they found it and to make sense of what they found. The mind of man was for them a legitimate means of discerning truth, and the minds of other wise men, whether past or present, could be summoned to test the worth of new ideas.

2

Ancient wise men were the forerunners of modern scientists and philosophers in that they ascertained truth by observation and reflection. By watching the movements of nature and the conduct of man recurring patterns could be discovered. These observations were formulated as axioms, parables or proverbs which captured the essence of reality and provided suitable guidelines for living. The wise believed that if they assiduously practised the proven principles of wisdom they would enjoy a happy and prosperous life. Underlying these principles and the persistent search of the wise to discern them, was the assumption that the universe is governed by an eternal order or design. This design was God's blueprint for creating the world and stands as the basic reality for all existence. It is the task of the wisdom student to search out the governing principle of the universe, otherwise known as 'wisdom'. To walk in the 'way of wisdom' is to live in accordance with the over-arching plan and principles exhibited in the construction of the universe.

To a large extent the early wisdom thinking in Israel was humanistic and practical. In the course of time, however, efforts were made to co-ordinate the relatively secular thinking of wisdom with the religious attitudes of the ardent followers of Yahweh, the God of Israel. The marriage of the two movements is reflected in the maxim, 'The fear of the LORD is the beginning of wisdom' (cp. Job 28: 28; Prov. 9: 10). The implication is that all wisdom, despite the relentless probing of the wise, is incomplete and fruitless without a prior commitment to the teachings and faith of Yahwism, the traditional religion of Israel. A later development of wisdom theology within the context of Yahwism revolves around the figure of Wisdom as a divine reality emanating from God prior to creation and attending him as counsellor in the work of designing the universe (Prov. 8: 22–31). The reader is directed to the discussion of wisdom by other commentators in this series (E. G. Clarke, *The Wisdom of Solomon*, pp. 8–12 and R. N. Whybray, *Proverbs*, pp. 3–6, 50–2).

One point at which wisdom philosophy and the theology of Yahwism converge is in the doctrine of reward and retribution. According to Deuteronomy, those Israelite believers who obey the covenant laws are promised the blessing of Yahweh, while those who violate his covenant and rebel against Yahweh are threatened with a divine curse. In wisdom teaching the expectation was similar: all who walked in the way of wisdom could anticipate a reward of happiness and prosperity, while those who ignored the maxims of wisdom would bring about their own destruction. A real dilemma arose when the assumption was made that those who suffered misfortune were being cursed for specific deeds of wickedness, or when flagrant sinners prospered in the community without ever facing the judgement of God. These issues are some of the major concerns of the book of Job. True to good wisdom tradition, the poet of Job challenges these and similar accepted teachings of Israelite theology by testing them in the crucible of human experience.

The wise were haunted by questions of meaning and purpose, injustice and evil. Why did the righteous suffer? What was the point of human existence when human beings experienced inner torment and endless doubts about the justice of God? Was there no integrity for the man oppressed by God or his fellow man? How does the human being find his true self amid the dehumanizing forces of a supposedly ordered universe? With these questions the book of Job is deeply involved.

These difficult issues were not confined to the scrutiny of Israelite wisdom disciples. Wise men throughout the ancient Near East recognized that actual experience challenged any simple belief that the world was governed by clear principles of cosmic justice. One example of this concern is a work popularly known as 'The Babylonian Job', more correctly described by its opening words as 'I will praise the Lord of Wisdom'; the original of this probably stems from about the fifteenth century B.C. The hero of the book complains about

4

the apparently arbitrary will of the gods who desert him in his hour of torment. 'Where have mortals ever learned the way of a god?' he cries. His friends abuse him as an outcast cursed by the gods; all his past piety, righteousness and good works are of no avail. He suffers turmoil of mind and body as he wallows in his own excrement. Yet he is innocent of any major crime and in no way deserves his fate. After several dreams and a healing ritual he is restored to life by Marduk, the 'Lord of Wisdom'. The ultimate purpose of the work is the exaltation of Marduk for his deliverance of the diseased sufferer.

Another relevant Babylonian parallel is the dialogue known as the 'Babylonian Theodicy', sometimes called 'A dialogue about human misery', a text dating back to about the time of David (about 1000 B.C.). Just as in Job, the friends of the sufferer present the traditional orthodox answers concerning the reason for suffering, while the sufferer counters with the realities of life as he has experienced them. Themes such as the prosperity of the wicked, the misfortune of the righteous, the absence of divine intervention for the oppressed and the inscrutability of the gods, are developed in a variety of ways. Both parties assume that the gods are responsible for maintaining justice among men, but that they created mankind prone to injustice. In the last analysis the friends agree that 'the divine mind, like the centre of the universe, is remote'. Other Near Eastern parallels could be cited, but these two examples illustrate that many of the questions posed by Job are treated in comparable literature prior to the writing of Job. While these similarities are important, Job's ultimate resolution of the problem is different. But more of that later!

THE LITERARY CHARACTER OF JOB

The book of Job surpasses any of its known Babylonian or Egyptian forerunners in literary beauty and insight. In bold outline its structure can be sketched as follows: prologue (chs. 1–2); Job's opening soliloquy (ch. 3); dialogue discourses (chs. 4–27); poem on wisdom (ch. 28); Job's closing soliloquy (chs. 29–31); speeches of Elihu (chs. 32–7); answer of God and response of Job (38: 1 – 42: 6); epilogue (42: 7–17).

The prologue and epilogue comprise a simple narrative story about a heroic figure similar to the patriarchs of ancient Israel. This story is probably a non-Israelite folk legend whose historical roots are lost in antiquity. In the book of Job this legend has been modified to provide an effective background and foil for the poetic discourses of the book. Precisely how the poet reworked the original narrative is debated; some scholars argue that the three comforters were introduced into the story as a device of the poet to provide a suitable wisdom context for debating the issues posed by the innocent sufferer. Others maintain that the scenes where Satan appears before the heavenly council were created by the author of Job to highlight the irrationality of Job's fate. Regardless of how the original folk legend was expanded, it now provides a dramatic and ironic arena within which the protagonists of the poem meet in theological combat.

The two 'soliloquies' of Job which frame the dialogue discourses bear strong similarities to features of the so-called lament psalms (e.g. Pss. 22 and 88) and the confessions of Jeremiah (e.g. Jer. 20: 7–18). The 'opening soliloquy' is a fierce complaint to God in which Job invokes a curse on the day of his birth. Typical of such complaints is the emotional exclamation 'Why?' which is evoked in response to the injustice of the sufferer's situation. Job's 'closing soliloquy' is similar to the summing up of a case at court. Elements typical of the protestation of innocence found in lament psalms have been expanded here into a lengthy defence of Job's personal integrity. He begins with a survey of his past life, follows with a vivid portrayal of his current agony and concludes with a bold oath of innocence in which he disclaims any impropriety of conduct.

The bulk of the poem is composed of three cycles of

speeches in which Job alternates with each of his three comforters, Eliphaz, Bildad and Zophar. The predominant literary form of these 'dialogue discourses' is that of the disputation in which one speaker addresses his opponent with oratory and arguments designed to discredit his position. In so doing the speaker may cite a teaching or truism which is held in common by both parties. This common ground, whether it be in the form of a proverb, a credal statement, a portion of a hymn or some other known tradition, provides the basis for the speaker's argument. The disputant may introduce his speech with sarcastic comments belittling his opponent's contentions or his capacity to think clearly. He may conclude with a forceful appeal to his opponent to change his ways and accept the superior thinking of the speaker. Job's own speeches, however, tend to fluctuate between arguments addressed to the friends in the dispute and violent outbursts against God. For Job the dilemma of his suffering can never be resolved by any kind of logical argument, however persuasive it may be. Job is demanding a direct confrontation with God. The third cycle of speeches is incomplete as it now stands. Most of Job's speech in ch. 26 should be added to Bildad's truncated address in ch. 25. (See the comment at that point.) Zophar's final speech has been completely lost although many scholars find portions of it among Job's speeches (see the comment at 27: 8).

Two segments of the book, the 'wisdom poem' and the 'Elihu speeches', are held by most scholars to be later additions inconsistent with its basic structure and outlook. The 'wisdom poem' of ch. 28 is not a disputation speech dealing with arguments previously raised, but a self-contained literary unit describing the inaccessibility of cosmic wisdom, and the futility of attempting to fathom the inscrutable ways of God. The mood of resignation reflected in this poem stands in direct contrast to the tone of Job's bold demands addressed to God. The theme of the inscrutability of God's wisdom does appear in the discourses of the friends and it is possible that ch. 28 was originally intended as the culminating speech of Zophar, the last of the friends (see the comment at the beginning of ch. 28). The problem with the 'Elihu speeches' lies in the fact that the figure of Elihu appears on the scene unexpectedly. He is nowhere introduced in the opening prose story along with the other characters. His arguments appear as a kind of appendix to the dialogue discourses and tend to anticipate many of the arguments put forward in the Yahweh speeches which follow. In addition there are certain stylistic differences between this unit and the rest of the discourses. Other scholars are inclined to view the Elihu speeches as genuine, but the later work of the poet himself. In either case, these speeches now stand as a bridge between the discourses of the friends and the majestic answer of God. The Elihu speeches are also a series of disputations which expand many of the arguments of the friends but pay special attention to the theme of God the Creator.

The 'answer of God' from the whirlwind which concludes the poem takes the form of a long series of riddles about creation. Such riddles are typical of certain kinds of wisdom literature. It seems likely that these questions were based on earlier lists of natural phenomena prepared by wisdom teachers. By responding with additional questions, God answers Job in a cryptic and indirect way; yet God too enters the dispute. 'Job's response' to God's answer is a brief expression of his new humility before his Creator.

THE DATE OF THE BOOK

When was this literary masterpiece written down? What specific audience was the writer addressing with his portrait of the righteous man crushed by God? Was there an historical or communal crisis in Israel to which this writer wished to speak an appropriate message from the context of the wisdom tradition? These questions are difficult to answer. The opening narrative of Job is probably based on an ancient legend whose roots may reach back to the patriarchal era. In Ezek. 14: 14, 20

Job is mentioned along with Noah and Danel (or Daniel), two other legendary figures from antiquity. The details of the story of Job are not inconsistent with what is known of the patriarchal period, while texts like 'The Babylonian Job' (cp. p. 4) illustrate that stories of this kind were prevalent as early as the patriarchal era. The original legend, moreover, was probably non-Israelite. The events of the story, as such, are probably set among the Edomites, a people whose ancestors are traced back to Esau, the brother of Jacob. For these and other reasons, ancient Jewish tradition favoured Moses as the author of the book of Job. This old legend provides the literary context for the later poet to create his work. Many elements within the poem itself, such as the retention of archaic divine names, illustrate that the poet was conscious of preserving the atmosphere of the patriarchal era throughout his work. It may be noted that the name Yahweh (rendered LORD in the N.E.B.) is used in prologue and epilogue, and in the headings of the final speeches of God and Job (chs. 38–42), but not in the remainder of the book except in 12: 9, probably as the result of a scribal alteration.

When was the poem of Job written? It is natural enough to think of the period of Israel's humiliation in exile as the time of writing. According to this view Job becomes a type of Israel. The questions of divine justice posed by Israel during her suffering are formulated and thrashed out vicariously in the person of Job. The difficulty with this hypothesis is that elsewhere in the Old Testament the exile of Israel is considered a well-deserved act of divine judgement upon her apostasy. Job is innocent; Israel is guilty. The second weakness of this theory is that an Edomite hero is employed to represent Israel. At the time of Israel's collapse the Edomites were rather unkind neighbours who helped to contribute to her downfall in 586 B.C. If we propose a date after the exile we are obliged to evaluate the relationship between Job and the teaching of Second Isaiah (the exilic prophet of Isa. 40–55 who was active about the middle of the sixth century B.C.). Here, particularly in Isa. 52: 13 – 53: 12, the suffering of one individual, who may represent a body of faithful prophets or a righteous remnant within Israel, is accepted by God as a vicarious atonement for the sins of Israel. Many scholars maintain, however, that the suffering servant poem of Isaiah is dependent on Job rather than *vice versa*. If we pose a date before the exile, we are forced to consider the probable literary connection between Job and the 'confessions of Jeremiah' (compare Job 3 and Jer. 20: 7–18). Here again, the priority of Job is as likely as the priority of Jeremiah. Similarities can also be discerned between certain expressions and forms in the Psalms and the rhetoric of Job, but nothing conclusive can be ascertained with regard to date. Dates as early as the eighth century B.C. and as late as the third century B.C. have been argued with great cogency.

The problem with many attempts to date Job is the tacit assumption that, as with prophetic books like Amos or Jeremiah, the author is addressing the Israelite community as it faces a public crisis or need. The viewpoint of the wisdom writer seems to be very different. He does not normally speak to a specific historical crisis, but rather to those recurring dilemmas and situations in life that plague all human beings. If his insights are true, they will be as welcome in Egypt as they are in Israel. Job, therefore, does not represent Israel as such, but any man or community who suffers without apparent reason and who searches for meaning and integrity in the face of the meaningless. Thus, while a date after 600 B.C. appears most probable because of the connections with Jeremiah, the specific historical situation in Israel is relatively secondary for interpreting the book. Obviously Job is using texts from Israel's worship life and is well acquainted with her wisdom traditions. Accordingly any date prior to the seventh century B.C. seems unlikely.

THE TEXT OF JOB

The Hebrew text of Job is probably more corrupt than that of any other biblical book. The N.E.B. footnotes to Job reflect but a small sample of the many textual difficulties and uncertainties with which the translator and interpreter of Job must wrestle if he begins with the Hebrew original. Recourse to early translations in Greek, Latin or Syriac often only compound the difficulties. The Septuagint (see the opening explanation of the N.E.B. footnotes), for example, is much shorter than the Hebrew original. In some cases the probable readings adopted are educated guesses based on principles of textual transmission while others are deduced from parallel readings or terminology found in related Semitic languages such as Canaanite, Aramaic or Accadian. Only some of the conjectured readings adopted by the N.E.B. translators have been included in the footnotes. Here as elsewhere differences of opinion sometimes exist between the translators and the commentator. Where these were significant the evidence for an alternative rendering has also been given. Space does not permit more than a selection of such cases for comment.

✻   ✻   ✻   ✻   ✻   ✻   ✻   ✻   ✻   ✻   ✻   ✻

Prologue

✻ The Prologue of Job is an old folk legend composed of four major scenes alternating between heaven and earth. The stage is set for these scenes by a preface which introduces the chief character and his life-style (1: 1–5). Job is presented as the greatest wise man of the ancient world and his deep piety is exemplified by his activities during the annual festivities in his community.

The opening scene is set in the court of heaven and consists primarily of a dialogue between the LORD and Satan (1:6–12). At the centre of their dispute is the figure of Job and the reason for his extraordinary goodness. The plot of the story is set in motion when Satan challenges the sincerity of Job's righteousness. God picks up the challenge and permits Job to be subjected to a series of curses that will strip him of all his possessions but leave his person whole. Job, meanwhile, is ignorant of the heavenly wager that is destined to turn his world upside down.

The second scene is divided into five short episodes on earth (1: 13–22). Without warning or provocation, Job is hit by a series of simultaneous catastrophes. Four escapers from four separate disasters overlap in reporting their tragic news and each closes with the haunting refrain, 'I am the only one to escape and tell the tale.' Two of these catastrophes are the work of foreign bandits and two are acts of God. In the process all Job's agricultural, pastoral and commercial interests are erased and his family killed. The closing episode depicts Job mourning his loss but piously blessing the name of the LORD. Job's faith rather than his patience is foremost in this scene.

The third scene is again located in the heavenly court where the dialogue between God and Satan is similar to that of the first scene (2: 1–6). God is proud of Job's integrity but Satan refuses to capitulate. He calls for even sterner measures to test Job's faith. Again permission is granted for Satan to smite Job, this time with bodily afflictions. The final scene portrays Job seated among the ashes suffering extreme physical anguish (2: 7–10). His wife picks up the suggestion of Satan to 'Curse God and die'. But Job's devotion remains undaunted; he accepts all the evils he has experienced as gifts of God. Job remains blameless to the bitter end.

The original conclusion of the story was probably some form of the Epilogue (found in 42: 7–17). However, an appendix has been added at this point to provide a bridge between the ancient legend and the poetic discourses of Job and his friends (2: 11–13). Three friends come to comfort Job in his plight, but his condition is so appalling that they do not even recognize him at first. For seven days they sit at his side in silence; once he breaks the silence the discourses can begin. ✶

THE LEGEND OF JOB

THERE LIVED in the land of Uz a man of blameless and **1**
upright life named Job, who feared God and set his
face against wrongdoing. He had seven sons and three ²
daughters; and he owned seven thousand sheep and three ³
thousand camels, five hundred yoke of oxen and five
hundred asses, with a large number of slaves. Thus Job
was the greatest man in all the East.

Now his sons used to foregather and give, each in turn, ⁴
a feast in his own house; and they used to send and invite
their three sisters to eat and drink with them. Then, when ⁵
a round of feasts was finished, Job sent for his children
and sanctified them, rising early in the morning and
sacrificing a whole-offering for each of them; for he
thought that they might somehow have sinned against
God and committed blasphemy in their hearts. This he
always did.

The day came when the members of the court of ⁶
heaven*a* took their places in the presence of the LORD,
and Satan*b* was there among them. The LORD asked him ⁷
where he had been. 'Ranging over the earth', he said,
'from end to end.' Then the LORD asked Satan, 'Have ⁸
you considered my servant Job? You will find no one
like him on earth, a man of blameless and upright life,
who fears God and sets his face against wrongdoing.'
Satan answered the LORD, 'Has not Job good reason to ⁹
be God-fearing? Have you not hedged him round on ¹⁰
every side with your protection, him and his family and
all his possessions? Whatever he does you have blessed,

[*a*] members of the court of heaven: *lit.* sons of God.
[*b*] *Or* the adversary.

11 and his herds have increased beyond measure. But stretch
out your hand and touch all that he has, and then he will
12 curse you to your face.' Then the LORD said to Satan, 'So
be it. All that he has is in your hands; only Job himself you
must not touch.' And Satan left the LORD's presence.

13   When the day came that Job's sons and daughters were
14 eating and drinking in the eldest brother's house, a messenger came running to Job and said, 'The oxen were
15 ploughing and the asses were grazing near them, when
the Sabaeans swooped down and carried them off, after
putting the herdsmen to the sword; and I am the only
16 one to escape and tell the tale.' While he was still speaking, another messenger arrived and said, 'God's fire
flashed from heaven. It struck the sheep and the shepherds
and burnt them up; and I am the only one to escape and
17 tell the tale.' While he was still speaking, another arrived
and said, 'The Chaldaeans, three bands of them, have
made a raid on the camels and carried them off, after
putting the drivers to the sword; and I am the only one
18 to escape and tell the tale.' While this man was speaking,
yet another arrived and said, 'Your sons and daughters
were eating and drinking in the eldest brother's house,
19 when suddenly a whirlwind swept across from the desert
and struck the four corners of the house, and it fell on the
young people and killed them; and I am the only one to
20 escape and tell the tale.' At this Job stood up and rent his
cloak; then he shaved his head and fell prostrate on the
21 ground, saying:

> Naked I came from the womb,[a]
> naked I shall return whence I came.

[a] *Lit.* my mother's womb (*cp. Eccles. 5: 15*).

The LORD gives and the LORD takes away;
blessed be the name of the LORD.

Throughout all this Job did not sin; he did not charge 22
God with unreason.

Once again the day came when the members of the 2
court of heaven took their places in the presence of the
LORD, and Satan was there among them. The LORD asked 2
him where he had been. 'Ranging over the earth', he
said, 'from end to end.' Then the LORD asked Satan, 'Have 3
you considered my servant Job? You will find no one
like him on earth, a man of blameless and upright life,
who fears God and sets his face against wrongdoing. You
incited me to ruin him without a cause, but his integrity
is still unshaken.' Satan answered the LORD, 'Skin for 4
skin! There is nothing the man will grudge to save himself. But stretch out your hand and touch his bone and 5
his flesh, and see if he will not curse you to your face.'

Then the LORD said to Satan, 'So be it. He is in your 6
hands; but spare his life.' And Satan left the LORD's 7
presence, and he smote Job with running sores from head
to foot, so that he took a piece of a broken pot to scratch 8
himself as he sat among the ashes. Then his wife said to 9
him, 'Are you still unshaken in your integrity? Curse
God and die!' But he answered, 'You talk as any wicked 10
fool of a woman might talk. If we accept good from God,
shall we not accept evil?' Throughout all this, Job did not
utter one sinful word.

When Job's three friends, Eliphaz of Teman, Bildad of 11
Shuah, and Zophar of Naamah, heard of all these calamities which had overtaken him, they left their homes and

arranged to come and condole with him and comfort
12 him. But when they first saw him from a distance, they
did not recognize him; and they wept aloud, rent their
13 cloaks and tossed dust into the air over their heads. For
seven days and seven nights they sat beside him on the
ground, and none of them said a word to him; for they
saw that his suffering was very great.

* 1: 1. *There lived* can be rendered 'once upon a time' thereby
indicating one mark of the legendary character of this Prologue. The location of the land of Uz seems to be somewhere
in the regions of Edom or Aram (cp. Gen. 10: 23; 36: 28). The
name *Job*, the meaning of which is disputed, was relatively
common in the second millennium B.C. The activities and
life-style of Job belong to the era of the patriarchs in the same
millennium. The hero of the legend is a figure from antiquity
to be ranked with 'blameless' Noah and righteous Danel, a
legendary wise king of ancient Canaan (Ezek. 14: 14; 28: 3).

blameless translates the Hebrew *tām*, a complete person who
exhibits integrity and piety in all aspects of life (cp. 9: 20–2).
An *upright* person is honest and righteous in all his dealings
(Prov. 21: 8; 14: 9). The individual who fears God has the
inner strength to shun wrongdoing (Prov. 3: 7). In Wisdom
literature 'the fear of the LORD' refers to the unique devotion
of those who follow the way of wisdom for their success
(Prov. 1: 7; 2: 5–8). As the perfect, upright hero who fears
God and avoids evil, Job is introduced as the perfect wise man.
He is an idealized figure from the past around whom the
legend revolves and who provides a perfect foil for the more
realistic, angry Job of the discourses. Within this framework
the stage is set for the listener to struggle with the irony of life
as exemplified in the conflict between the two Job figures, the
Job of the legend and the Job of real life.

2–3. Job's family and possessions are also given in terms of
the ideal. *Seven* and *three* are symbols of perfection. Each pair

16

of numbers adds up to a multiple of ten, the symbol of totality. Job possesses the wealth of a patriarchal chieftain involved in trade, agriculture and pastoral pursuits (cp. Gen. 12: 16; 26: 12–14). As *the greatest man in all the East* Job equals or exceeds Solomon in wisdom and riches (1 Kings 3: 12–13).

4–5. The *feast* is probably an annual seven-day harvest festival at the end of the year (cp. Exod. 23: 14–17). On the eighth day Job offers a sacrifice to sanctify his household, not because of flagrant sins, but because of possible curses that *might somehow* have been expressed in the heart. As the perfect priest Job goes beyond the requirements of any Israelite law.

6. *The day* of the heavenly council meeting was probably simultaneous with the annual festival in Job's household. Job's pious sacrifices, like those of Noah, had apparently attracted the attention of heaven (cp. Gen. 8: 20–1). The *members of the court of heaven* are lesser heavenly beings known as 'sons of the gods' (Gen. 6: 2), 'holy ones' (Job 5: 1), 'sons of the Most High' (Ps. 82:6), and similar designations (cp. Ps. 89: 6–8). They appear as servants and attendants of El in Canaanite mythology and of Yahweh in the Old Testament. Yahweh, the ancient name of the God of Israel (see the N.E.B. footnote on Exod. 3: 15), is regularly translated 'the LORD' in the Prologue and Epilogue of Job. Alternate names for God appear in the poetic sections of Job.

6b–7. *Satan* is not a proper name but a title meaning 'the adversary'. Here Satan is not equivalent to the devil of later Christian theology, but functions like a prosecuting attorney in a court of law (cp. Zech. 3: 1–2). He also seems to be engaged in espionage activities, ranging the entire earth to check on the lives of men (cp. Zech. 1: 10–11).

8. The LORD honours Job by calling him *my servant* (cp. 2 Sam. 7: 5), but he opens himself to Satan's cynicism by raising Job's case as unique. His record is clean and the LORD is happy to boast about his prize servant before the court. Job, like Adam before him, is the one perfect man in all the earth.

9–11. Satan takes immediate advantage of the LORD's boasting by challenging the sincerity and depth of Job's faith. Job is a devout man, suggests the adversary, because he has been surrounded by the blessings of God. Job's good conduct has been motivated by self-interest not deep conviction. A true test of faith would reveal whether Job could fear God without expecting any rewards and for no other reason than that God is God. This theme is probed repeatedly in the poem of Job. The first test Satan proposes is the removal of all Job's possessions.

12. The LORD, convinced of Job's sincerity, accepts the challenge on Job's behalf. Job, however, remains ignorant of the reasons for his misfortunes.

13-15. In a single day Job goes from riches to rags. Each calamity has but one survivor with the same sad tale to tell (cp. 1 Kings 18: 22). The Sabaean marauders, whose identity remains uncertain, wipe out Job's agricultural activities.

16. Celestial fire terminates Job's pastoral pursuits. *God's fire* may refer to lightning (as in 1 Kings 18: 38), or to a supernatural fire typical of ancient legends (cp. Gen. 19: 24; Num. 16: 35). Ironically it is Satan who uses God's fire to curse God's servant. The fugitive, however, interprets the calamity as an act of God, not of Satan.

17. *The Chaldaeans* here seem to be semi-nomadic bandits who attack Job's camel caravan while on a trading mission. In the Old Testament the term is most often used for the Babylonians, the conquerors of Judah in the sixth century B.C.

18-19. The *whirlwind* that annihilates Job's family is, like God's fire, a special intervention of God. This destructive wind is the counterpart to the 'tempest' (of 38: 1) from which God later announces his creative power.

20-2. Job mourns according to the customs of his day (cp. Gen. 37: 34). He confesses that he emerged *naked* from mother earth and will return to her in the same condition. Like the Psalmists he blesses the name of Yahweh recognizing his right to give or take blessings at his discretion. Job's faith remains unshaken and his integrity unsullied. God has won the first round.

2: 1–3. The third scene opens with God making a pointed comment about Job's unshaken integrity. Even more pointed is the remark that Satan *incited* God to act in such a way that Job was ruined *without a cause* (cp. 1 Chron. 21: 1). The question is thereby raised as to whether the LORD was goaded into compromising his justice to win a wager. On earth Job ignorantly accepts his fate.

4–6. Satan refuses to admit defeat; he knows the weakness of human beings and demands a final test. *Skin for skin* seems to be a terse proverbial saying which is explained by the words that follow. Human beings will do anything to save their lives if they are tortured with enough diseases. In spite of his previous comment about Job's ruin being 'without a cause' (in verse 3), the LORD agrees to the new test.

7–8. The *running sores* with which Satan afflicts Job are probably a repulsive skin disease similar to one of plagues experienced by the Egyptians (Exod. 9: 8–10). His new home among the ashes of the local dump suggests that he was excluded from his community like a leper.

9–10. Job's wife is a realist; she echoes the suggestion of Satan to '*Curse God and die!*'. Cursing God would force him to show his hand and put Job out of his misery. Job's response is one of absolute trust; he fears God without 'good reason'. He accepts the evil he has endured as a valid expression of God's sovereign will. The LORD wins the wager and Satan is discredited.

11–13. This appendix to the legend introduces the disputants in the poetic discourses. The three friends are professional wise men from areas generally associated with Edom (cp. Jer. 49: 7; Gen. 25: 2). They come as friends ready to *comfort* Job, or, as the original implies, to sympathize with him in his suffering (see the note on 6: 14). Their seven days of mourning are true expressions of silent sympathy, but as soon as they speak, their human compassion is replaced by professional pride. *

Job's complaint to God

✶ Job's opening soliloquy is a violent lament over his own life (cp. Pss. 69; 88). Gone is the patient Job of the Prologue. 'Why?' cries the angry Job of the poet. His 'Why?' is not a question for information but the explosion of a frustrated human being. Job sees no reason to be born if life is devoid of all meaning, especially if it is God himself who has blocked all vision of hope (3 : 20–3). Job's life is one of sheer torture at the hands of God (verses 24–6). In the face of such futility Job curses his origins and longs to erase the night of his conception from the calendar of heaven (verses 3–6). He summons those familiar with the forces of chaos to destroy the night of his own creation (verses 7–10). For Job birth is a disaster, unless it is a still-birth or an abortion. Life is worthless when death is the only place of true rest and equity for all (verses 11–19). Job does not actually curse God as his wife had advocated (2: 9), but he comes close to it. Nor does he commit suicide, although he is tempted to do so. He does, however, force God to face the ugly reality of human torment with the hope that God might be moved to compassion. But no compassion is forthcoming, either from God or from Job's friends. Job suffers alone. ✶

WHY BE BORN?

3 1–2 After this Job broke silence and cursed the day of his birth :

3   Perish the day when I was born
      and the night which said, 'A man is conceived'!

4   May that day turn to darkness; may God above not look for it,
      nor light of dawn shine on it.

5   May blackness sully it, and murk and gloom,
      cloud smother that day, swift darkness eclipse its sun.

Blind darkness swallow up that night;   6
count it not among the days of the year,
reckon it not in the cycle of the months.
That night, may it be barren for ever,   7
no cry of joy be heard in it.
Cursed be it by those whose magic binds even the   8
   monster of the deep,
who are ready to tame Leviathan himself with spells.
May no star shine out in its twilight;   9
may it wait for a dawn that never comes,
nor ever see the eyelids of the morning,
because it did not shut the doors of the womb that   10
   bore me
and keep trouble away from my sight.
Why was I not still-born,   11
why did I not die when I came out of the womb?
Why was I ever laid on my mother's knees   12
or put to suck at her breasts?
Why was I not hidden like an untimely birth,   16
like an infant that has not lived to see the light?
For then I should be lying in the quiet grave,   13
asleep in death, at rest,
with kings and their ministers   14
who built themselves palaces,
with princes rich in gold   15
who filled their houses with silver.
There the wicked man chafes no more,   17^a
there the tired labourer rests;
the captive too finds peace there   18
and hears no taskmaster's voice;

[*a*] *Verse 16 transposed to follow verse 12.*

2   21   H J O

19 high and low are there,
    even the slave, free from his master.

20 Why should the sufferer be born to see the light?
    Why is life given to men who find it so bitter?

21 They wait for death but it does not come,
    they seek it more eagerly than*a* hidden treasure.

22 They are glad when they reach the tomb,
    and when they come to the grave they exult.

23 Why should a man be born to wander blindly,
    hedged in by God on every side?

24 My sighing is all my food,
    and groans pour from me in a torrent.

25 Every terror that haunted me has caught up with me,
    and all that I feared has come upon me.

26 There is no peace of mind nor quiet for me;
    I chafe in torment and have no rest.

✻ 1. *After this* refers to the seven days of sympathetic silence
in 2:13.

   3. Job damns both his birthday and the night of his conception, not because they are evil in themselves, but because
they became the vehicles for his entry into a life of bitterness.
Jeremiah expressed a similar curse during his persecutions
(Jer. 20: 14–18).

   4–5. Light symbolizes the beginnings of creation and life
when God first said, 'Let there be light' (Gen. 1: 3). Job longs
to reverse his own creation by returning to the darkness of
primeval chaos (Gen. 1: 2). Darkness symbolizes death, chaos
and the underworld. Reflecting this the opening words of
verse 4 can be translated, 'That day – let there be darkness!'

   6–7. Job calls for the night of his conception to be annihilated by darkness and erased from the calendar.

[*a*] *Or* seek it among. . .

8. *monster of the deep* renders the reading 'sea'. Prince Sea and Leviathan are chaos monsters from Canaanite mythology who were defeated by Baal in a great cosmic battle (see the comment on 41:1). These forces were thought to threaten the existing creation periodically and therefore had to be kept under control. Yahweh is also said to have conquered Leviathan in primeval times (Ps. 74:13–14; Isa. 27:1). Job calls upon incantation experts who have the power to curse, or awaken the forces of chaos to use their skill in cursing the night of his conception.

10. Job's reason for invoking the preceding curses is that he was born into a world of *trouble*; this renders the Hebrew *'āmāl*, a term which implies severe hardship and oppression. It is used a number of times in the book; elsewhere for Israel's sufferings in Egypt (Deut. 26:7) and the affliction of the Servant (Isa. 53:11).

11–12, 16. Verse 16 is relocated at this point because of the common theme of death at birth. When birth is a calamity, abortion is preferable. To be nursed and fondled as a child is to be deluded into believing that there is a reason for living. The *Why* of Job's cry is typical of lament Psalms (e.g. 22:1). It is an exclamation of agony in the face of insurmountable difficulties and uncertainties.

13–19. If Job had died at birth he would now be enjoying complete rest in the underworld where the rich and poor of the earth are one.

17–19. This passage provides a portrait of those liberated by death. Job, it seems, identifies himself with the *labourer*, the *captive* and the *slave*. He views life as slavery (see at 7:1), and God as the *taskmaster*. The term *taskmaster* is used for the Egyptian overseers who oppressed the Israelites in slavery (Exod. 5:6). To die is to be liberated from the bondage of life under God.

20. *'āmēl*, the word for *sufferer*, is derived from the same root word as *'āmāl* ('trouble' in verse 10). This connection suggests the idea of a sufferer who is oppressed and abused.

There is no point in living if brutality and bitterness are the order of the day. On *light* see at verse 4.

21-2. Those tortured by the agony of life hunt for death as if it were the greatest *treasure* to be found. When they find it they celebrate their homecoming.

23. This verse is the key to Job's torment. His dilemma is not merely that life is oppressive and meaningless, but that God is the cause of the problem. The hedge with which God surrounds Job is not a hedge of blessings as Satan claimed (1: 10), but a prison wall that prevents Job from finding any direction or hope in life. He is born to *wander blindly*, or, as the Hebrew suggests, his 'way' is hidden. In wisdom literature 'the way' (*derek*) means direction for living, the prescribed pattern of conduct, and the ultimate destiny for those who follow the principles of wisdom (cp. Prov. 4: 10-19). God has blocked Job's 'way'; he is completely lost.

24-6. Job's suffering is worse than oppression; it is a life-time of continuous terror and fear with no chance of relief.   ✶

First cycle of speeches

The First Discourse of Eliphaz

✶ The opening discourse of Eliphaz is a disputation designed to convince Job of the reasons for his suffering and bring him to his knees in submission. This disputation as such focuses on four axioms about man:

What innocent man ever perished? (4: 7)
Can mortal man be righteous before God? (4: 17)
Man is born to trouble. (5: 7)
Happy the man whom God rebukes! (5: 17)

The teaching implied behind the discourse of Eliphaz, and especially the opening axiom about man (4: 7), is the so-called doctrine of reward and punishment, a version of which is found in Deuteronomy (e.g. 7: 12–16; 11: 13–17). In its popular form, that doctrine teaches that all who are righteous will be rewarded with good things while all who are wicked will suffer divine retribution. The distorted implication of that teaching is that all who actually suffer must be guilty of some wickedness, while those who are blessed are apparently good people. The inference of the friends is that Job, who is on the verge of perishing, is far from innocent, but that if he acknowledges his guilt he may survive.

The second and third axioms offer uncomplimentary portraits of man (4: 17; 5: 7). Instead of hailing him as 'a little less than the angels' or a 'little less than a god' (Ps. 8: 5), Eliphaz emphasizes the weakness of the angels and the corrupt earthbound character of man. Instead of acclaiming him as a creature crowned 'with glory and honour' (Ps. 8: 5), Eliphaz views him as composed of clay, imperfect and unrighteous, born to suffer misfortune, destined to perish and devoid of the wisdom that brings true life. The fourth axiom moves beyond the character of man as such to the lot of man under the corrective discipline of God (5: 17).

DO INNOCENT MEN PERISH?

Then Eliphaz the Temanite began: **4**

    If one ventures to speak with you, will you lose 2
        patience?
    For who could hold his tongue any longer?
    Think how once you encouraged those who faltered, 3
    how you braced feeble arms,
    how a word from you upheld the stumblers   4
    and put strength into weak knees.
    But now that adversity comes upon you, you lose 5
        patience;
    it touches you, and you are unmanned.

6   Is your religion no comfort to you?
    Does your blameless life give you no hope?
7   For consider, what innocent man has ever perished?
    Where have you seen the upright destroyed?
8   This I know, that those who plough mischief and sow
        trouble
    reap as they have sown;
9   they perish at the blast of God
    and are shrivelled by the breath of his nostrils.
10 The roar of the lion, the whimpering of his cubs, fall
        silent;
    the teeth of the young lions are broken;
11 the lion perishes for lack of prey
    and the whelps of the lioness are abandoned.

* 2. Many of the speeches in Job begin with a sarcastic comment that does not further the argument but merely serves to belittle the opposition with remarks of a personal nature. The first such remark of Eliphaz is rather subdued (but cp. 15: 2–6).

3–6. These verses offer a preliminary analysis of Job's condition. Job had been considered a righteous and wise man (cp. 1: 1; 29: 7ff.) whose *word* strengthened the weak and helped the unfortunate. When he himself suffers misfortune, however, his alleged piety offers him no support and he is *unmanned*, or, as the Hebrew original suggests, he 'panics'.

6. The analysis of Job's condition concludes with a jibe about the hypocrisy of Job's faith. Job's comforters consider Job a secret sinner, not a pious hero. *religion* translates the word 'fear' which is shorthand for 'the fear of God' or 'fear of the LORD' (1: 1; 5: 4; Prov. 1: 7). In wisdom literature 'the fear of God' is an expression which epitomizes the religious way of life for the wise. Job had been *blameless* in pursuing that way. (On the 'way' see the comments on 3: 23.) *hope* in the

26

book of Job involves the possibility and power for a new beginning (14: 7).

7–9. Here Eliphaz presents his first argument designed to demonstrate Job's guilt. His argument has two sides: the innocent do not perish, whereas the wicked do. The first contention of this argument is grounded in an accepted tradition which Job should be willing to recognize. Eliphaz bases his second assertion on personal experience (verse 8).

7. 'Perish' is a recurring term in this chapter (verses 9, 11, 20). By dwelling on this expression Eliphaz draws attention to the opening word of Job's cry in the previous chapter (3: 3). Eliphaz is obsessed with the question of man's destruction.

8. *trouble* is another theme Eliphaz picks up from Job's opening outburst (see at 3: 10, 20). The Hebrew term for trouble usually implies arduous toil and agony (cp. 3: 10). That kind of trouble is the normal fate of man according to Eliphaz in a later axiom (5: 7). In 4: 8, however, the trouble that people *reap* is also determined by their evil intentions (cp. Hos. 8: 7; Prov. 22: 8).

9. The wicked die beneath God's wrath. It is ironical that the word used for the death-giving *blast* of God in this verse is the same as the word for the life-giving 'breath' of God in the creation of man (in Gen. 2: 7).

10–11. An argument from nature, perhaps based on an old proverb, is appended to amplify the idea of verses 8–9. Even the ferocious *lion perishes* eventually. The lion is often a metaphor for the wicked (cp. Prov. 28: 15; Pss. 7: 2; 10: 9).   ✳

HUMAN BEINGS ARE CORRUPT CLAY

A word stole into my ears,   12
and they caught the whisper of it;
in the anxious visions of the night,   13
when a man sinks into deepest sleep,
terror seized me and shuddering;   14

the trembling of my body frightened me.

15 A wind brushed my face
    and made the hairs bristle on my flesh;

16 and a figure stood there whose shape I could not discern,
    an apparition loomed before me,
    and I heard the sound of a low voice:

17 'Can mortal man be more righteous than God,
    or the creature purer than his Maker?

18 If God mistrusts his own servants
    and finds his messengers at fault,

19 how much more those that dwell in houses whose walls
        are clay,
    whose foundations are dust,
    which can be crushed like a bird's nest

20 or torn down between dawn and dark,
    how much more shall such men perish outright and
        unheeded,

21 *a*die, without ever finding wisdom?'

✻ 12–16. Eliphaz claims to have gained his insight into the
following axiom (verse 17) through an uncanny mode of
revelation comparable to a nightmare. Both 'word' (verse 12)
and 'wind' (verse 15) are prophetic vehicles of divine communication (Jer. 1: 4; 2: 1; Isa. 61: 1). It is surprising, however,
that Eliphaz, who like his friends normally depends on accepted wisdom axioms from tradition, should claim direct divine
revelation.

13. The word *anxious* can be rendered 'nightmares'. Adam
experienced a similar deep *sleep* when Eve was created (Gen.
2: 21).

16. *the sound of a low voice* is an expression which occurs in a

[a] *Prob. rdg.,* transposing Their rich possessions are snatched from them
to follow 5: 4.

similar form in 1 Kings 19: 12. Eliphaz seems to be claiming an experience of revelation comparable to that of Elijah.

17. According to this axiom the fundamental relationship of man, as creature, to God, as Creator, involves the condition of man as impure or unrighteous and of God as pure or righteous. *man* and *creature* are two of several terms for human beings used in these axioms. While the translation *creature* for *geber* captures the implications of the context, this Hebrew term usually implies the idea of a 'strong man'. Job speaks of himself as a *geber* whose way has been blocked by God (3 : 23). Later God challenges Job to gird up his loins and act like a true man (*geber*) (38: 3; 40: 7). *man* here renders *'enōsh*, another term for man, perhaps intended to provide a pun on another word of the same form meaning 'weak'. In the axiom of Eliphaz, man, whether weak or strong, is impure before his *Maker*. The term *Maker* is typical of wisdom contexts and expresses a primary aspect of man's relationship to God (see Prov. 17: 5; 22: 2). The parallel axioms about man in 15: 14 and 25: 4 (cp. 9: 2) support an alternative translation for this verse which reads, 'Can a mortal man be righteous before God. . .?' The question is not whether man can be superior to God in righteousness, but whether man as creature can ever be righteous in the presence of God. On *righteous* see the comment at 9: 2.

18. The *servants* and *messengers* of God are heavenly beings (cp. 15: 15). In the prose narrative of Job, Satan acts as a messenger in the court of heaven after roaming the earth (1: 6–7; 2: 1–2). There are several traditions about how some of these figures rebelled and suffered eternal consequences (Gen. 6: 1–4; Isa. 14: 12–15). Eliphaz implies that in the last analysis even celestial beings cannot be considered completely trustworthy. It follows then that if the angels are imperfect, man must be even further from being a paragon of purity.

19. *those that dwell in houses whose walls are clay* are human beings whose bodies are but crumbling clay. Like the first man they are made of *dust* (Gen. 2: 7) and will return to dust

(Gen. 3: 19). *like a bird's nest*: or possibly 'a moth'; in either case the image is one of man's extreme fragility.

20. *unheeded* renders a widely accepted emendation which literally means 'without name'. To die without perpetuating one's name meant the total perishing of an individual (Ruth 4: 5, 10; 1 Sam. 24: 21).

21. N.E.B. footnote explains that the first part of this verse fits better after 5: 4. But it may be rendered, 'Is their tent cord not pulled up?', an image that would vividly describe death in everyday terms. To die *without ever finding wisdom* is the ultimate disaster for adherents of the wisdom school. Wisdom is the impetus, guide and goal of life for all who follow its way (Prov. 4: 7–13). Wisdom implies an entire system of ideas which differs from other Israelite schools of thought. The guidelines for living the way of wisdom are preserved by tradition through the great wise men of the past (cp. 8: 8; Prov. 4: 1–4). ✳

MEN ARE BORN LOSERS

5 Call if you will; is there any to answer you?
   To which of the holy ones will you turn?

2 The fool is destroyed by his own angry passions,
   and the end of childish resentment is death.

3 I have seen it for myself: a fool uprooted,
   his home in sudden ruin about him,[a]

4 his children past help,
   browbeaten in court[b] with none to save them.

5 [c]Their rich possessions are snatched from them;
   what they have harvested others hungrily devour;
   the stronger man seizes it from the panniers,

[a] ruin about him: *prob. rdg.; Heb. obscure.*
[b] in court: *lit.* in the gate.
[c] *Line transposed from 4: 21.*

panting, thirsting for their wealth.
Mischief does not grow out of the soil   6
nor trouble spring from the earth;
man is born to trouble,   7
as surely as birds fly[a] upwards.

✻ The climax to this section is an axiom which asserts that
man is 'born to trouble' (verse 7). Eliphaz leads up to this
point with an opening taunt (verse 1), a proverb about fools
(verse 2), examples of folly from human experience and a
quotation about the origin of trouble (verse 6). For Eliphaz
man is a born loser; he cannot avoid a life of agony and
disaster.

1. The *holy ones* are heavenly beings in God's court whom
Eliphaz has previously classified as potentially untrustworthy
(4: 18; cp. 15: 15). Elsewhere in the Old Testament the holy
ones are synonymous with the 'sons of God' or 'the angels'
(Ps. 89: 7; Zech. 14: 5). By challenging Job to find a mediator
among the lesser divine beings the taunt of Eliphaz anticipates
Job's later yearning for just such a figure (9: 32–3; cp. 16: 19).

2. This verse is a typical proverb classifying the *fool*, that is,
the person uninitiated in the principles of wisdom. *The fool is
destroyed by his. . .passions*, the wise man controls them (cp.
Prov. 14: 30). By quoting this proverb Eliphaz seems to accuse
Job of being a fool.

3–4. Eliphaz confirms the truth of his proverb about fools
by citing examples from his own experience.

4. *with none to save* can be rendered 'with no liberator'. In
the Old Testament a 'liberator' may free another individual
from his accuser in court or from his oppressor in life. Job
later complains that he has no such liberator in his court case
against God (10: 7).

5. On 5*a* see the comment on 4: 21. The translation of the
whole verse remains uncertain.

[a] *Or* as sparks shoot.

6. This quotation recalls the sowing and reaping of *trouble* in 4: 8, and sets the stage for the following axiom about man. *soil* and *earth* render Hebrew words for 'the dust' of 'the ground' from which man is made (Gen. 2: 7). According to Gen. 3: 18 'thorns and thistles' *spring from the earth* to give man a life of hardship. Verse 6, therefore, should perhaps be considered a rhetorical question which reads, 'Does not mischief grow out of the soil...?'

7. According to this axiom man is destined to face a life of *trouble* or 'agonizing misfortune'. (On *trouble* see the comments at 3: 10 and 4: 8.) The word for *man* here is the same as the word for Adam, another reason for assuming that verses 6–7 may reflect the creation traditions of Gen. 2–3. *birds* renders a Hebrew expression 'sons of Resheph'. Resheph is the name for the northwest semitic god of pestilence who seems to have dwelt in the underworld. The children of Resheph were apparently supposed to have brought disease and suffering from the underworld to the earth. N.E.B. footnote 'as sparks shoot' offers an alternative, based on the idea that pestilence is connected with a god of fire. The point of the reference here is that once man is born the forces of disease and misfortune will inevitably fly forth from the netherworld to plague his life. It is possible that the words 'soil' or 'dust' in verse 6 also refer to the underworld (cp. 17: 16); this would mean that both verses make a similar point. ✶

HYMN TO THE LORD OF JUSTICE

8 For my part, I would make my petition to God
   and lay my cause before him,

9 who does great and unsearchable things,
   marvels without number.

10 He gives rain to the earth
    and sends water on the fields;

11 he raises the lowly to the heights,

the mourners are uplifted by victory;
he frustrates the plots of the crafty, 12
and they win no success,
he traps the cunning in their craftiness, 13
and the schemers' plans are thrown into confusion.
In the daylight they run into darkness, 14
and grope at midday as though it were night.
He saves the destitute from their greed,[a] 15
and the needy from the grip of the strong;
so the poor hope again, 16
and the unjust are sickened.

✵ This doxology on divine justice is not offered by Eliphaz as a vehicle for worship, but as the motivation for Job to make a formal confession of his guilt (cp. Amos 5: 6–9). If Job repents he can expect the pattern of divine justice expressed in this hymn to materialize in his own life. Hannah's prayer presents a comparable portrait of God as the Lord of universal justice (1 Sam. 2: 1–10). One major difference between her prayer and Eliphaz's hymn is the wisdom language used in the latter. Terms like 'unsearchable', 'crafty', 'success', 'cunning' and 'schemers' plans' belong to the jargon of the wisdom school. In short, Job 5: 9–16 has the characteristics of a wisdom hymn.

8. When Eliphaz exhorts Job to *make. . .petition* he is recommending a formal rite of confession. The implication, of course, is that Job is guilty of some undisclosed sin (cp. John 9: 24).

9. The expression *who does* is the same word as the title 'Maker', before whom man is impure (4: 17). The mysteries of the Maker's world are the object of the wise man's research; the affirmation of this wisdom hymn is that there are innumerable mysteries of God which are literally 'beyond discovery' or *unsearchable* (cp. 11: 7).

[a] *Lit.* mouths.

33

10. The first example of God's great deeds is the gift of rain, a mysterious commodity essential to the survival of mankind (cp. 36: 26–8). A reference to God's activity in nature may appear out of place in a catalogue of divine acts of justice. In wisdom theology, however, the way God orders nature corresponds to the way he executes justice among men (cp. Prov. 8).

11–14. God's justice is demonstrated when the less fortunate and oppressed are rescued from their plight and when those who seek power by unscrupulous means are brought to nought.

15–16. The outcome of God's justice is *hope*, that is, the impetus for a new beginning with him (cp. 4: 6). An accompanying issue is the thwarting of the unjust, or, as the Hebrew text reads, 'the silencing of injustice itself'. ✵

DISCIPLINED MEN ARE FORTUNATE

17 Happy the man whom God rebukes!
therefore do not reject the discipline of the Almighty.

18 For, though he wounds, he will bind up;
the hands that smite will heal.

19 You may meet disaster six times, and he will save you;
seven times, and no harm shall touch you.

20 In time of famine he will save you from death,
in battle from the sword.

21 You will be shielded from the lash of slander,[a]
and when violence comes you need not fear.

22 You will laugh at violence and starvation
and have no need to fear wild beasts;

23 for you have a covenant with the stones to spare your
fields.

[a] from. . .slander: *or* when slander is rife.

and the weeds have been constrained to leave you at peace.
You will know that all is well with your household, 24
you will look round your home and find nothing amiss;
you will know, too, that your descendants will be 25
many
and your offspring like grass, thick upon the earth.
You will come in sturdy old age to the grave 26
as sheaves come in due season to the threshing-floor.

We have inquired into all this, and so it is; 27
this we have heard, and you may know it for the truth.

☆ 17. The final axiom in chs. 4–5 asserts that men who experience the punitive discipline of God are fortunate. The implication of this axiom is that suffering and disaster may be due to the corrective punishment of God rather than the inevitable misfortunes men are born to endure. *Happy*: a term which in wisdom literature and in the Psalms designates someone fortunate or blessed. The 'rebuke' of God is more than a verbal rebuff; it involves the kind of intense instruction and criticism that will prove to be a corrective discipline (cp. Prov. 3:11–12). In Job 13:10 the N.E.B. happily translates the same verb as 'expose', thereby capturing the connotation of radical chastisement. *discipline* renders a Hebrew term which may refer to intensive instruction in the principles of wisdom (Prov. 1:2f., 7f.), or to harsh chastisement (Prov. 23:13). Job is expected to acknowledge his pathetic condition as a medium of instruction from *the Almighty*.

Almighty translates the title 'Shaddai', an archaic name for God prevalent among the patriarchs (Gen. 17:1; Exod. 6:2–3). The use of this title throughout Job suggests that the author wanted to preserve the atmosphere of the patriarchal setting even in the poems and to address the human dilemma by re-interpreting ancient and cherished traditions of his people.

18. The ground for the exhortation of verse 17 is an old doctrine about the God of Israel as the Lord of death and life who kills and makes alive, wounds and binds, smites and heals (see Deut. 32: 39; Hos. 6: 1–2). Israelite theology in general leaves no room for a dualism in which the god of death or evil is distinct from the god of life and good. Yahweh, not Satan or some other figure, was ultimately responsible for calamities and sickness. Job, therefore, had to come to terms with God and why he had crushed him.

19–21. These verses develop the doctrine of verse 18 in relation to possible crisis situations in Job's life. Job is assured that if he accepts his own crisis as due to divine discipline, he can be confident that God will *save* him. The two terms for *save* in verses 19 and 20 are often linked with God's mighty deliverance of his people from historical foes (e.g. Exod. 18: 8; Deut. 7: 8). In Job and the Psalms, however, 'salvation' frequently means emergence from the realm of death. For Job, death was both inviting and threatening, a reality with which he lived constantly. He saw no one who could save him, no liberator (10: 7; see on 5: 4).

19. *six times. . .seven times*: a numerical idiom for 'innumerable times' (cp. Amos 1: 3 where N.E.B. renders the Hebrew 'three crimes, four' as 'crime after crime').

22–6. Eliphaz expands his portrait of how God intervenes on man's behalf with promises of what Job can expect as a result of his personal liberation by God. This description by Eliphaz reflects a common ideal of well-being (*shālōm*) which faithful wise men envisage for their lives. When the wise man achieves a harmonious relationship with God through the obedient pursuit of wisdom, he can expect to experience a comparable bond with nature (cp. also on verse 10). By contrast Job describes the good life of the wicked in similar terms (21: 7–13).

23. The term *weeds* is usually translated 'wild beasts'. The

covenant of peace is a pact between man and nature, including both the stones of the field and the 'wild beasts' of the field. The *stones* will not hinder agriculture any more than 'wild beasts' will interfere with pastoral pursuits. The idea of a covenant of peace with nature harks back to ancient Near Eastern myths of a tranquil primal paradise. Israel envisaged the new age as a similar era of peace with all creation (cp. Hos. 2: 18; Isa. 11: 6–8).

27. This self-assured conclusion balances Eliphaz's sarcastic opening comment (4: 2). He claims that he, along with his companions in the wisdom school, has *inquired into* the teachings he has enunciated and found them to be true, despite the assertion that the great mysteries of God are ultimately 'unsearchable' (5: 9).   *

Job's First Response to Eliphaz

* Job's response does not take up the arguments of Eliphaz point for point. Instead, Job opens with an outburst of intense anger against God. He is the great hunter of heaven pursuing a pitiful target called Job (6: 2–7). Job's anguish turns to a death wish as his resistance to suffering flags. For God to terminate Job's misery would be a welcome act of divine mercy (8–13). Even his friends, who might be expected to show genuine human compassion, are exposed by Job as nothing but traitors and hypocrites. Their covenant of friendship with Job means nothing to them (verses 14–23). After this fierce castigation of his friends Job challenges them to stop arguing and specify his guilt. 'Show me where I have erred', he pleads. But his pleas are lost on men who do not have the integrity of Job (24–30). *

LET GOD CRUSH ME

Then Job answered: **6**

    O that the grounds for my resentment might be ₂
      weighed,

and my misfortunes set with them on the scales!

3   For they would outweigh the sands of the sea:
what wonder if my words are wild?[a]

4   The arrows of the Almighty find their mark in me,
and their poison soaks into my spirit;
God's onslaughts wear me away.

5   Does the wild ass bray when he has grass
or the ox low when he has fodder?

6   Can a man eat tasteless food unseasoned with salt,
or find any flavour in the juice of mallows?

7   Food that should nourish me sticks in my throat,
and my bowels rumble with an echoing sound.

8   O that I might have my request,
that God would grant what I hope for:

9   that he would be pleased to crush me,
to snatch me away with his hand and cut me off!

10   For that would bring me relief,
and in the face of unsparing anguish I would leap for
joy.[b]

11   Have I the strength to wait?
What end have I to expect, that I should be patient?

12   Is my strength the strength of stone,
or is my flesh bronze?

13   Oh how shall I find help within myself?
The power to aid myself is put out of my reach.

✻ 2–3. Were it possible to weigh suffering, Job's misery and
anger would outweigh *the sands of the sea*.

    4. *the Almighty*, or rather Shaddai (see at 5: 17), is no longer
the guardian of the helpless, but a celestial archer pursuing his

[a] what. . .wild?: *or* therefore words fail me.
[b] *Prob. rdg.; Heb. adds* I have not denied the words of the Holy One,

38

human victim with poisoned arrows. Job is left to cry out like a wounded animal, terrified by his God.

5. Job's cry is clear evidence of his torture, not his prosperity. An old proverb is quoted to prove the point: *the wild ass* does not *bray* while he is feeding, but only when he is deprived or desperate.

6–7. The proverb of verse 6 seems to declare that some foods are too nauseating to swallow. For Job the counsel he receives is so revolting he cannot stomach it.

8–10. Job has one final hope in life: that God would *crush* him into the dust (cp. 4: 19–20) and cut him off from the land of the living (cp. 3: 11–19). Job's death wish, however, is not morbid or suicidal. He wants God to be both the agent of a merciful end and the instrument of judgement. The cruelty of God is that he leaves Job hanging without relief and without a verdict.

11–13. Job's complaint intensifies and his resistance to divine torture fades as all prospect of future divine compassion or vindication disappears. Job lacks the *strength of stone* to endure endless oppression. He is but human, after all. ✻

MY FRIENDS ARE TRAITORS

Devotion is due from his friends 14
to one who despairs and loses faith in the Almighty;
but my brothers have been treacherous as a mountain 15
    stream,
like the channels of streams that run dry,
which turn dark with ice 16
or are hidden with piled-up snow;
or they vanish the moment they are in spate, 17
dwindle in the heat and are gone.
Then the caravans, winding hither and thither, 18
go up into the wilderness and perish;[a]

[a] *Or* and are lost.

39

19 the caravans of Tema look for their waters,
  travelling merchants of Sheba hope for them;
20 but they are disappointed, for all their confidence,
  they reach them only to be balked.
21 So treacherous have you now been to me:[a]
  you felt dismay and were afraid.
22 Did I ever say, 'Give me this or that;
  open your purses to save my life;
23 rescue me from my enemy;
  ransom me out of the hands of ruthless men'?

24 Tell me plainly, and I will listen in silence;
  show me where I have erred.
25 How harsh are the words of the upright man!
  What do the arguments of wise men[b] prove?
26 Do you mean to argue about words
  or to sift the utterance of a man past hope?
27 Would you assail an orphan[c]?
  Would you hurl yourselves on a friend?
28 So now, I beg you, turn and look at me:
  am I likely to lie to your faces?
29 Think again, let me have no more injustice;
  think again, for my integrity is in question.
30 Do I ever give voice to injustice?
  Does my sense not warn me when my words are wild?

✻ 14. With no sympathy forthcoming from God, Job could at least expect some sympathy from his human companions. 'A despairing man', says Job, 'needs the loyalty of a friend when he *loses faith in the Almighty*.' According to this render-

[a] So. . .to me: *prob. rdg.; Heb. obscure.*
[b] wise men: *prob. rdg.; Heb. unintelligible.*
[c] *Or* a blameless man.

ing of verse 14, a friend is loyal to his covenant of friendship, especially in times of despair. A friend is a compassionate fellow human being even when faith in God has vanished. Faith, religion and God himself are not basic to the nature of true friendship. To be a friend is to be a co-human in a de-humanized situation; it means assuming a common posture on the dust and ashes.

15–20. After Job's three friends had broken their sympathetic silence (see 2: 13), they proved to be no friends at all. Their betrayal provokes Job to vent a lengthy tirade in which he describes his friends as treacherous streams like the wadis of Palestine which run dry in the summer and provide no refreshment for parched travellers. *Tema*: An important trading-centre in N. Arabia; *Sheba*: cp. 1 Kings 10: 1–13.

21–3. Job's friends took one look at him and ran scared; he bore the ominous marks of divine wrath. Job made no demands of their friendship; he solicited no heroic acts of deliverance from his foes. He longed for sympathy in his struggle to understand what was happening, but found none.

24. Job now changes his approach and confronts his friends with the accusation of Eliphaz that Job must be guilty of some sin. He calls on his accusers to avoid vague insinuations about his guilt and to specify his crime.

25–6. The arguments of Job's friends are but a battle over words; they are quite insensitive to Job's real plight.

28–30. Job closes this speech with a plea for his friends to set aside all prejudice and face honestly the question of whether Job has ever been guilty of injustice. Ultimately his *integrity* and God's justice are at stake. *

Job's First Response to Eliphaz (*continued*)

* This speech (ch. 7) is one of the bitterest complaints Job addresses to God. Its vehemence is reflected in the way Job appropriates three themes concerning the lot of man. Eliphaz had given his pessimistic portrait of the nature and destiny of

man. Job offers an even more appalling picture. He sees man as a slave oppressed by God, as subject to the relentless scrutiny of a heavenly Watchman, and as destined to return to oblivion in Sheol, the underworld. If Job is a slave then God is his slavemaster imposing an endless life of hardship on his work-man (7: 1-4). Before God, the heavenly Watchman, Job also feels like a dangerous monster who needs to be guarded con-stantly (verses 11-12). God, however, is not satisfied with watching Job; he torments Job by invading his sleep with nightmares (verses 13-16). In the mouth of Job the beautiful confession of Ps. 8: 4-5 that God honours and remembers man becomes a biting satire. God cares for man by finding endless ways of testing and torturing him (verses 17-20). Despite his testimony that life is but a fleeting journey to Sheol, the land-of-no-return (verses 5-10), Job contemplates with delight his rest in the grave, far from the seeing eye of the heavenly Watchman. There God will no longer be able to torment his victim (verses 8 and 21).

BORN TO BE A SLAVE

7 Has not man hard service on earth,
  and are not his days like those of a hired labourer,

2 like those of a slave longing for the shade
  or a servant kept waiting for his wages?

3 So months of futility are my portion,
  troubled nights are my lot.

4 When I lie down, I think,
  'When will it be day that[a] I may rise?'
  When the evening grows long and I lie down,[b]
  I do nothing but toss till morning twilight.

5 My body is infested with worms,

[a] day that: *so Sept.; Heb. om.*
[b] and I lie down: *prob. rdg., cp. Pesh.; Heb. om.*

42

and scabs cover my skin.[a]

My days are swifter than a shuttle[b]   6
and come to an end as the thread runs out.[c]

Remember, my life is but a breath of wind;   7
I shall never again see good days.
Thou wilt behold me no more with a seeing eye;   8
under thy very eyes I shall disappear.
As clouds break up and disperse,   9
so he that goes down to Sheol never comes back;
he never returns home again,   10
and his place will know him no more.[d]

✻ 1–2. The opening axiom describes man as a slave oppressed
in the service of life. *hard service* suggests the practice of con-
scripting forced labour common in the ancient Near East (cp.
1 Sam. 14: 52; 1 Kings 9: 15–22). Man's very existence is
slavery; he is born into bondage and longs for the freedom of
death (cp. 3: 13–19). The slavemaster of life is apparently God
himself. The concept of man created to be a servant of the
gods is also found in Mesopotamian mythology.

3–4. Job's life as a slave is completely empty. His *troubled
nights* are, as the original Hebrew implies, nights of agony and
unjust oppression (on 'trouble' see 3: 10; 4: 8). Job is dehumanized by God day and night.

6. The Hebrew words for *thread* and 'hope' (see footnote)
are identical. The double meaning implied in the use of this
word is reflected in the translation 'life-thread' in 8: 13.

7–8. These verses revolve around a threefold use of the
word 'eye'. Job pleads for God to *Remember* that once his brief
life is over his 'eye' will never *see good days* of prosperity. In

[a] *Prob. rdg.; Heb. adds* it is cracked and discharging.
[b] *Or* a fleeting odour.
[c] as...out: *or* without hope.
[d] *Or* and he will not be noticed any more in his place.

43

the grave the *seeing eye* of El, the heavenly Watchman, will no longer be privileged to spy on his slave. Under the *very eyes* of the Almighty watcher he will vanish and then it will be too late to vindicate or condemn him.

9–10. Sheol as the netherworld of the dead from which there is no return is a common concept of the ancient Near East (cp. 10: 21). For Job, Sheol is also the land of refuge from God. ✳

AM I A MONSTER?

11   But I will not hold my peace;
       I will speak out in the distress of my mind
       and complain in the bitterness of my soul.

12   Am I the monster of the deep, am I the sea-serpent,
       that thou settest a watch over me?

13   When I think that my bed will comfort me,
       that sleep will relieve my complaining,

14   thou dost terrify me with dreams
       and affright me with visions.

15   I would rather be choked outright;
       I would prefer death to all my sufferings.

16   I am in despair, I would not go on living;
       leave me alone, for my life is but a vapour.

17   What is man that thou makest much of him
       and turnest thy thoughts towards him,

18   only to punish him morning by morning
       or to test him every hour of the day?

19   Wilt thou not look away from me for an instant?
       Wilt thou not let me be while I swallow my spittle?

20   If I have sinned, how do I injure thee,
       thou watcher of the hearts[a] of men?

[a] of the hearts: so *Sept.*; *Heb. om.*

Why hast thou made me thy butt,
and why have I become thy*a* target?
Why dost thou not pardon my offence
and take away my guilt?
But now I shall lie down in the grave;
seek me, and I shall not be.

21

✷ 12. The imagery shifts from that of God the oppressive watchman to God the guardian of chaos. Job feels he is one of the chaos monsters of Canaanite mythology who were conquered and controlled by Baal. Job is like a dangerous *monster* under constant guard and therefore less than human in the sight of God.

13–16. In his yearning for compassion Job turns to sleep as his last resort. But God penetrates his subconscious with terrifying *dreams* that intensify his longing for the final sleep of death.

17–18. This axiom about man is a parody on Ps. 8: 4 which reads, 'what is man that thou shouldst remember him, mortal man that thou shouldst care for him?' In Job's version of that axiom, the special attention God pays to man is sadistic rather than salutary. He probes man's life to find excuses for visiting afflictions upon him every morning. His care is the cruel oppression of a taskmaster, not the magnanimous remembering of a Creator who enjoys honouring mortals (see Ps. 8: 5).

20. Job names his God a Man-Watcher whose perpetual surveillance makes him a spy rather than a guardian. Job is the target and God the hunter, watching, waiting and toying with his prey.

21. Job does not relinquish his claim of innocence. He suggests that if God does see some *guilt* in Job he should forgive Job and end his agony. That would be more consistent with God's character. Soon Job will return to the dust and it will be too late for God to display his love. ✷

[a] *So some MSS., cp. Sept.; others* my.

45

The First Discourse of Bildad

✻ Bildad's speech exhibits features typical of a wisdom teacher. He begins by posing the central question about God's justice (verse 3), cites a pointed example from Job's life (verse 4), appeals to ancient tradition (verses 8–19) and calls on Job to implore God's mercy (verses 5–7). The God of Israel was above all a God of justice. For God to pervert justice would be to act contrary to his nature. Yet the arguments of Job raised the possibility that God was actually not being true to himself. For Bildad that thought is intolerable. The death of Job's own children is clear evidence of God's punitive justice. If Job were innocent he need only beg God's favour and he would also experience the other side of God's justice. Job would be restored to his rightful estate.

Bildad is also a man steeped in tradition. For him the collective wisdom of the fathers offers far greater authority than any of his own arguments. Bildad follows a wisdom teaching-device of probing the distant past for normative answers to crucial questions; for the wise man antiquity means authority. Bildad's word from the ancient fathers was a proposition based on a proverb: just as reeds need water to survive so men need communion with God. Those who forget God lose contact with the source of life and hope. ✻

ASK THE FATHERS!

8 Then Bildad the Shuhite began:

2   How long will you say such things,
      the long-winded ramblings of an old man?

3   Does God pervert judgement?
      Does the Almighty pervert justice?

4   Your sons sinned against him,
      so he left them to be victims of their own iniquity.

5   If only you will seek God betimes

and plead for the favour of the Almighty,
if you are innocent and upright,   6
then indeed will he watch over you
and see your just intent fulfilled.
Then, though your beginnings were humble,   7
your end will be great.

Inquire now of older generations   8
and consider the experience of their fathers;
for we ourselves are of yesterday and are transient;   9
our days on earth are a shadow.
Will not they speak to you and teach you   10
and pour out the wisdom of their hearts?
Can rushes grow where there is no marsh?   11
Can reeds flourish without water?
While they are still in flower and not ready to cut,[a]   12
they wither earlier than[b] any green plant.
Such is the fate of all who forget God;   13
the godless man's life-thread breaks off;
his confidence is gossamer,   14
and the ground of his trust a spider's web.
He leans against his house but it does not stand;   15
he clutches at it but it does not hold firm.
His is the lush growth of a plant in the sun,   16
pushing out shoots over the garden;
but its roots become entangled in a stony patch   17
and run against a bed of rock.
Then someone uproots it from its place,   18
which[c] disowns it and says, 'I have never known you.'
That is how its life withers away,   19

[a] and. . .cut: *or* they are surely cut.
[b] *Or* wither like. . .   [c] *Or* and.

47

and other plants spring up from the earth.

20   Be sure, God will not spurn the blameless man,
       nor will he grasp the hand of the wrongdoer.

21   He will yet fill your mouth with laughter,
       and shouts of joy will be on your lips;

22   your enemies shall be wrapped in confusion,
       and the tents of the wicked shall vanish away.

✽ 3. Job's previous speech implied that God does *pervert judgement* (cp. 9: 19–20). His personal experience ran counter to the traditional Israelite doctrine of justice. The Psalmist affirmed that God's cosmic 'throne is built upon righteousness and justice' (Ps. 89: 14). God's justice and righteousness are the guarantee of all cosmic, communal, and cultic order. To pervert justice would be to revert to chaos.

4. The death of Job's children (1: 18–19) is cited as evidence of divine justice in Job's own life. Job may appear to be perfect but the sinfulness of his children was a truth recorded in his own heart (1: 5).

5–7. Bildad does not yet condemn Job as wicked, but argues that if he is *innocent*, as he claims, he need merely implore *the favour of the Almighty* to discover God's providence.

6c. *just intent fulfilled*: a more literal translation – 'rightful estate restored' – is preferable. Bildad assumes that if Job were to receive back his lost estate he would be satisfied. Far from it! Job is not agonizing over the loss of his goods, but over the apparent injustice and violence of his God. Job wants answers, not estates.

8. This verse reflects the custom of appealing to ancient authority to establish a truth or doctrine. The same practice is found in 20: 4 (cp. also Isa. 40: 21). The *older* or 'first' *generations* were closer to the beginning of things when truth was first discerned. The 'beginnings' are the time when truth was established. To *Inquire* of the beginnings is to return to the original truths of life mediated through the *fathers*.

9–10. The reasons given for citing ancient tradition are twofold. Each individual is an ephemeral creature who during his lifetime can gain no depth of understanding. Through the accumulated mind of the past, however, he can receive true instruction in the ways of wisdom.

11–12. Bildad cites this proverb to substantiate the arguments that follow.

13–14. Here Bildad emphasizes the ancient truth that *the fate of all who forget God* is like that of reeds without water. To forget God means more than a lapse of memory; it involves breaking with God and relying on a power other than God for support (cp. Deut. 8: 11–20). The future of any who make this break is as flimsy as a *gossamer* or as weak as *a spider's web*. On *life-thread* see at 7: 6.

15–18. A poetic portrayal of people whose life is not rooted in God, the source of all life.

19. As it stands the text of verse 19 reads, 'Behold, that is the joy of his way, and from the dust another sprouts.' Taken in this sense this verse provides a sarcastic finale to Bildad's portrait of the godless man. He returns to the dust to be replaced by another from the dust.

20–2. Job was previously declared *blameless* (1: 1) and subsequently insisted that he was innocent of any wrong-doing (31: 6). His condition, however, belied the assertion of Bildad that the blameless enjoy a life of exuberance and success. If Job is a wrongdoer there is no way he can expect God to *grasp* his *hand*, that is, to select him as the agent of his special divine purposes (cp. Isa. 42: 6; 51: 18). ✻

Job's First Response to Bildad

✻ In this response Job contemplates taking God to court even though he knows that no case against God has a chance. God is both judge and defendant, witness and executioner. The injustice of the situation is compounded by God's arbitrary use of his power and his unwillingness to stand trial or give

Job a hearing. God is elusive and almighty; there is no way Job can force him to appear in court. Even if he did, Job could only expect another violent display of unjustified fury (verses 2–4, 11–20). This frustrating dilemma provokes Job to recite a hymn to his God as the King of chaos (verses 5–10). Yet Job persists in his search for a way to vindicate his integrity even though he believes that God is blind in his dispensation of justice and would reverse any court decision favourable to Job. He even dreams of a powerful arbiter who could guarantee a fair trial with God, but Job knows that no such higher authority exists (verses 32–5).   ✳

NO CASE AGAINST GOD HAS A CHANCE

9 Then Job answered:

2   Indeed this I know for the truth,
    that no man can win his case against God.

3   If a man chooses to argue with him,
    God will not answer one question in a thousand.[a]

4   He is wise, he is powerful;
    what man has stubbornly resisted him and survived?

5   It is God who moves mountains, giving them no rest,
    turning them over in his wrath;

6   who makes the earth start from its place
    so that its pillars are convulsed;

7   who commands the sun's orb not to rise
    and shuts up the stars under his seal;

8   who by himself spread out the heavens
    and trod on the sea-monster's back;[b]

9   who made Aldebaran and Orion,

[a] If a man. . . thousand: *or* If God is pleased to argue with him'
man cannot answer one question in a thousand.
[b] *Or* on the crests of the waves.

the Pleiades and the circle of the southern stars;
who does great and unsearchable things,   10
marvels without number.

He passes by me, and I do not see him;   11
he moves on his way undiscerned by me;
if he hurries on,^a who can bring him back?   12
Who will ask him what he does?
God does not turn back his wrath;   13
the partisans of Rahab lie prostrate at his feet.
How much less can I answer him   14
or find words to dispute with him?
Though I am right, I get no answer,   15
though I plead with my accuser for mercy.
If I summoned him to court and he responded,   16
I do not believe that he would listen to my plea –
for he bears hard upon me for a trifle^b   17
and rains blows on me without cause;
he leaves me no respite to recover my breath   18
but fills me with bitter thoughts.
If the appeal is to force, see how strong he is;   19
if to justice, who can compel him^c to give me a
    hearing?
Though I am right, he condemns me out of my own   20
    mouth;
though I am blameless, he twists my words.
Blameless, I say; of myself   21
I reck nothing, I hold my life cheap.
But it is all one; therefore I say,   22
'He destroys blameless and wicked alike.'

[a] *So some MSS.; others* seizes.
[b] *Lit.* a hair.   [c] *So Sept.; Heb.* me.

23   When a sudden flood brings death,
       he mocks the plight of the innocent.

24   The land is given over to the power of the wicked,
       and the eyes of its judges are blindfold.[a]

✽ 2. Job picks up the axiom of Eliphaz that man cannot be righteous before God (see at 4: 17) and sets it in a court context. According to Job 'man can never be vindicated before God' when he brings his case against God into court. For although Job may have a legitimate case, God is both judge and defendant.

3–4. *argue* renders the Hebrew *rīb* which involves arguing a case in court. Even if God were brought to trial and put on the witness stand, Job claims that God would never answer any of the questions put to him. No matter how persistent the interrogator, God is too ingenious and too powerful to be convicted by human arguments (cp. 33: 12–13).

5–10. Job's reference to a wise and powerful God (verse 4) provokes a satirical hymn to the Creator. Acts of chaos are linked with acts of creation as examples of the unsearchable mysteries of the Maker. In the midst of his own personal chaos, Job views God as the grand disturber of the universe (cp. Jer. 4: 23–8).

5–6. To overthrow the *mountains* and disturb the eternal *pillars* of the earth means to shake the very foundations of the world, and ultimately of all cosmic order and justice (see Pss. 82: 3–5; 96: 10).

7. God not only creates light, but returns the world to primeval darkness, devoid of sun and stars. He is the God of earthquakes and eclipses.

8. God *spread out the heavens* as a cosmic tent in which he reigns and displays his celestial might (cp. Isa. 40: 21–2; Ps. 104: 2–4). If inclined he can also control chaos, here symbolized by the *sea-monster* and known in Canaanite mythology as Prince Sea (see the note on 7: 12).

[a] *Prob. rdg.; Heb. adds* if not he, then who?

9. Job cannot blame the *stars* for his destiny, for God governs the constellations and is therefore responsible for Job's fate. The precise identification of the constellations remains uncertain (cp. also 38: 31f.).

10. For Job the *unsearchable* mystery of God lies in the tension between his creative power and his destructive tendencies. As a victim of the latter Job can find no reassurance in this hymnic refrain as it was cited earlier by Eliphaz (5: 9). This Creator is also Job's judge and accuser.

11–13. When this Creator is angry (cp. verse 5), he moves on a relentless path of devastation. He is invisible but violent; there is no way for Job to confront him without being annihilated like the followers of *Rahab. Rahab*, like Prince Sea (verse 8), is a name for the great dragon who symbolizes the primordial chaos forces overthrown by the Creator (see 26: 12).

14–15. An orderly trial procedure is impossible with an angry, elusive opponent like God. Job claims to be in the *right*, or 'righteous', but he has no way of forcing God to be the defendant and take the stand. God seems to have reversed the roles so that Job is all but compelled to plead for mercy from God as if God were the just accuser.

16–18. Not only is it impossible to compel God to testify, but this Judge would never heed anything Job said. He is intent on abusing Job, not on handling his case.

17a. An alternative reading is, 'he would hit me with a tempest'. This suggestion anticipates what actually happens to Job when God finally speaks from the 'tempest' (38: 1).

19–20. These verses pose Job's dilemma as sharply as any. He does not have the power to subpoena God as an equal and force him into courts (cp. 40: 9–14). If Job appeals for justice he has no assurance of getting a fair hearing. God is more interested in finding ways to make Job appear guilty. God, moreover, is so biased in his use of power that he would coerce the innocent to confess his guilt or reverse any legal decision favourable to Job.

21-4. Job cries out in utter despair. He lives in a world (better than *land*, verse 24) without moral order, where the innocent are mocked and the wicked are mighty. But although he rejects life as worthless and futile, he clings to his integrity as the last vestige of meaning, even if God's righteousness is threatened in the process. Some interpreters argue that this tenacity was the great sin of Job, the sin of self-righteousness; others hail it as the evidence of a deep but realistic faith (cp. 2: 3; 32: 8-13; 40: 8). ✳

WHERE CAN ONE FIND AN ARBITER?

25   My days have been swifter than a runner,
        they have slipped away and seen no prosperity;
26   they have raced by like reed-built skiffs,
        swift as vultures swooping on carrion.
27   If I think, 'I will forget my griefs,
        I will show a cheerful face and smile',
28   I tremble in every nerve;[a]
        I know that thou wilt not hold me innocent.
29   If I am to be accounted guilty,
        why do I labour in vain?
30   Though I wash myself with soap
        or cleanse my hands with lye,
31   thou wilt thrust me into the mud
        and my clothes will make me loathsome.

32   He is not a man as I am, that I can answer him
        or that we can confront one another in court.
33   If only there were one to arbitrate between us
        and impose his authority on us both,
34   so that God might take his rod from my back,

[a] *Or* I am afraid of all that I must suffer.

and terror of him might not come on me suddenly.

I would then speak without fear of him;   35

for I know I am not what I am thought to be.

✻ 25–9. Job laments his sad plight, the brevity of his pathetic life, the futility of any attempt to escape the burden of his apparent guilt, and the pointless struggle to prove his innocence. He cannot escape, he cannot win and yet he refuses to compromise his integrity; his lot is intolerable.

30–1. Job's judge has another inhuman trait: he enjoys plunging the pure into a filthy pit to make them unclean. Instead of the defendant being given clean clothes as the mark of his acquittal (cp. Zech. 3: 3–5), Job expects God to make certain that Job appears guilty, regardless of the evidence Job produces to the contrary.

32–5. In a moment of desperation Job reaches for the impossible to resolve his dilemma. He entertains the dream that somewhere in the universe an arbiter would intervene and mediate between himself and God.

32. God and man are so different that any normal court confrontation between them is excluded.

33. In spite of this, Job contemplates a figure who is so powerful or so persuasive that he could *impose his authority* on both God and man, thereby forcing them into court to face each other honestly. This figure would *arbitrate*, that is, decide the case fairly and correct the guilty party. Whether Job had in mind a member of the heavenly council (see 1: 6; 5: 1), or a personal god who would be his advocate before the council, is relatively secondary. No such independent mediator exists for Job; he knows that he must ultimately deal directly with the Almighty (cp. 10: 7).

34–5. There can be no justice or equity when the slave is intimidated by the *rod* of his taskmaster and thereby prevented from giving true testimony before the court. God's oppression fosters perjury not justice. Concerning *terror* see the comment on 13: 21. ✻

Job's First Response to Bildad (continued)

✳ This lament revolves around the theme of God as Job's personal Creator whose ultimate plans for Job's future are exposed as a sinister plot to create in order to condemn. Job's words are more than an angry complaint; they seem designed to provoke the Creator to sympathy for his creations or to immediate rage against them. Job wants some action, at least, that will break God's deathly silence. He therefore proceeds to speculate to God's face about his motives for condemning an innocent man like Job. Why should God spurn what he had laboured so hard to create? Either he is sadistic, devoid of sympathy, or finite like man (verses 1–7). Job then turns from speculations to memories. He takes God back to experience again his ecstasy in moulding Job from almost nothing into a human being who was precious, perfect, and lovable. Why would God want to mutilate his own masterpiece (verses 8–12)? In the wake of this poetic nostalgia Job erupts with vitriolic indictments. He accuses God of duplicity and insincerity. God the Creator is really God the spying destroyer. God the Artist, who moulds men like a human potter, is really an inhuman hunter (verses 13–17). Life with this God is meaningless. The only recourse is to plead for a few final hours of relief from the hands of God, the Enemy (verses 18–22). ✳

REMEMBER HOW YOU MADE ME, GOD?

10 I am sickened of life;
    I will give free rein to my griefs,
    I will speak out in bitterness of soul.

² I will say to God, 'Do not condemn me,
    but tell me the ground of thy complaint against me.

³ Dost thou find any advantage in oppression,
    in spurning the fruit of all thy labour

and smiling on the policy of wicked men?
Hast thou eyes of flesh   4
or dost thou see as mortal man sees?
Are thy days as those of a mortal   5
or thy years as the life of a man,
that thou lookest for guilt in me   6
and dost seek in me for sin,
though thou knowest that I am guiltless   7
and have none to save me from thee?

'Thy hands gave me shape and made me;   8
and dost thou at once turn and destroy me?
Remember that thou didst knead me like clay;   9
and wouldst thou turn me back into dust?
Didst thou not pour me out like milk   10
and curdle me like cheese,
clothe me with skin and flesh   11
and knit me together with bones and sinews?
Thou hast given me life and continuing favour,   12
and thy providence has watched over my spirit.
Yet this was the secret purpose of thy heart,   13
and I know that this was thy intent:
that, if I sinned, thou wouldst be watching me   14
and wouldst not acquit me of my guilt.
If I indeed am wicked, the worse for me!   15
If I am righteous, even so I may lift up my head;[a]
if I am[b] proud as a lion, thou dost hunt me down   16
and dost confront me again with marvellous power;
thou dost renew thy onslaught upon me,   17
and with mounting anger against me

[a] *Prob. rdg.; Heb. adds* filled with shame and steeped in my affliction.
[b] *So Sept.; Heb.* if he is.

bringest fresh forces to the attack.

18 Why didst thou bring me out of the womb?
O that I had ended there and no eye had seen me,

19 that I had been carried from the womb to the grave
and were as though I had not been born.

20 Is not my life short and fleeting?
Let me be, that I may be happy for a moment,

21 before I depart to a land of gloom,
a land of deep darkness, never to return,

22 a land of gathering shadows, of deepening darkness,
lit by no ray of light,*a* dark*b* upon dark.'

✲ 1. Job's inner fury is so intense he can no longer suppress it
(cp. Jer. 20: 8–9).

2–3. The Hebrew word for 'good' can be translated *advantage* as here or 'enjoyment'. Either God is sadistic or he is self-indulgent; he oppresses victims like Job for his own self-satisfaction and not for any discernible noble purpose. *the fruit of all thy labour* refers to God's personal creation of a human being whom he is now rejecting as worthless.

4. Is God incomplete by being only God? Could he sympathize with Job better if he were human like Job?

5–6. Is God's life span also limited? Is his time so short that he must now concentrate his search for sin into the lifetime of one man?

7. Job is trapped by a sinister God. His motives must be base for he knows Job is innocent. And regardless of Job's vision of a mighty arbiter (9: 32–5), God knows that there is no 'deliverer' for Job (see notes on 5: 4, 19).

8–12. Job develops the motif of personal creation (from verse 3) by depicting the mysteries of human birth in the poetic language of ancient Near Eastern thought-patterns.

[a] lit...light: *or* a place of disorder.
[b] *Prob. rdg.; Heb. obscure.*

The purpose of his imaginative description, it would seem, is to help God re-live his initial rapture over creating this man and to stir again the original compassion of the Creator for this unique work.

8. The thought that God, who worked so intimately in the creation of Job, would destroy his own work of art should be revolting to God.

9. God is like a potter moulding human beings with select *clay* (cp. Gen. 2: 7; Jer. 18: 6). But is the only purpose of this delicate operation to return his special creations to the *dust* from which they came (cp. 4: 19; Gen. 3: 19)?

10–11. These verses offer an unusual poetic description of human conception and pre-natal growth as an intimate labour of God himself. Semen, poured *like milk* into the mother's womb, is wrapped in *flesh* and woven together by God into a human embryo (cp. Ps. 139: 13–16).

12. Prior to his debacle at the hands of God, Job had experienced a rich measure of divine *providence* and love. The Hebrew word *ḥesed*, rendered *continuing favour* here and 'devotion' in 6: 14, refers to a deep loyalty motivated by a selfless love that is not destroyed by disruptions in the relationship. It is this love which Job longs to revive by this nostalgic portrait of God's previous presence in Job's life.

13–14. While God was supposed to be 'watching' over Job with genuine providence and concern (verse 12), he was actually *watching* like a spy to discover a sin that would lead to Job's conviction and condemnation (see on 7: 7–8, 18–20). That was God's *secret* and sinister *purpose* from the beginning.

15*b*. The final phrase may be better rendered: 'I cannot lift up my head', and to this the clause which appears in N.E.B. footnote adds the explanation that Job has no chance of acquittal when God smothers him with shame and the appearance of guilt.

16–17. Job is like a wild animal subjected to the ugly exploits of an angry hunter from heaven. God appears inhuman and Job feels less than human (see on 6: 4).

18–19. Job returns to the dilemma of his opening lament
(3: 11–26). If God's purposes are indeed sinister and demonic
(as in verses 13–17), there is no meaning to life and no reason
to exist. Non-being is far more appealing than being.

20–2. Finally, Job pleads for mercy before his enemy. He
begs for a momentary reprieve from God's persistent persecution. After all, Job has but a few days to live before he must
travel to Sheol, the land of gloom, death and oblivion (cp.
on 7: 9–10). *

The First Discourse of Zophar

* Zophar, who seems to have less acumen and resources than
his two friends, is also much less sensitive to Job's dilemma.
After accusing Job of talking volumes of nonsense he tries to
summarize Job's entire position in two short sentences: 'My
doctrine is true! My life is clean!' (verses 2–4). Zophar accuses
Job of seeing only one side of the question. The other side is
hidden in the mysterious wisdom of God and lies far beyond
the grasp of limited human minds (verses 7–9). Is Job too big a
fool to realize that the invisible God can see all sin? Or is Job
as stupid as the wild ass of the old proverb (verses 10–12)?
Finally Zophar summons Job to repent of his wrongs and
thrust all evil from his life. The expected result is a spectacular
reversal of fortunes; Job will be renowned as a great wise man
once again (verses 13–20). *

THE WISDOM OF GOD IS UNSEARCHABLE

11 Then Zophar the Naamathite began:

2   Should this spate of words not be answered?
     Must a man of ready tongue be always right?
3   Is your endless talk to reduce men to silence?
     Are you to talk nonsense and no one rebuke you?
4   You claim that your opinions are sound;

you say to God, 'I am spotless in thy sight.'
But if only he would speak   5
and open his lips to talk with you,
and expound to you the secrets of wisdom,   6
for wonderful are its effects!
[Know then that God exacts from you less than your
     sin deserves.]
Can you fathom the mystery of God,   7
can you fathom the perfection of the Almighty?
It is higher than heaven;*a* you can do nothing.   8
It is deeper than Sheol; you can know nothing.
Its measure is longer than the earth   9
and broader than the sea.
If he passes by, he may keep secret his passing;   10
if he proclaims it, who can turn him back?
He surely knows which men are false,   11
and when he sees iniquity, does he not take note of it?*b*
Can a fool grow wise?   12
can a wild ass's foal be born a man?
If only you had directed your heart rightly   13
and spread out your hands to pray to him!
If you have wrongdoing in hand, thrust it away;   14
let no iniquity make its home with you.
Then you could hold up your head without fault,   15
a man of iron, knowing no fear.
Then you will forget your trouble;   16
you will remember it only as flood-waters that have
     passed;
life will be lasting, bright as noonday,   17

[*a*] It is...heaven: so *Vulg.; Heb.* The heights of heaven.
[*b*] does...of it?: *or* he does not stand aloof.

and darkness will be turned to morning.

18   You will be confident, because there is hope;

sure of protection, you will lie down in confidence;[a]

19   great men will seek your favour.

20   Blindness will fall on the wicked;

the ways of escape are closed to them,

and their hope is despair.

✻ 2–3. Zophar, who lacks the opening tact of his companions, begins with a sarcastic retort belittling Job's cries of agony as glib verbosity that must be exposed as such.

4. Zophar hears Job making two distinct claims: his teaching is true and his conduct blameless (cp. 9: 20–1). The words *to God* are an uncertain addition by the N.E.B. translators.

5. Zophar wishes God would speak and convict Job; Job longed for God to speak and end his endless misery (cp. 9: 3, 15).

6. *the secrets of wisdom* are the focus of Zophar's speech These 'secrets' are literally things hidden from human scrutiny (cp. 28: 11). Zophar rebukes Job for arguing from the obvious and not probing the deeper mystery of divine wisdom where the true answer to his suffering lies. The N.E.B. translation *for wonderful are its effects* is based on a conjectured reading. The original can be rendered 'there are two sides to effective discernment'. According to Zophar, Job has only considered the surface side of his problem; the reverse side reflecting God's mysterious ways must also be discerned.

6c. This comment, which seems to be inappropriate at this point, does not help Job to grasp the mystery of God. If it is original, it would merely reveal Zophar's insensitivity to Job's affliction; probably it is a later scribal comment.

7–9. *the mystery of God* refers to deep matters explored and probed by the wise (cp. 5: 9; 38: 16). Ultimately the full depth of God's wisdom cannot be fathomed; there is a limit to

[a] *Prob. rdg.; Heb. adds* and you will lie down unafraid.

man's understanding of God's mysteries. This idea is high-lighted if we translate the Hebrew for *perfection* by 'farthest limit' as in 28: 3. The extremities of God's mysterious wisdom are higher than the heavens where he dwells and deeper than Sheol where the dead disappear. His ways reach beyond the boundaries of the universe he created. In short, God is trans-cendent and man is limited. To comprehend the hidden side of God's wisdom is beyond human capabilities (cp. 28: 12–27; Prov. 30: 3–4).

10–11. Zophar modifies Job's earlier complaint about an angry and elusive God (from 9: 11–12) to illustrate his mys-terious movements as he executes his judgements. He knows the identity of all sinners even if Job's mind is too dull to discern them.

12. A very obscure verse, probably a proverb suggesting the impossibility of change in some creatures. Job, like the fool, will apparently never be able to understand his own guilt or the mysteries of God (cp. Prov. 14: 7–9).

13–14. Zophar assumes that Job is an impenitent sinner who could name his iniquities if he chose to do so. He therefore repeats the appeals of Eliphaz and Bildad (5: 8; 8: 5) for Job to clarify his thinking, amend his ways and humbly pray for mercy. Again Zophar exhibits a total lack of appreciation for Job's struggle with the problem of divine justice.

15–20. If Job repents he can expect a new and beautiful life free from fear. The *trouble* or 'oppression' he has experienced (see on 3: 10, 20) will soon be a mere memory. The darkness of death will be transformed into the light of life (see on 3: 4–5). Job's faith will return and his *hope* will revive (cp. 14: 7–9). He will again know the full life of a respectable and beloved wise man to whom people come for counsel (cp. 29: 7–10, 21–5). ✶

'' *Job's First Response to Zophar*

✳ Job's answer to Zophar seems to be a response to all three friends whose one-sided analysis of God's wisdom and justice was tantamount to lies and whose ugly insinuations about Job's mind and guilt were callous and unwarranted. Job's chief concern in the opening chapter of this response is to accent those destructive, arbitrary and illogical acts of the Creator in nature and life whereby the guardians of justice are crushed and the forces of chaos allowed to run rampant. Unfortunately, the memories of the aged wise recall only those traditions which support their favoured doctrines. But the animals know better. Human experience and the observation of nature verify the presence of catastrophes from God which reduce the ordered world and its communities to a shambles, irrespective of individual guilt or innocence (verses 7–12). In hymnic majesty Job enumerates these outrageous acts of God as the true signs of his mysterious wisdom and spectacular power. These are the violent mysteries of life he has let loose on a trusting world. Chaos is also a work of God (verses 13–25). ✳

ASK THE ANIMALS

12 Then Job answered:

2   No doubt you are perfect men[a]
and absolute wisdom is yours[b]!

3   But I have sense as well as you;
in nothing do I fall short of you;
what gifts indeed have you that others have not?

4   Yet I am a laughing-stock to my friend –
a laughing-stock, though I am innocent and blameless,
one that called upon God, and he answered.[c]

[a] *Prob. rdg.; Heb.* No doubt you are people.
[b] *So Aq. and Symm.; Heb.* and wisdom will die with you.
[c] *Or* and he afflicted me.

64

Prosperity and ease look down on misfortune,   5
on the blow that fells the man who is already reeling,
while the marauders' tents are left undisturbed   6
and those who provoke God live safe and sound.[a]

Go and ask the cattle,   7
ask the birds of the air to inform you,
or tell the creatures that crawl to teach you,   8
and the fishes of the sea to give you instruction.
Who cannot learn from all these   9
that the LORD's own hand has done this?
(Does not the ear test what is spoken   11[b]
as the palate savours food?
There is wisdom, remember, in age,   12
and long life brings understanding.)

In God's hand are the souls of all that live,   10
the spirits of all human kind.

✳ 2–3. Job's opening words are a biting response to Zophar's
sarcastic and insensitive comments. The heart, which is the
base of both emotional and mental activities in Hebrew
thought, is here rendered *sense*. Zophar contended that Job
was a fool whose 'heart' was confused, that is, he could not
think clearly (11: 12–13) or grasp both sides of a question
(11: 5–6). Job insists that he is as intelligent as these famous
wise men who call themselves his friends.

4–6. Job attempts to explain his dilemma to Zophar. Job
has not led a life of crime. He has always been *blameless* like
Noah (cp. Gen. 6: 9) and accustomed to hearing God's answer
when he summoned him in prayer. But now, for no apparent
reason, he has become an object of derision to his friends.

[a] *Prob. rdg.; Heb. adds* He brings it in full measure to whom he will
(*cp. 21: 17*).
[b] *Verse 10 transposed to follow verse 12.*

Meanwhile the wicked *live safe and sound*, untouched by God's wrath. God's capricious power is the terrifying mystery which Job intends to emphasize in this speech. The translation of verse 5 remains uncertain, as does that of 6c (see N.E.B. footnote).

7–8. Job's appeal to ask the animals for instruction in the way of wisdom is a serious but satirical response to Bildad's earlier call to ask the fathers (8: 8–10). The animals are as knowledgeable as the fathers in learning how to face the harsh facts of life before an arbitrary God. Wisdom teachers often turn to nature for lessons in wisdom (cp. Prov. 6: 6; 30: 15–33).

9. Animals know that catastrophes are the arbitrary work of God. The misfortunes they suffer are not the result of sins they have committed against God. *the LORD*: probably an error for 'God' (Eloah), see p. 9.

10. The N.E.B. editors have transposed verse 10 to follow verse 12. If kept as part of the thought-sequence of verses 7–9, this verse seems to introduce the claim that since all creatures, including human beings, are endowed with the spirit of the Almighty, they are capable of discerning these uncomfortable truths about God. Elihu makes a similar claim (32: 7–9).

11. Job quotes an old proverb to prove that truth can be learned through critical observation (cp. 34: 3). The verb *savours*, when used in its noun form, can mean mental discernment or judgement (as in verse 20).

12. In the light of verses 7–11, verse 12 is either to be taken as a sarcastic comment or framed as a question. Job is clearly repudiating the argument of Bildad that age is the true source of wisdom (8: 8–10; cp. 15: 9–10). In verses 8–12 Job challenges the very foundation of wisdom teaching that truth is revealed in the ancient past, tested and transmitted through the fathers. For Job experience is as authoritative as tradition. *

HYMN TO THE GOD OF CHAOS

Wisdom and might are his,   13
with him are firmness and understanding.

If he pulls down, there is no rebuilding;   14
if he imprisons, there is no release.

If he holds up the waters, there is drought;   15
if he lets them go, they turn the land upside down.

Strength and success belong to him,   16
deceived and deceiver are his to use.

He makes counsellors behave like idiots   17
and drives judges mad;

he looses the bonds imposed by kings   18
and removes the girdle of office from their waists;

he makes priests behave like idiots   19
and overthrows men long in office;

those who are trusted he strikes dumb,   20
he takes away the judgement of old men;

he heaps scorn on princes   21
and abates the arrogance of nobles.

He leads peoples astray and destroys them,   23 [a]
he lays them low, and there they lie.

He takes away their wisdom from the rulers of the   24
   nations
and leaves them wandering in a pathless wilderness;

they grope in the darkness without light   25
and are left to wander like a drunkard.

He uncovers mysteries deep in obscurity   22
and into thick darkness he brings light.

[a] *Verse 22 transposed to follow verse 25.*

✻ Job employs a hymnic form to portray the truth which, he claimed (in verses 7–12), was known to man and nature through observation and experience. That truth is the sovereignty of God evident in disruptive forces throughout the universe. In nature and society God discloses himself as the lord of chaos. His unpredictable destructive tendencies are the real mystery of his wisdom.

13. Eliphaz had shown how God used his power for good (5: 10–16) and Zophar had extolled the unfathomable mystery of God's wisdom (11: 5–9). Job now intends to expose the alien side of God's wisdom and power.

14–15. Chaos and drought themes are intertwined in these verses. To 'rebuild' means to re-create what has been reduced to chaos (cp. Jer. 1: 10). Much of the language of these verses is also found in the flood story (Gen. 6–8). When God *holds up the waters* above the heavens (cp. Deut. 11: 17), there can be *no release* of the rains; *drought* is inevitable. If God does open the skies, chaos waters overwhelm the earth as in the days of Noah. God is apparently a God of death and cosmic extremes.

16. *Strength and success* are parallel to the 'might and wisdom' of God hailed in verse 13. Job's negative interpretation of these divine attributes is made explicit by the complementary assertion that *deceived and deceiver* also belong to him, as if they were also his attributes or companions. In the mind of Job, the success of God is not achieved by a consistent application of true justice, but by using whatever forces he wills in whatever way he chooses. The N.E.B. words *to use* are not part of the Hebrew original.

17–19. God destroys the very foundations of justice and order in government, court and temple.

20. As well as challenging the adequacy of the aged fathers to teach wisdom (verses 7–12), Job argues that God actually removes their faculties of judgement (see on verses 7–8, 12).

23–5. God's destructive activities extend to whole nations and peoples. The expression *a pathless wilderness* is literally 'in chaos without a way'. God reduces nature and nations to 'chaos', a term used to describe the condition of the world before creation (Gen. 1: 2). The terror of this situation parallels that of Job himself (see on 3: 23). God provides no 'way' whereby those enveloped in chaos can find hope or direction; they are smothered by primeval darkness.

22. Job contradicts Zophar (11: 6–9) by maintaining that these chaotic deeds are the ugly mysteries which God makes known to men. *

Job's First Response to Zophar (continued)

* Job is now ready to argue his case with God and end the pointless dialogue about God with his friends. Before he begins, however, Job unleashes a lengthy tirade against his companions, chiding them for trying to defend God with obvious lies. Soon the tables will be turned, he predicts, and their devious arguments will appear ludicrous as they stand trial before this same God (verses 4–12). With fierce courage Job announces his readiness to defend his own integrity, even if it kills him. He insists that if he could face God in court he would be vindicated completely because no one would be able to withstand or silence his forceful testimony (verses 13–19). He then sets down two conditions which would make it possible for him to confront God in court: that God would withhold his terror and that he would remove his oppressive hand. But God does not answer. Job attempts to begin the trial anyway by soliciting the specific charges against him. Again there is no answer and Job breaks into a fresh lament accusing God of ruthless acts of violence. Job has become an enemy, a condemned criminal and a marked slave for God to track down at will (verses 20–7). *

I AM READY TO ARGUE MY CASE

13   All this I have seen with my own eyes,
       with my own ears I have heard it, and understood it.

2   What you know, I also know;
       in nothing do I fall short of you.

3   But for my part I would speak with the Almighty
       and am ready to argue with God,

4   while you like fools are smearing truth with your falsehoods,
       stitching a patchwork of lies, one and all.

5   Ah, if you would only be silent
       and let silence be your wisdom!

6   Now listen to my arguments
       and attend while I put my case.

7   Is it on God's behalf that you speak so wickedly,
       or in his defence that you allege what is false?

8   Must you take God's part,
       or put his case for him?

9   Will all be well when he examines you?
       Will you quibble with him as you quibble with a man?

10   He will most surely expose you
       if you take his part by falsely accusing me.

11   Will not God's majesty strike you with dread,
       and terror of him overwhelm you?

12   Your pompous talk is dust and ashes,
       your defences will crumble like clay.[a]

13   Be silent, leave me to speak my mind,
       and let what may come upon me!

14   I will[b] put my neck in the noose[c]

[a] your defences. . .clay: *lit.* the bosses of your shields are bosses of clay.
[b] *So Sept.; Heb.* Why shall I. . .   [c] *Lit.* take my flesh in my teeth.

and take my life in my hands.
If he would slay me, I should not hesitate;   15
I should still argue my cause to his face.
This at least assures my success,   16
that no godless man may appear before him.
Listen then, listen to my words,   17
and give a hearing to my exposition.
Be sure of this: once I have stated my case   18
I know that I shall be acquitted.
Who is there that can argue so forcibly with me   19
that he could reduce me straightway to silence and death?

Grant me these two conditions only,   20
and then I will not hide myself out of thy sight:
take thy heavy hand clean away from me   21
and let not the fear of thee strike me with dread.
Then summon me, and I will answer;   22
or I will speak first, and do thou answer me.
How many iniquities and sins are laid to my charge?   23
let me know my offences and my sin.
Why dost thou hide thy face   24
and treat me as thy enemy?
Wilt thou chase a driven leaf,   25
wilt thou pursue dry chaff,
prescribing punishment[a] for me   26
and making me heir to the iniquities of my youth,
putting my feet in the stocks[b]   27
and setting a slave-mark on the arches of my feet?[c]

[a] *So Pesh.; Heb.* bitter things.
[b] *Prob. rdg.; Heb. adds* keeping a close watch on all I do.
[c] *Prob. rdg.; Heb. adds verse 28,* he is like...have eaten, *now transposed to follow 14: 2.*

✻ 1–2. Job claims to have observed the destructive works of God depicted in the preceding chapter. Job's acumen is no less than that of Eliphaz who makes a counter claim (5: 3, 27).

3. In the last analysis Job is not interested in a dialogue about God with his friends. He wants a direct encounter with God so that he can *argue* his case against the Almighty. The friends only argue about God; they never wrestle with God as Job is doing.

4–5. Job accuses his friends of being hypocrites whose pious teachings are lies that neither illuminate nor heal. (The second part of verse 4 may be understood to refer to 'useless doctors', 'quacks'.) Their complete silence would demonstrate more wisdom than anything they have said to date.

6–12. Job addresses his friends with a series of rhetorical questions and comments couched in court language. Does God need the help of your falsehoods to defend his actions? Will you presume to argue his case for him in court? Will you use the same lies when he examines you? Your secret conniving against me will be exposed. Or are you never afraid of his terror and dread? Before his awesome majesty *your defences will crumble like clay* and your position will be denounced. In the Epilogue Job's predictions are confirmed (42: 7). Verse 12 can be rendered 'your cherished arguments are but proverbs of ashes, your answers are but dusty answers', a pointed rebuke for wisdom teachers.

13–15. In contrast to his friends, Job plans to speak the truth regardless of the consequences. He has nothing to lose and refuses to be intimidated by the terror of God (cp. verse 21). Even under the threat of execution, Job will argue his *cause*, that is, the 'way' which he has followed with integrity and devotion throughout his life (on 'way' see at 3: 23).

16. The Hebrew for the word *success* is often translated 'salvation' or 'deliverance' (as in Isa. 12: 3). Job boasts to his friends that his bold innocence is still his guarantee of being vindicated or 'saved', even though he had previously ruled out the possibility of a fair trial before a fickle judge like God (ch. 9).

17–19. Job has a sudden surge of new confidence. He contends that if he can finally bring his case to court God will acquit him. The insurmountable difficulty of ever compelling God to appear in court is momentarily ignored (cp. 9: 16–19). With a final display of bravado Job declares that no amount of evidence or arguments could be produced to silence or crush him. God alone, it seems, can silence Job (40: 4–5).

20–1. Job now requests God to establish the conditions upon which it would be possible for Job to appear before God in court. Earlier Job had envisaged an arbiter with sufficient authority to restrain God's overwhelming terror and remove the rod of oppression from Job's back (9: 34). Without an arbiter to guarantee a fair trial, God himself would have to honour Job's requests by withdrawing his terror and his heavy hand voluntarily. The 'terror' or *dread* of God is a mysterious force emanating from God which renders helpless all with whom it comes in contact (cp. Exod. 23: 27; Josh. 2: 9). The *heavy hand* of God refers to those unjustified sufferings of Job which prevent him from speaking freely.

22. If these conditions are met Job is willing to be defendant (*22a*) or plaintiff (*22b*).

23. With no directives from God, Job opens his case with a public appeal for anyone to specify his sins and to bring formal charges against him. Later Eliphaz attempts to do so (22: 5–9). Job, however, is really flinging this challenge into the face of God to goad him into action.

24. When God does not respond, Job's anger returns. He had only just set up the conditions upon which he would no longer hide and harbour hostility against God (verse 20). Now God is hiding and treating Job as if he were an *enemy* to be ambushed rather than a plaintiff to be faced in court.

25. God's brutality extends to the tormenting of the helpless and insignificant, like Job.

26. Job is condemned before the trial begins; his punishment has been prescribed in advance. No justice is now possible.

27. Job is treated like a criminal and a slave. His feet are placed in *stocks* or 'fetters' so that his path can be followed easily as he drags his burden with him. Job's mark of slavery (cp. Isa. 44: 5) is engraved into the soles of his feet so that every step he takes can be traced. On the motif of Job as slave and God as slavemaster see the comments on ch. 7.

28. This verse is transposed to follow 14: 2 where its theme belongs. ✻

Job's Soliloquy on Mortality

✻ In this soliloquy (ch. 14) Job makes no effort to answer any charges or points made by the three friends. He focuses on the mortality of man by developing two axioms about man similar to those which appear earlier (in 4: 17; 5: 1; 7: 1, 17). The first of these accents the brevity and turmoil of mortal life (verse 1) and the second contemplates the awful finality of human death (verse 10). Analogies from nature are drawn to highlight both of these truths (verses 2, 11, 18–19). Man, unlike the tree, has no real hope, no inner capacity to endure and overcome his mortality and return to life (verses 7–12). The first axiom, according to Job, should motivate God to show mercy and allow his harassed servants to enjoy their brief life. But God remains a tyrannical taskmaster (verses 3–6). The second axiom provokes Job to contemplate Sheol as a land of refuge instead of death, a land from which he could return when God's anger had subsided. But God remains a relentless pursuer (verses 13–17). In the last analysis he is also the God of death and mortal man can never escape his hand (verses 20–2). ✻

LIFE IS BUT A PRELUDE TO DEATH

14 Man born of woman is short-lived and full of disquiet.
2   He blossoms like a flower and then he withers;
     he slips away like a shadow and does not stay;

[a]he is like a wine-skin that perishes
or a garment that moths have eaten.
Dost thou fix thine eyes on such a creature,   3
and wilt thou bring him into court to confront thee?[b]
The days of his life are determined,   5
and the number of his months is known to thee;
thou hast laid down a limit, which he cannot pass.
Look away from him therefore and leave him alone[c]   6
counting the hours day by day like a hired labourer.

If a tree is cut down,   7
there is hope that it will sprout again
and fresh shoots will not fail.
Though its roots grow old in the earth,   8
and its stump is dying in the ground,
if it scents water it may break into bud   9
and make new growth like a young plant.
But a man dies, and he disappears;[d]   10
man comes to his end, and where is he?
As the waters of a lake dwindle,   11
or as a river shrinks and runs dry,
so mortal man lies down, never to rise   12
until the very sky splits open.
If a man dies, can he live again?[e]
He shall never be roused from his sleep.
If only thou wouldst hide me in Sheol   13
and conceal me till thy anger turns aside,

[a] he is like...have eaten: *13: 28 transposed here.*
[b] *So one Heb. MS.; others add* (4) Who can produce pure out of
unclean? No one.
[c] and leave him alone: *so one MS.; others* that he may cease.
[d] *Or* and is powerless.
[e] *Line transposed from beginning of verse 14.*

if thou wouldst fix a limit for my time there, and then
  remember me!

14   *a*Then I would not lose hope, however long my service,
      waiting for my relief to come.

15   Thou wouldst summon me, and I would answer thee;
      thou wouldst long to see the creature thou hast made.

16   But now thou dost count every step I take,
      watching all my course.

17   Every offence of mine is stored in thy bag;
      thou dost keep my iniquity under seal.

18   Yet as a falling mountain-side is swept away,
      and a rock is dislodged from its place,

19   as water wears away stones,
      and a rain-storm scours the soil from the land,
      so thou hast wiped out the hope of frail man;

20   thou dost overpower him finally, and he is gone;
      his face is changed, and he is banished from thy sight.

22*b* His flesh upon him becomes black,
      and his life-blood dries up within him.*c*

21   His sons rise to honour, and he sees nothing of it;
      they sink into obscurity, and he knows it not.

✻ 1. *Man* is identical with the name Adam, and therefore
representative of all mankind from the beginning. The brevity
of human life is a common concern of Job, especially when it is
associated with intense *disquiet* (cp. 7: 4; 10: 20). The Hebrew
term for *disquiet* is rendered 'torment' in 3: 26 where it concludes and summarizes the inner torture of a man cursing
his abortive life before God. Human beings are born to be

[*a*] *See note on verse 12.*
[*b*] *Verses 21 and 22 transposed.*
[*c*] His flesh...within him: *or* His own kin, maybe, regret him, and his
slaves mourn his loss.

tortured by the terrifying reality of their impending death. Their own mortality haunts them.

2. Man's life is as transient as *a flower*, *a shadow*, *a wine-skin* or a robe. 13: 28 has been transposed to follow verse 2.

3. God the Watchman spies on man to uncover sufficient evidence to convict him in court (cp. 7: 7, 17–20).

5–6. Why should man be badgered by God when he knows the brevity and limit of human life? Job has used this argument several times to plead for divine compassion (7: 7, 19; 10: 18–20). *hired labourer* reiterates the theme of man living as an oppressed servant of God (see on 7: 2).

7–9. The human life-span is fixed and brief with no future beyond the grave. A tree, however, has *hope*, that is, the inner resources for a new beginning beyond disaster or death. A stump may 'die in the dust', but it can rise again at the scent of life-giving water. This condition suggests an underlying in-justice in the divine ordering of creation. Why should a tree have greater hope than man? On *hope* see also 4: 6; 5: 16; 11: 18.

10. This axiom emphasizes the finality of human death. Once dead, man lacks the resources to revive himself, or, as the rendering of the N.E.B. footnote indicates, 'he is powerless'. Human beings live with the spectre of their own future help-lessness hanging over their lives.

11. Man's life ebbs away like *a lake* or stream that *runs dry*.

12. Job's view of death is consistent with that of ancient Israel. In spite of Near Eastern myths which suggest a con-trary view, Israel rejected the idea of a human resurrection from the dead until well after the time of Job (cp. Ps. 41: 8; Eccles. 3: 19–20). At that time the expressions rendered *rise*, *live*, and *roused* became technical terms for resurrection from the dead (Isa. 26: 19; Dan. 12: 2).

13. Although Job acknowledges death as the terminal point of all human existence, he gropes for the impossible to relieve his present plight (compare the note on 9: 32–5). He dreams of *Sheol* as a pleasant asylum from God's fury rather than a

land of death, darkness and oblivion (cp. 7: 9–10). At the
appointed time, when God's rage had subsided, Job could see
himself returning to earth for a fair trial. Job's idea was born
out of his deep frustration over the inequity of his situation.
His idea anticipates, in part, the later belief that a resurrection
was necessary to vindicate innocent martyrs and convict
blatant persecutors at a judgement after death (Dan. 12: 2;
2 Macc. 7: 9).

14–17. Job feels that he could tolerate his oppressive *service*
as God's labourer (cp. on 7: 1), if he had this *hope* to strengthen
him. Eventually God's compassion for his personal creation
would return (cp. on 10: 3, 8–12), and Job would then be
willing to appear before God in court. God, however, will
grant Job no such privilege. As a vigilant watchman and a
meticulous scribe, God observes and records every false step
of his enemy (cp. verse 3; 13: 26–7).

18–19. After this interlude of wishful thinking (in verses
13–17), Job returns to the harsh reality of man's inevitable lot.
A tree may have limited *hope*, but in the end even mountains
and *stones* are eroded by the elements sent from heaven. Simi-
larly, it is God who also erases the 'hope' of mortal man (cp.
on verses 6–9). God keeps forcing man to face his mortality.

20–2. Job closes his soliloquy with a portrait of the God of
death who transforms his victims into grotesque creatures
racked with pain and oblivious to any future happenings that
might ease their pathetic condition. Misery and mortality are
strange works of God.   ✳

Second cycle of speeches

The Second Discourse of Eliphaz

✶ The tone of Eliphaz' second disputation is harsher than his first and coloured with overtones of righteous anger. Job's speeches have threatened the very heart of traditional wisdom teachings; he is tantamount to a heretic. In response Eliphaz argues on the basis of several themes ranging from the nature of the original wise man to the inner character of the truly wicked man. With bitter sarcasm Eliphaz compares Job with a perfect first man who claims to have a monopoly on wisdom by virtue of his privileged position in the heavenly council. But if, as Eliphaz has previously argued, the members of that celestial court are not trustworthy, Job can hardly claim to be superior to any other human being. In reality he is nothing short of a presumptuous fool. Instead of encouraging Job to reassess his position, Eliphaz gleefully analyses the internal feelings and ultimate fate of the wicked man. In so doing he brands Job rather than edifying him. The supposition that the wicked who prosper live in constant anxiety is perhaps to be regarded as a piece of wishful thinking on the part of the pious. The problem is deeper than Eliphaz perceives. ✶

JOB, THE IRRELIGIOUS FOOL

Then Eliphaz the Temanite answered: **15**

Would a man of sense give vent to such foolish notions 2
and answer with a bellyful of wind?
Would he bandy useless words 3
and arguments so unprofitable?
Why! you even banish the fear of God from your 4
mind,
usurping the sole right to speak in his presence;

5   your iniquity dictates what you say,
     and deceit is the language of your choice.
6   You are condemned out of your own mouth, not by
        me;
     your own lips give evidence against you.

※ 2–6. Eliphaz began his first discourse with a sarcastic analysis of Job's dilemma implying that his prior faith as a wise man was a sham (4: 2–6). Now Eliphaz goes a step further in trying to discredit Job's position by bluntly accusing him of being an irreligious fool. Everything that Job has said, according to Eliphaz, is a repudiation of the accepted conduct and religious principles of a true wise man.

2. *man of sense* renders the Hebrew for 'wise man'. Instead of Job debating with the cool logic of a wise man his words are nothing but 'hot air'.

3. *bandy* reflects the sarcastic connotation which Eliphaz seems to give to the normal Hebrew word 'instruct'. Job's 'instruction' in wisdom is but a futile game for fools.

4. The *fear of God* is the beginning of wisdom according to the proponents of wisdom theology (Job 28: 28; Prov. 1: 7). It is precisely this religious attitude which according to Eliphaz' opening speech should have been Job's source of strength (see on 4: 6). Now Eliphaz accuses Job of abandoning the very cornerstone of popular wisdom theology by approaching God without any sense of devotion or piety.

5–6. Job is a public sinner and his speeches are the incontrovertible evidence. They are proof that Job is motivated by *iniquity* and *deceit*. From his own mouth he is *condemned*, that is, the verdict 'wicked' rests on his head and he lies outside the pale of the religious community.   ※

JOB, THE ORIGINAL MAN

Were you born first of mankind?   7
were you brought forth before the hills?
Do you listen in God's secret council   8
or usurp all wisdom for yourself alone?
What do you know that we do not know?
What insight have you that we do not share?   9
We have age and white hairs in our company,   10
men older than your father.
Does not the consolation of God suffice you,   11
a word whispered quietly in your ear?
What makes you so bold at heart,   12
and why do your eyes flash,
that you vent your anger on God   13
and pour out such a torrent of words?
What is frail man that he should be innocent,   14
or any child of woman that he should be justified?
If God puts no trust in his holy ones,   15
and the heavens are not innocent in his sight,
how much less so is man, who is loathsome and rotten   16
and laps up evil like water!

☆ 7. *mankind* renders the Hebrew *'ādām* which can mean
'man', 'mankind' or Adam. This reference to *first* man makes
it clear that Job is being compared to some kind of Adam-
figure *born* before the creation of the world was completed.
Wisdom, too, is said to be 'born...long before the hills'
(Prov. 8: 25). *brought forth* translates a Hebrew verb which
implies the labour pains of birth. Primordial birth rather than
the act of creation out of dust or chaos is reflected in the
language of this passage. Man, born of God, is apparently
superior to man 'born of woman' (15: 14) and capable of

appropriating primordial wisdom directly rather than attempting to steal it like Adam and Eve in the garden (Gen. 3).

8. The *secret council* refers to the council of divine beings present at creation (38: 7). That council is the celestial arena where divine decisions are made about the destiny of earth and its inhabitants (cp. 1: 6–12). Some prophets claimed to have attended heavenly council sessions when decisions were made about Israel (Jer. 23: 18, 23). *wisdom* was apparently accessible prior to creation when she dwelt alone with God (Prov. 8: 22–31). Traditions about a wise first man dwelling on the primordial cosmic mountain lie behind Ezekiel's taunt of the king of Tyre (Ezek. 28: 12–19). Some wisdom theologians of Israel insisted that true wisdom was inaccessible to ordinary man (Job 28). Only if Job were the original man could he sit in the divine council, possess true wisdom and thus be superior to wise men like his friends.

9–10. Job's prior arguments challenging the traditional teachings of wisdom theology seem to presuppose that he had secret knowledge or revelations which the friends did not enjoy. *age and white hairs* mean that the wise men of Job's community were not only older than he, but also wiser.

11–16. Eliphaz returns to the argument about man he propounded in 4: 17–21. This argument serves as a corrective to the preceding comment which posed the possibility of man being wise and the heavenly council being the reservoir of wisdom. The *holy ones* of the celestial assembly are not to be trusted, while man as man is nothing but a loathsome creature with an avid thirst for evil. Eliphaz introduces his argument by chiding Job for not relying on the consolation of God to resolve his problems.

11. *the consolation of God* refers to the message of divine compassion and goodness which may be *quietly* or 'gently' offered. The consolations of Eliphaz had been far from gentle, especially in the face of Job's fierce refusal to affirm the compassion of God in his peculiar crisis.

12–13. Instead of meekly accepting words of comfort Job explodes with rage against God. For Eliphaz such an approach is intolerable.

14. Before God, man as creature is unclean and un-righteous (see on 4: 17). *child of woman* renders 'born of a woman' (as in 14: 1), a designation for man which may stand in contrast to the previous portrait of the first man as 'born' in some unique way (verse 7).

15. *holy ones* is an alternative name for divine beings. If the heavenly beings are not *innocent*, how much less an earthly creature like man.

16. Here Eliphaz goes beyond 4: 17–21 by emphasizing the disgusting nature of man and his propensity for drinking *evil like water*. *loathsome* reproduces a verb which is often used to depict how abominable certain idolatrous practices are in the sight of God (cp. Deut. 7: 26). Job is as revolting as an idolater in the sight of Eliphaz. ✳

THE AGONY AND FATE OF THE WICKED MAN

I will tell you, if only you will listen,   17
and I will describe what I have seen
[what has been handed down by wise men   18
and was not concealed from them by their fathers;
to them alone the land was given,   19
and no foreigner settled among them]:
the wicked are racked with anxiety all their days,   20
the ruthless man for all the years in store for him.
The noise of the hunter's scare rings in his ears,   21
and in time of peace the raider falls on him;
he cannot hope to escape from dark death;   22
he is marked down for the sword;
he is flung out as food for vultures;   23
such a man knows that his destruction is certain.

24   Suddenly a black day comes upon him,
        distress and anxiety overwhelm him
        [like a king ready for battle];

25   for he has lifted his hand against God
        and is pitting himself against the Almighty,

26   charging him head down,
        with the full weight of his bossed shield.

27   Heavy though his jowl is and gross,
        and though his sides bulge with fat,

28   the city where he lives will lie in ruins,
        his house will be deserted;
        it will soon become a heap of rubble.

29   He will no longer be rich, his wealth will not last,
        and he will strike no root*a* in the earth;*b*

30   scorching heat will shrivel his shoots,
        and his blossom*c* will be shaken off by the wind.

31   He deceives himself, trusting in his high rank,
        for all his dealings will come to nothing.

32   His palm-trees*d* will wither*e* unseasonably,
        and his branches will not spread;

33   he will be like a vine that sheds its unripe grapes,
        like an olive-tree that drops its blossom.

34   For the godless, one and all, are barren,
        and their homes, enriched by bribery, are destroyed by
            fire;

35   they conceive mischief and give birth to trouble,
        and the child of their womb is deceit.

[a] root: *prob. rdg., cp. Vulg.; Heb. unintelligible.*
[b] *Prob. rdg.; Heb. adds* he will not escape from darkness.
[c] *So Sept.; Heb.* mouth.
[d] His palm-trees: *prob. rdg., cp. Sept.; Heb. om.*
[e] *So Sept.; Heb.* will be filled.

✻ The section 15: 17–35 is a lengthy characterization of the wicked, the first portion of which focuses primarily on their inner anguish (verses 20–6), while the second emphasizes their ultimate fate (verses 27–35). Verse 20 appears to be an axiom about the wicked man which Eliphaz derives from wisdom tradition and which he himself confirms from personal experience. He contends that the wicked man has a deep and agonizing consciousness of his evil character and imminent fate. He lives in constant terror of death; he is acutely aware of his headlong onslaught on God. The wicked man's disaster is inevitable and he knows it (cp. Ps. 73: 18–20).

18–19. These verses may be taken as genuine. The teaching which follows is not merely the opinion of Eliphaz. He has the backing of the *fathers*, that is, the revered teachers of past wisdom tradition (cp. on 8: 8–10). That tradition, moreover, is the unadulterated wisdom of the local community, that has been kept free from alien philosophies.

20. This axiom about the *wicked* man emphasizes the internal turmoil he suffers throughout his life. Job's agony, therefore, can be interpreted as the pangs of a guilty conscience as much as physical discomfort. *all the years* can be better translated 'the few years' *in store for him*. Job, however, insists that the wicked enjoy a long life (21: 7).

21–3. Because he is so racked with fear the sound of the hunt is an omen in his ears and the *dark* a foreboding of his death. *vultures* await his imminent end.

24. The *black day* of death which the wicked man has always feared finally overtakes him and the *anxiety* with which he has lived overwhelms him. The final clause may be original and underlines the theme of death ready to attack.

25–6. The ground for the doom of the wicked man is his high-handed revolt against God. The image is that of a warrior in full battle array assaulting his enemy. The implied conclusion is that Job, by virtue of his frontal attacks on God, deserves the fate he is experiencing.

27. Obesity is employed as a metaphor for the prosperity typical of those with a rebellious spirit (cp. Deut. 32: 15).

29. An alternative rendering of 29*b* is 'his possessions will not extend into the underworld'. The intent of the verse is that no matter how many goods the wicked man annexes he 'cannot take them with him'. The words placed in the N.E.B. footnote as an addition may then be seen as linked to this theme; the wicked man cannot escape that 'darkness' of death which he has feared throughout his life (cp. verses 22 and 24).

30. The image of man as a plant or tree is common in wisdom literature (cp. 14: 2; Ps. 1: 3). The theme is continued in verses 32–3.

31. This verse not only breaks the sequence of images about the wicked man as a plant that dies prematurely, but also presents several translation difficulties. The key word for *nothing* or 'vanity' appears twice in the original, the first instance of which the N.E.B. emends to *high rank*. The idea of this verse is that those who trust in something worthless become worthless.

34. *the godless, one and all* is literally 'the assembly of ungodly', an idiom which stands in contrast to the divine 'council' of verse 8. Even as an organized gang the godless are impotent; their homes will be consumed *by fire*. Fire is regularly a symbol of direct divine intervention (1: 16; 20: 26). The 'fire of God' which struck Job's property would naturally be interpreted by his friends as a plain sign of God's wrath on a wicked man.

35. Eliphaz introduced this theme in 4: 8–9. *trouble* means painful misfortune and grievous toil. In spite of the fact that man is born to suffer oppressive trouble (5: 7), the abnormal suffering of the wicked is due to his evil schemes and machinations. Thus 'man born to trouble' may also *conceive* and *give birth to trouble*. Job begins his next speech by accusing his friends of being the 'trouble makers'. ✳

Job's Second Response to Eliphaz

✵ Job's passion and fury give rise to another fervent lament over the bitterness of his life. He rails on his friends as oppressive comforters who have neither the compassion nor the intellect to understand his condition. They are false witnesses who lie blatantly and intensify his bitterness. Job feels himself the object of an irrational mockery and persecution at the hands of God and his vicious cohorts. Job is all but dead, his life an endless ritual of mourning. The only possible escape from this living hell is a friend or witness of a different kind, an anonymous heavenly being who can sympathize with Job and testify boldly to his innocence. Job dreams of an unusual situation in which this heroic mediator would defend Job against God before the council of heaven. But Job's hopes die with Job; no witness arises to force the council into session. ✵

PERSECUTED BY MAN AND GOD ALIKE

Then Job answered: **16**

I have heard such things often before, 2
you who make trouble, all of you, with every breath,
saying, 'Will this windbag never have done? 3
What makes him so stubborn in argument?'
If you and I were to change places, 4
I could talk like you;
how I could harangue you
and wag my head at you!
But no, I would speak words of encouragement, 5
and then my condolences would flow in streams.
If I speak, my pain is not eased; 6
if I am silent, it does not leave me.

7   Meanwhile, my friend wearies me with false sympathy;
8   they tear me to pieces,*a* he and his*b* fellows.
     He has come forward to give evidence against me;
     the liar*c* testifies against me to my face,
9   in his wrath he wears me down, his hatred is plain to
        see;
     he grinds his teeth at me.

     My enemies look daggers at me,
10   they bare their teeth to rend me,*d*
     they slash my cheeks with knives;
     they are all in league against me.
11   God has left me at the mercy of malefactors
     and cast me into the clutches of wicked men.
12   I was at ease, but he set upon me and mauled me,
     seized me by the neck and worried me.
     He set me up as his target;
13   his arrows rained upon me from every side;
     pitiless, he cut deep into my vitals,
     he spilt my gall on the ground.
14   He made breach after breach in my defences;
     he fell upon me like a fighting man.

✻ 2–6. Job begins his response to Eliphaz with a biting indictment of his friends as ludicrous opponents without the brains
or the heart to help.

2*b* may be rendered 'you are all oppressive comforters'.
Instead of sympathizing with Job as genuine friends (see on
2: 11; 6: 14), these three companions only add to Job's
oppression or *trouble* (see on 3: 10; 4: 8).

[a] So some MSS.; others they seize me.
[b] Prob. rdg.; Heb. my.
[c] So Vulg.; Heb. my falsehood.
[d] Lit. they open their mouth at me.

4. Job claims that if he changed places with his friends he could 'bewitch them with words'. But words are worthless when a man is being tortured.

5–6. Out of his own experience of human suffering Job claims to know the appropriate expressions of sympathy to ease the burden of others. But his own agony is so fierce and so unwarranted that no words or silence can offer him solace. Eliphaz had glibly proposed 'divine consolations' as adequate balm for Job's inner wounds (15: 11).

7–8. The consolations of God and man are futile when the sufferer is being persecuted as ferociously as Job. The text of verses 7–8 remains uncertain, but the central idea seems to be that of a false 'witness' who crushes Job's morale and injures his case with repeated lies. This untrustworthy witness has his counterpart in the reliable heavenly witness whom Job expects to arise on his behalf (verse 19).

9*a–b*. The imagery shifts to that of a wild beast rending its prey and gnashing its teeth. Such is the character of the witness against Job. The word for *wears down* can also be rendered 'tears down'.

9*c–10*. Job's enemies are experts in the ugly art of calumny and derision. The word for *knives* can also be translated 'insults'.

11. God, who was once Job's protector (10: 12), has surrendered him to evil men for their sport. Job's persecution is not due to the tolerance of a disinterested deity, but is the direct result of his personal intervention against Job, who knows nothing of Satan as any mediating agent of doom (as in 1: 12).

12–14. These verses develop the theme of God the heavenly hunter (see on 6: 4; 7: 20). God is a *fighting man* or 'mighty hero' (like Nimrod, the mighty hunter, cp. Gen. 10: 9), who has surrounded his prey with sufficient forces to maintain a perpetual onslaught of abuses. Job is mauled and mangled by a violent warrior-God and set up as a *target* for his celestial archers (cp. Lam. 3: 12–13). Job's passion history is one of mockery, injustice, violence and despair. Unlike Jesus Christ (cp. Mark 15: 4f.), Job refuses to remain silent. He wants to expose God for what he is and to make him see himself as Job does. God is the ultimate enemy. ✳

BEFRIENDED BY AN UNKNOWN WITNESS

15 I stitched sackcloth together to cover my body
and I buried my forelock in the dust;

16 my cheeks were flushed with weeping
and dark shadows were round my eyes,

17 yet my hands were free from violence
and my prayer was sincere.

18 O earth, cover not my blood
and let my cry for justice find no rest!

19 For look! my witness is in heaven;
there is one on high ready to answer for me.

20 My appeal will come*a* before God,
while my eyes turn again and again to him.

21 If only there were one to arbitrate between man and God,
as between a man and his neighbour!

22 For there are but few years to come
before I take the road from which I shall not return.

✳ 15–16. Job is like a man performing fitting rites in memory of his own pathetic life. He has been humiliated to the point of being one with *the dust*, with death itself. He is nothing.

17. Job insists that his barrage of accusations against God is honest and true. He may have called God a ferocious hunter or an unfeeling slavedriver, but his prayer was pure. God is the violent one, not Job. *violence* refers to destructive evil

[a] My ... come: *so Sept.; Heb.* My intercessors are my friends.

forces that may result in chaos (cp. Gen. 6: 11, 13). Job, like the suffering servant, claims to have no history of violence (cp. Isa. 53: 9). He is innocent and God knows it (10: 7).

18. Job's annihilation by God is nothing short of murder. Job therefore adjures the earth to keep his blood uncovered and free to scream. The blood of a murdered individual was thought to have the power to cry to heaven for vengeance (Gen. 4: 10; Ezek. 24: 8). Job wants his blood to plead for justice to God, his accuser and murderer.

19. Here Job offers another of his unrealistic dreams (cp. on 9: 33–5; 14: 13) in which he announces a heavenly witness who can testify to Job's innocence before the heavenly council. Presumably this witness is a member of that council and could plead for Job in much the same way that Satan had prosecuted the case against Job (1: 6–12; cp. Zech. 3: 1–5). Job's dilemma is compounded by the fact that he sees God as his accuser and his judge. God, then, cannot be Job's 'witness' or 'arbiter' as some scholars contend.

20. This verse can be rendered, 'my interpreter, my friend before God when my eye is weeping'. Job describes this heavenly witness as his one true friend (cp. 6: 14), someone who can interpret his sufferings to God with genuine sympathy and force a just decision. The same expression for 'interpreter' appears in Gen. 42: 23 and in Job 33: 23 where it is translated 'mediator'.

21. The role of the 'witness' is similar to that of the arbiter in Job's earlier hope (9: 33). Job saw that figure as a powerful being capable of forcing God into court to process Job's case. The authority of this new heavenly mediator apparently lies in his honest testimony to the truth of what happened. Armed with this evidence he could take up the cudgels for a disenfranchised human being like Job.

22. Job wishes his acquittal would come soon since his life is so short and no judgement is possible after death. But all of Job's hopes for a mediator before God are futile (cp. 10: 7). No one actually arises to defend him.   *

Job's Second Response to Eliphaz (continued)

✻ Job continues his lament over the sickening and scandalous nature of his existence. In this complaint he reflects a heightened consciousness of the presence and potential of death in his life. But death is no longer liberation; the grave offers no opportunity for redress or vindication. Life in the underworld is as devoid of hope as life on earth. Yet Job's hope persists; he explores every possible avenue that might lead to an honest consideration of his case before God. He is even willing to appeal to the justice of God and ask his heavenly accuser also to be his 'pledge' and guarantor. In the end he finds no one to defend him; there is no righteous or wise man who is even disturbed by the gross injustice Job has suffered. ✻

BOTH LIFE AND DEATH ARE HOPELESS

17 My mind is distraught, my days are numbered,
and the grave is waiting for me.

2 Wherever I turn, men taunt me,
and my day is darkened[a] by their sneers.

3 Be thou my surety with thyself,
for who else can pledge himself for me?

4 Thou wilt not let those men triumph,
whose minds thou hast sunk in ignorance;

5 if such a man denounces his friends to their ruin,
his sons' eyes shall grow dim.

6 I am held up as a byword in every land,
a portent for all to see;

7 my eyes are dim with grief,
my limbs wasted to a shadow.

8 Honest men are bewildered at this,

[a] my ... darkened: *lit.* my eyes are weary.

and the innocent are indignant at my plight.
In spite of all, the righteous man maintains his course,   9
and he whose hands are clean grows strong again.

But come on, one and all, try again!   10
I shall not find a wise man among you.

My days die away like an echo;   11
my heart-strings*a* are snapped.
Day is turned into night,   12
and morning*b* light is darkened before me.
If I measure Sheol for my house,   13
if I spread my couch in the darkness,
if I call the grave my father   14
and the worm my mother or my sister,
where, then, will my hope be,   15
and who will take account of my piety?
I cannot take them down to Sheol with me,*c*   16
nor can they descend with me into the earth.

✻ 1–2. Job's spirit is broken and *the grave* a beckoning solution to life.

3. Job, it would seem, can find no third party to be his *surety* in court; no 'arbiter' (cp. 9: 33), 'witness' (16: 19) or 'friend' has arisen to defend him. He therefore challenges God himself to stand as his 'pledge' or 'guarantor'. Job is apparently appealing to a hidden justice and compassion of God which he has not experienced in his current crises. To date God has been his accuser, oppressor, watchman and judge. The custom of an individual giving a pledge for another party was common in legal and commercial contexts (Gen. 38: 17; Deut. 24: 6–17).

[a] *Prob. rdg.; Heb.* the desires of my heart.
[b] morning: *prob. rdg.; Heb.* near.
[c] to Sheol with me: *so Sept.; Heb. obscure.*

4–5. In desperation Job returns to the traditional understanding of divine justice as a possible assurance of hope. He
cannot imagine that his friends, who lack the ability to think
clearly, will be exalted by God for their part in Job's case.
Surely God will punish those who denounce *friends* for personal profit as Job's companions have done.

6–7. Job again laments his physical and mental misery. His
condition is so ugly and ominous that he has become a scandal
to his community. He is a disgusting *byword* or 'proverb' on
everyone's lips.

8–10. These verses interrupt Job's lament and clash with his
basic position. If they are original here they are probably
satirical. Job, like Jeremiah, would then be saying that no
righteous or wise man exists in his community (cp. Jer. 5:
1–5). If there were such a man he would stand aghast at Job's
fate and rise up in righteous indignation against God. If this
man were to maintain his *course* with integrity he would
support Job publicly and testify on his behalf. Job taunts his
friends into being righteous wise men worthy of the name,
but he knows the situation is hopeless; he must prosecute his
case alone.

11–12. Job resumes his lament stressing the futility of his
lifeless life. The darkness and gloom of death are the order of
the day (cp. 3: 3–6; 10: 21).

13–16. Job realizes that even death is not the answer. If he
welcomes death (cp. 3: 21–2), whether by suicide or not, he
will have no future chance of being vindicated. There is no
second chance beyond *the grave*; hoping for the grave is no
hope at all (on 'death' and 'hope' see at 14: 7–12). No witnesses, judge or jury can be summoned to meet in the underworld. Job's *hope* here is his yearning for the strength to win
acquittal and subsequently begin life anew. Alas, the situation
in heaven and on earth is no better than that in the underworld of *Sheol*. The universe is totally devoid of hope.   ✳

The Second Discourse of Bildad

✶ After a brief sarcastic remark about Job's arrogance, Bildad
follows the lead of Eliphaz and launches into a lengthy description of the agony and fate of the wicked (cp. 15: 17–35).
The wicked, according to Bildad, are the inevitable victims of
their own evil schemes. They live in perpetual fear of their
own downfall; the terrors of death stalk their lives. They die
childless and forgotten, except for comments of disgust by
travellers who pass the ruins of the wicked. Bildad apparently
classifies Job, who is now childless, as one of the wicked, but
he makes no appeal for Job to repent or any effort to comprehend Job's problems. He wants Job to meet the terrors of
Death and draw his own conclusions.   ✶

MEET THE TERRORS OF DEATH

Then Bildad the Shuhite answered: **18**

How soon will you bridle[a] your tongue?   2
Do but think, and then we will talk.
What do you mean by treating us as cattle?   3
Are we nothing but brute beasts to you?[b]
Is the earth to be deserted to prove you right,   4
or the rocks to be moved from their place?

No, it is the wicked whose light is extinguished,   5
from whose fire no flame will rekindle;
the light fades in his tent,   6
and his lamp dies down and fails him.
In his iniquity his steps[c] totter,   7
and his disobedience trips him up;

[a] bridle: *prob. rdg.; Heb. unintelligible.*
[b] *Prob. rdg.; Heb. adds* rending himself in his anger.
[c] In ... steps: *so Pesh.; Heb.* The steps of his iniquity.

8 he rushes headlong into a net
  and steps through the hurdle that covers a pit;

9 his heel is caught in a snare,
  the noose grips him tight;

10 a cord lies hidden in the ground for him
  and a trap in the path.

11 The terrors of death suddenly beset him
  and make him piss over his feet.

12 For all his vigour he is paralysed with fear;
  strong as he is, disaster awaits him.

13 Disease eats away his skin,
  Death's eldest child devours his limbs.

14 He is torn from the safety of his home,
  and Death's terrors escort him to their king.[a]

15 Magic herbs lie strewn about his tent,
  and his home is sprinkled with sulphur to protect it.

16 His roots beneath dry up,
  and above, his branches wither.

17 His memory vanishes from the face of the earth
  and he leaves no name in the world.

18 He is driven from light into darkness
  and banished from the land of the living.

19 He leaves no issue or offspring among his people,
  no survivor in his earthly home;

20 in the west men hear of his doom and are appalled;
  in the east they shudder with horror.

21 Such is the fate of the dwellings of evildoers,
  and of the homes of those who care nothing for God.

[a] *Or* and you conduct him to the king of terrors.

✲ 2–3. Bildad rebukes Job for not reflecting on his answers and giving his friends ample opportunity for response before he makes rash comments. To call one's friends *brute beasts* is intolerable and crude (see comment at 16: 9). The phrase in the N.E.B. footnote is considered a late addition by some editors. If included, it suggests that Job himself is the wild animal doing the rending, not his congenial companions.

4. Bildad charges Job with unlimited arrogance. He wants the entire world to revolve around his will, and the very foundations of cosmic justice to be shaken on his behalf. The Hebrew for 'moving the rocks' recalls 9: 5–6 (see the comment there).

5–6. Contrary to the claims of Job (21: 7ff.), the wicked are destined to die without hope or happiness (cp. Prov. 13: 9).

7–10. The wicked are eventually caught in their own devices, like animals snared into traps. Iniquity is often considered a force with the inherent power to destroy the sinner who commits it (cp. Prov. 26: 27; Jer. 2: 19).

11. Not only do the wicked eventually fall prey to their own machinations, they live in constant dread of their impending death. They hear *terrors* dogging their steps and they panic. These *terrors*, which the N.E.B. has rendered *The terrors of death*, are personified in the following verses.

12. For this uncertain text we suggest the translation, 'The Hungry One meets him, Calamity stays at his side.' 'Calamity' and 'The Hungry One', which is another name for Death (as in Ps. 33: 19), are the first two terrors the wicked must face.

13. *Disease*, the first born child of *Death*, is one more terror sent to make the life of the wicked miserable.

14. The wicked are torn from their homes and taken to *Death*, 'king of terrors' (see N.E.B. footnote), and ruler of the underworld (cp. Ps. 49: 13–14). This vision haunts the wicked; they know a battery of terrors will fly from the underworld to return them to the dusty abode of death (cp. note on 5: 6–7).

15. The N.E.B. rendering of this obscure text suggests that

the wicked follow various superstitious rites to ward off the terrors of death.

16–21. The fate of the wicked man is worse than death. He dies without progeny or name. His memory disappears from the earth. From *the east* to *the west* horrified men make the comment: those are the ruins of the wicked. Bildad is apparently insinuating that Job is destined to suffer the same fate; after all, he has lost all his children. ✻

Job's Second Response to Bildad

✻ This great speech has often been viewed as the highpoint in Job's profession of faith. The redeemer figure he foresees here has been hailed as clear evidence of his faith in a coming Messiah comparable to the royal figure in Isaiah (9: 2–7; 11: 1–10). The constellation of ideas and the broader context of Job's own discourses, however, suggest a different kind of hope. Job is not drawing upon a widespread Israelite tradition about a great national leader to come. He needs a personal vindicator. He is on the verge of a total breakdown, his time has all but expired and he has nowhere to turn. No one has stepped forward to assume his case, no friends, no heavenly witness, no arbiter, no compassionate God. He is dying alone, condemned by God. His friends are no longer impartial; they have taken God's side. No one from on high comes to his rescue when he cries: 'bloody murder'; for murder it is! God is the assailant and Job the victim, God is the hunter and Job the dangerous beast (verses 2–12). Understandably none of Job's friends or relatives is inclined to identify with God's prey. They prefer to disown him. Job is cursed by God and ostracized from society. He cannot expect human sympathy for he is now to be considered less than human (verses 13–21).

In the depths of his desperation Job refuses to surrender his faith completely. From his broken soul there rises a final vision of hope, a frantic but beautiful dream of liberation. Even though he feels like a wounded animal under attack by

human scavengers, he clings to the hope that someone will
intervene at the last minute to rescue his life from oblivion and
vindicate his name before God. His hope is based on the cer-
tainty of his own integrity and the belief that compassionate
justice must exist somewhere. He is so sure of his own
rightness that he cannot imagine dying for ever without a
redeemer arising to force a confrontation with God and a
genuine acquittal in court. The identity of this heroic vindicator remains a mystery to Job (verses 21–7).   ✳

HOUNDED BY GOD

Then Job answered: **19**

How long will you exhaust me   2
and pulverize me with words?
Time and time again you have insulted me   3
and shamelessly done me wrong.*a*
If in fact I had erred,   4
the error would still be mine.
But if indeed you lord it over me   5
and try to justify the reproaches levelled at me,
I tell you, God himself has put me in the wrong,   6
he has drawn the net round me.
If I cry 'Murder!' no one answers;   7
if I appeal for help, I get no justice.
He has walled in my path so that I cannot break away,   8
and he has hedged in the road before me.
He has stripped me of all honour   9
and has taken the crown from my head.
On every side he beats me down and I am gone;   10
he has pulled up my tent-rope*b* like a tree.

[a] done me wrong: *so some MSS.; others* are astonished at me.
[b] *Or* he has uprooted my hope.

11   His anger is hot against me
        and he counts me his enemy.

12   His raiders gather in force[a]
        and encamp about my tent.

✻ 2–3. Job throws some of Bildad's sarcasm back in his face by asking him *How long* he intends to insult Job with a barrage of meaningless words (cp. 8: 2; 18: 2).

4. Job is not admitting to any wrongdoing. He is presenting a hypothesis about his case. He may be saying that if he has indeed *erred* it is no concern of his friends; or more probably that if he is accounted guilty the fault is not really his, and verse 4*b* would then be taken as a question. Verse 6 makes it clear that Job blames God for his apparently guilty condition.

5–6. *try to justify* renders the same Hebrew word as 'arbitrate' in 16: 21 (cp. 9: 33). Job accuses his friends of being arrogant and partial arbiters who present a biased case against him instead of recognizing God as the real culprit. God has perverted justice by making Job the guilty party in the dispute. God, the hunter, has trapped Job like a wild animal (cp. 10: 16). Job's friends are deluded by his pitiful condition and their blind adherence to the traditional doctrine of reward and punishment (see the opening comments to Eliphaz' first discourse). Job looks guilty!

7. Job claims that his attack by God is tantamount to murder (cp. note on 16: 18). Jeremiah sent a similar cry heavenward during his persecution (Jer. 20: 8; cp. Hab. 1: 2). Earlier Job had hoped for a witness to present his case before the heavenly council, testify to his murder and demand redress from God (see on 16: 18–21). Now God, it seems, has prevented Job's cry from being heard. He calls out to a deaf universe.

8–12. Job maintains that he has been ambushed by a murderous God and his troops, who throw a net around Job, block his route of escape and proceed to humiliate him. He

[a] *Prob. rdg.; Heb. adds* they raise an earthwork against me.

has been dehumanized; the honour and glory of being a human being crowned by God have been removed (cp. Ps. 8: 5; Prov. 4: 8–9). He is not only beaten like an animal, but his inner resources of hope are also uprooted (as the N.E.B. footnote to verse 10 suggests). On *hope* see the notes at 14: 7–9.

11. Job is a vicious enemy whom God hunts with his net (verse 6) like some ancient chaos dragon (see the note on 7: 12).

12. The imagery of this verse shifts to that of a city or fortress under siege. By retaining the words in the N.E.B. footnote this metaphor is heightened. Job is so formidable that God summons his heavenly raiders to help him subdue his foe. Job has become the symbol of all that is chaotic, evil and less than human; he is God's personal enemy and the object of an organized campaign to assassinate his character and annihilate his humanity. ✳

DISOWNED BY ALL

My brothers hold aloof from me,	13
my friends are utterly estranged from me;	
my kinsmen and intimates fall away,	14–15
my retainers have forgotten me;	
my slave-girls treat me as a stranger,	
I have become an alien in their eyes.	
I summon my slave, but he does not answer,	16
though I entreat him as a favour.	
My breath is noisome to my wife,	17
and I stink in the nostrils of my own family.	
Mere children despise me	18
and, when I rise, turn their backs on me;	
my intimate companions loathe me,	19

and those whom I love have turned against me.

20   My bones stick out through[a] my skin,[b]

and I gnaw my under-lip with my teeth.

✻ Job is considered less than a human being by God and all who knew him personally. He has become an obnoxious creature even to his inner circle of friends and relatives. This theme is more fully developed in ch. 30.

13. His *friends* are unlike the ideal compassionate friend Job described earlier (see on 6: 14; 16: 20).

14–16. God's ugly involvement in Job's life has caused his alienation from all his relatives. They disown him as one accursed. Job's slaves, who should be able to sympathize with Job's suffering and oppression, do not recognize him (cp. on 3: 17–19).

17. Job's sickness is so revolting that he has become repulsive even to his own family.

18–19. Those who once respected Job now despise him and those whom he loved deeply treat him with disdain. Job stands alone, a marked man facing a murderous God. At that moment no one is willing to identify with him. He is a total outcast.

20. The translation of this verse remains uncertain.   ✻

VINDICATED AT LAST

21   Pity me, pity me, you that are my friends;

for the hand of God has touched me.

22   Why do you pursue me as God pursues me?

Have you not had your teeth in me long enough?

23   O that my words might be inscribed,

O that they might be engraved in an inscription,

[a] stick out through: *lit.* cling to.
[b] *Prob. rdg.; Heb. adds* and my flesh.

cut with an iron tool and filled with lead   24
to be a witness[a] in hard rock!
But in my heart I know that my vindicator lives   25
and that he will rise last to speak in court;
and I shall discern my witness standing at my side[b]   26
and see my defending counsel, even God himself,
whom I shall see with my own eyes,   27
I myself and no other.

My heart failed me when you said,   28
'What a train of disaster he has brought on himself!
The root of the trouble lies in him.'[c]
Beware of the sword that points at you,   29
the sword that sweeps away all iniquity;
then you will know that there is a judge.[d]

✽ 21. Job pleads with his *friends* to be genuine friends, that is,
human, compassionate and loyal during his conflict with God
(see on 6: 14). Job has been *touched* by God like a man cursed
with a plague (cp. 1: 11). The *hand of God* is the oppressive
destructive power under which Job is writhing (cp. 12: 9).

22. Job assails his friends for stalking and mauling him like
a wounded beast. God is the hunter and they are the scavengers feasting on his flesh.

23–4. Job's final hope of a vindicator is prefaced by a desire
to record his grand vision for posterity. Job expects to be
acquitted at the last minute, but he wants posterity to know
that he *inscribed* his own testimony to his innocence and his
hope. That *inscription* is to be permanent and personal,
according to the proper procedures of the time (cp. Jer. 32: 14).

[a] to ... witness: *or* for ever.
[b] my witness ... side: *prob. rdg.; Heb. unintelligible.*
[c] *So many MSS.; others* me.
[d] *Or* judgement.

25a. This verse is notoriously difficult. The preceding context makes it clear that all of Job's efforts to stir God's compassion have failed; he remains adamant as Job's accuser. No
heavenly witness has arisen to assume Job's case before the
council of heaven. Yet amid his despair Job's faith in his own
integrity moves him to expect someone more than a witness
(16: 19) and greater than an arbiter (9: 33), who will vindicate
him in the end. Job's yearnings for a liberator are not a prophetic prediction of a Messiah. Rather, they are cries of a
frantic faith welling forth from the abyss of utter desperation.
They are impossible dreams from the soul of a destroyed
human being (cp. on 9: 33-5; 14: 13; 16: 19-21). With God,
friends and the council of heaven against him, Job gives birth
to the absurd belief that there must be someone who can
vindicate him, someone who can be his *gō'ēl*, his *vindicator* or
'redeemer'. A 'redeemer' in Israel was bound up with the
living kinship unity. He could redeem those sold into slavery
(Lev. 25: 47-55), re-acquire property for the family line (Lev.
25: 23-4), avenge the blood of a kinsman (Num. 35: 19), or
preserve the line of a relative through marriage (Deut. 25:
5-10). The basic idea is that of preserving the life-force and
integrity of the family line. The 'redeemer' prevented the
family from becoming extinct. Elsewhere God was praised as
the Redeemer who liberated and protected his people (Exod.
6: 5; 15: 13). Job saw himself as unjustly oppressed and murdered by God (see on 16: 18; 19: 7) and therefore in need of a
redeemer.

25b. The N.E.B. translates the Hebrew word 'rise' (*qūm*)
as *rise . . . in court*. Job looks for a fair trial when his vindicator
will prove his rightness. *last* probably means at the last minute,
before the very end when Job has almost returned to dust.
Job's redeemer will snatch him from the mouth of the grave.
It is also possible that Job imagines his vindication happening
after death, perhaps in the underworld, just as he contemplated being hidden in the land of death until God's anger had
passed and a fair hearing was possible (14: 13-15). In either

case Job is reaching for a hope that contradicts all he has learned about God as his accusing enemy and death as the place of permanent annihilation.

26–7. The text of these verses is corrupt and their interpretation hotly disputed. One rendering proposes that Job will see God face to face even though Job is dead and stripped of human flesh. A second translation reflects the idea that Job will rise from the dead with a new flesh to behold God and be vindicated. The N.E.B. rendering has *God himself* as the *witness* and *defending counsel* whom Job will behold face to face as his redeemer. The difficulty with the N.E.B. interpretation is that Job's previous heroes of hope were figures quite distinct from God (9: 33–5; 16: 19–21). God, moreover, is viewed by Job as nothing less than a relentless hunter, slavemaster and murderer from whom Job needs to be delivered. It seems more likely that Job is clinging to the hope of a last-minute intervention by a redeemer who will rescue his life and vindicate his integrity before he is destroyed by God, the heavenly destroyer. Like the former heroes of Job, this redeemer remains a mysterious heavenly stranger, a forerunner of the New Testament Christ. After death Job knows of nothing but oblivion (10: 21–2); resurrection is impossible (14: 10–12). If Job expects to see his vindicator in person, their meeting would need to take place before he dies. Although Job is not vindicated by God or a redeemer at the end, he does *see* God and repent in the 'dust' (42: 5–6).

28*a* is actually 27*c* in the Hebrew original. After his glorious cry of hope Job falls back into his former depression: 'my heart fails within me'.

28–9. Job's friends interpret his plight as the result of God's judgement. Job warns them that the same sword of punishment will be pointed at them. ✳

The Second Discourse of Zophar

✳ Eliphaz and Bildad had both given portraits of the fate and agony of the wicked man (15: 17–35; 18: 5–21). Zophar's analysis, however, is a characterization of the wicked tyrant, the mighty ruler who lusts to be like God and threatens to rival God. He is like the king of Babylon who longed to set his 'throne high above the stars of God' (Isa. 14: 4–21) or the mighty prince of Tyre who in his arrogance said, 'I sit throned like a god on the high seas' (Ezek. 28: 1–10). The weakness of Zophar's despot is his insatiable greed. In the end he will consume the property of even the poorest subject. Then God will move against him with a powerful display of cosmic weapons from his heavenly storehouse. The universe itself will rise up to declare this tyrant guilty and he will return to the dust from which he arose. Zophar seems to imply that Job's arrogance matches that of this tyrant, for Job is experiencing the very disasters appointed for this rebel. ✳

PRIDE AS HIGH AS HEAVEN

20 Then Zophar the Naamathite answered:

2   My distress of mind forces me to reply,
     and this is why[a] I hasten to speak:
3   I have heard arguments that are a reproach to me,
     a spirit beyond my understanding gives me the answers.
4   Surely you know that this has been so since time began,
     since man was first set on the earth:
5   the triumph of the wicked is short-lived,
     the glee of the godless lasts but a moment?
6   Though he stands high as heaven,
     and his head touches the clouds,

[a] this is why: *prob. rdg.; Heb. obscure.*

he will be swept utterly away like his own dung,   7
and all that saw him will say, 'Where is he?'
He will fly away like a dream and be lost,   8
driven off like a vision of the night;
the eye which glimpsed him shall do so no more   9
and shall never again see him in his place.
The youth and strength which filled his bones   11[a]
shall lie with him in the dust.
His sons will pay court to the poor,   10
and their[b] hands will give back his wealth.
Though evil tastes sweet in his mouth,   12
and he savours it, rolling it round his tongue,
though he lingers over it and will not let it go,   13
and holds it back on his palate,
yet his food turns in his stomach,   14
changing to asps' venom within him.
He gulps down wealth, then vomits it up,   15
or God makes him discharge it.
He sucks the poison of asps,   16
and the tongue of the viper kills him.
Not for him to swill down rivers of cream[c]   17
or torrents of honey and curds;
he must give back his gains without swallowing them,   18
and spew up his profit undigested;
for he has hounded and harassed the poor,   19
he has seized houses which he did not build.
Because his appetite gave him no rest,   20
and he cannot escape his own desires,

[a] *Verses 10 and 11 transposed.*
[b] *Prob. rdg.; Heb.* his.
[c] rivers of cream: *prob. rdg.; Heb. obscure.*

21   nothing is left for him to eat,
      and so his well-being does not last;
22   with every need satisfied his troubles begin,
      and the full force of hardship strikes him.
23   [a]God vents his anger upon him
      and rains on him cruel blows.
24   He is wounded by weapons of iron
      and pierced by a bronze-tipped arrow;
25   out at his back the point comes,
      the gleaming tip from his gall-bladder.[b]
26   Darkness unrelieved awaits him,[c]
      a fire that needs no fanning will consume him.
      [Woe betide any survivor in his tent!]
27   The heavens will lay bare his guilt,
      and earth will rise up to condemn him.
28   A flood will sweep away his house,
      rushing waters on the day of wrath.
29   Such is God's reward for the wicked man
      and the lot appointed for the rebel[d] by God.

    ✷ 2–3. Although distressed by Job's tirades, Zophar's spirit compels him to speak (cp. 32: 7–9).

    4. Zophar here follows the lead of Bildad in appealing to ancient tradition as the normative source of truth (see on 8: 8–10). The time when *man was first set on the earth* reflects the 'setting' of Adam in the primeval garden (Gen. 2: 8) and represents the original era of God's revelations to man (see on Job 15: 7–8; cp. Deut. 4: 32). The first man enjoyed the pristine truth.

        [a] *So one Sept. MS.; Heb. prefixes* Let it be for filling his belly.
        [b] *So some MSS. of Sept.; Heb. adds* terrors upon him.
        [c] *So Sept.; Heb.* awaits his stored things.
        [d] the rebel: *prob. rdg.; Heb.* his word.

5. This axiom, which Zophar is quoting as a verity from ancient tradition (cp. 8: 11–13), emphasizes that the celebrations of the wicked are fleeting. Zophar grants, with Job, that the wicked may prosper, but only for a short time.

6–11. Man who is made 'little less than a god' (Ps. 8: 5) also has the impulse to become like God and assume his position on high (cp. Gen. 3: 5, 22; Ezek. 28: 2). This *hybris*, or arrogance, is balanced by the repeated divine reminder that man, in spite of his honour and glory as a human being (Ps. 8: 5), is nevertheless dust and must return to the underworld (Gen. 3: 19; Isa. 14: 9–11; 26: 13–14). Zophar contends that this god-like tyrant will perish *like his own dung*, vanish *like a dream* and lie lifeless in the earth. His surviving children will be forced to make amends for his misdeeds. Zophar seems to be saying that Job's pride in his own unblemished integrity, maintained at the expense of God's eternal justice, is an arrogance comparable to that of presumptuous rulers who claim to be gods.

6*a* can also be translated, 'Though his pride stand as high as heaven'.

12–14. Evil is described as a delicacy that causes food-poisoning in the stomach (cp. Prov. 20: 17).

15–16. He who gorges ill-gotten wealth will be forced by God to disgorge it; he who swallows the poison of evil will die from it (cp. Deut. 32: 33–5).

17–19. *torrents of honey and curds* symbolize a life of great plenty and ease (cp. Exod. 3: 8). The wicked ruler will never be permitted to enjoy that kind of life because he has committed the ultimate crime, namely, the oppression of *the poor* (cp. Mic. 2: 1–2; Ezek. 16: 49).

20–2. This wicked man is no petty criminal; he is an arrogant overlord whose insatiable greed matches his exalted pride. Absolute greed, says Zophar, eventually leads to a shortage that affects even the ruler of the land. Then he, like Job, experiences oppressive *hardship*, or, as it is rendered elsewhere, 'trouble' (see on 3: 10; 5: 6–7).

23–5. There are several obscure sections in these verses, the N.E.B. editors opting for an abbreviated text. The imagery is that of God the warrior venting his anger on this tyrant from a full arsenal of celestial forces. God's weapons are often identified with elements of a massive thunderstorm (cp. Hab. 3: 9-11). Job claims to be the repeated target of this heavenly archer (see on 6: 4; 7: 20; 16: 12).

26. The *Darkness* of the underworld and the special fire of God are prepared as judgement for this despot (see on 1: 16; 3: 4–5). Verse 26c is considered a late addition by the N.E.B. editors; it underlines the theme of relentless doom.

27–8. *The heavens* and the *earth will rise up* like witnesses in court against the tyranny of this wicked man. His wickedness has reached cosmic proportions (verse 6), and so the powers of the universe are ready to testify against him. Cosmic forces, including heaven and earth, were summoned as witnesses to ancient Near Eastern treaties (cp. Deut. 30: 19; 32: 1; Mic. 6: 1–2).

29. A statement referring back to verse 5 and summarizing the points of the entire chapter. ✶

Job's Second Response to Zophar

✶ Job suppresses his personal laments against God and proceeds to answer the contentions of his opponents. On several occasions he cites their position before he gives his own opinion (e.g. verses 16, 19, 22, 28). The subject under dispute is the fate of the wicked and especially of wicked rulers. Contrary to the claim of his friends, Job sees the wicked prospering in every aspect of their life. God, who refrains from punishing them, allows them to live as if he did not exist. The wicked ruler has the additional advantage of dying in peace and being buried in splendour. The cherished doctrine of wisdom teachers that the wicked bring about their own downfall seems to be contradicted by real life. ✶

THE WICKED ENJOY LONG LIFE

Then Job answered: **21**

Listen to me, do but listen,   2
and let that be the comfort you offer me.
Bear with me while I have my say;   3
when I have finished, you may mock.
May not I too voice*a* my thoughts?   4
Have not I as good cause to be impatient?
Look at my plight, and be aghast;   5
clap your hand to your mouth.
When I stop to think, I am filled with horror,   6
and my whole body is convulsed.

Why do the wicked enjoy long life,   7
hale in old age, and great and powerful?
They live to see their children settled,   8
their kinsfolk and descendants flourishing;
their families are secure and safe;   9
the rod of God's justice does not reach them.
Their bull mounts and fails not of its purpose;   10
their cow calves and does not miscarry.
Their children like lambs run out to play,   11
and their little ones skip and dance;
they rejoice with*b* tambourine and harp   12
and make merry to the sound of the flute.
Their lives close in prosperity,   13
and they go down to Sheol in peace.
To God they say, 'Leave us alone;   14

[*a*] May . . . voice: *prob. rdg.; Heb. obscure.*
[*b*] with: *so some MSS.; others* as to.

III

we do not want to know your ways.
15   What is the Almighty that we should worship him,
      or what should we gain by seeking his favour?'

✷ 2-3. Job has repeatedly chided his friends for lack of compassion (6: 14-23; 16: 4-9). Now he asks for at least the kindness of being silent listeners (cp. on 2: 11-13).

4-6. Verse 4a can be rendered 'Is my dispute about man?' Job is appalled at this detached debate about 'man' in which his friends are engaged. For Job the crisis is personal; his life is at stake. His friends should be as horrified as he is at his *plight*. Yet in the verses that follow Job sets aside his own anguish and argues the points made by his opponents.

7-9. Job counters the arguments of Bildad and Zophar about the agony and fate of the wicked (18: 5-21; 20: 5-29). Instead of fleeting triumphs they enjoy a *long life* of power, instead of a bleak future without progeny they know a flourishing and happy household (cp. Jer. 12: 1-2). The only experience they miss is *the rod* of God's oppressive judgement, a 'rod' that Job has felt constantly against his back (9: 34). Job is experiencing what should be the lot of the wicked, and they in turn are enjoying what should be Job's portion.

10-12. The wicked have fertile flocks, their children are healthy and their household a continuous festival. At a festival Job's family and flocks were destroyed without warning (1: 13-19).

13. The consummation of a long and blessed life is to die swiftly and peacefully. The wicked enjoy that privilege.

14-15. The *ways* of God are guidelines for life under the tutelage of wisdom (see on 3: 23; Prov. 4: 10-19). Faithful adherence to these 'ways' of wisdom was believed to ensure prosperity and honour (cp. Prov. 3: 13-18; 4: 7-9). The wicked, however, laugh at these principles; life is more profitable without God's help. If God is but another source of material blessings he is unnecessary.   ✷

WHY SHOULD THE CHILDREN SUFFER?

Is not the prosperity of the wicked in their own hands?　16
Are not their purposes very different from God's[a]?
How often is the lamp of the wicked snuffed out,　　17
and how often does their ruin come upon them?
How often does God in his anger deal out suffering,
bringing it in full measure to whom he will?[b]
How often is that man like a wisp of straw before the　18
　wind,
like chaff which the storm-wind whirls away?
You say, 'The trouble he has earned, God will keep for　19
　his sons';
no, let him be paid for it in full and be punished.
Let his own eyes see damnation come upon him,　　20
and the wrath of the Almighty be the cup he drinks.
What joy shall he have in his children after him,　　21
if his very months and days are numbered?
Can any man teach God,　　　　　22
God who judges even those in heaven above?

One man, I tell you, dies crowned with success,　　23
lapped in security and comfort,
his loins full of vigour　　　　24
and the marrow juicy in his bones;
another dies in bitterness of soul　　　25
and never tastes prosperity;
side by side they are laid in earth,　　　26
and worms are the shroud of both.

[a] God's: *prob. rdg.*; *Heb.* mine.
[b] *Line transposed from 12: 6.*

✲ 16. Job seems to be quoting the position of his friends who piously say, 'Their prosperity is not in their own hands, the purposes of the wicked are not mine!' The N.E.B. rendering is based on several conjectured readings.

17–18. Job answers the previous quotation from his friends with a series of rhetorical questions. The future of *the wicked* is not *snuffed out* like a light (cp. 18: 5–6), his reward is not God's angry judgement (cp. 20: 29), and his life does not vanish like *straw before the wind* (cp. 15: 30). The N.E.B. editors have chosen to transfer 12: 6c to make verse 17 of this chapter a normal four-line poetic unit.

19a. Job quotes another traditional axiom of his opponents. The belief existed in Israel that the children of the wicked would be punished for the sins of their parents (Exod. 34: 7; Jer. 31: 29–30). Job's opponents had interpreted that doctrine to mean that even if the wicked did not know God's wrath in this life, their children would experience it. God was hiding his anger for them (cp. Matt. 27: 25).

19b–21. This position Job condemns as totally unjust. A sinner should pay for his own crimes and understand why he is being condemned (cp. Ezek. 18: 1–4). The words *and be punished* can be rendered 'so that he understands'. Each man should knowingly confront his own *damnation*; what happens to *his children* is of no concern to him once he is dead (cp. 14: 21).

22. Job may again be citing a charge of his companions. Eliphaz had accused Job of 'usurping all wisdom' for himself (15: 8) and claiming to be more righteous than God who finds fault even with his heavenly messengers (cp. 4: 17–18; 15: 14–15). Job knows that God is unteachable; he will not even listen to Job's concerns.

23–6. All men die equal, the prosperous and the poverty-stricken. All lie helpless in the same dust (cp. 3: 13–19). A fuller treatment of this theme appears in Eccles. 9: 2–6. ✲

TYRANTS ENJOY A GLORIOUS DEATH

I know well what you are thinking   27
and the arguments you are marshalling*a* against me;
I know you will ask, 'Where is the great man's home 28
    now,
what has become of the home of the wicked?'
Have you never questioned travellers?   29
Can you not learn from the signs they offer,
that the wicked is spared when disaster comes   30
and conveyed to safety before the day of wrath?
No one denounces his conduct to his face,   31
no one requites him for what he has done.
When he is carried to the grave,   32–33
all the world escorts him, before and behind;
the dust of earth is sweet to him,
and thousands keep watch at his tomb.
How futile, then, is the comfort you offer me!   34
How false your answers ring!

* 28. This quotation summarizes the contention of Zophar
about the tyrant (20: 4ff.). Where are the great houses of the
mighty rulers now? Zophar could point to Job as one such
mighty ruler whose house and property were annihilated.

29. Bildad followed tradition and asked the fathers (8:
8–10); Eliphaz insisted their tradition had not been con-
taminated by foreign influence (15: 17–19). Job appeals to the
tales of *travellers* as more truthful than these local traditions of
his companions.

30–3. Travellers can testify to the glory of evil monarchs
who are *spared* disaster throughout their lives. Their subjects
are too afraid to condemn them for their conduct or take

[a] *So Pesh.; Heb.* you do violence.

action against them. When they die they are borne to a tomb with great pomp and ceremony. Their body is guarded against grave robbers and *the dust of earth* becomes an abode of peaceful repose.

34. The compassion of Job's friends is as insipid as their arguments (cp. verses 2–3).   ✲

Third cycle of speeches

The Third Discourse of Eliphaz

✲ In his third discourse Eliphaz moves in for the kill. He confronts Job with God as an impartial and righteous judge, who would not stand to gain from anything Job might offer, no matter how righteous he were. In point of fact Job belongs to the camp of the outcasts. He has not only challenged the leading doctrines of wisdom, but has also denied its moral foundations. There is therefore no escape from the great celestial overseer. Job's only hope is to come to terms with this judge by demonstrating a radical change of attitude. Such repentance, argues Eliphaz, will lead to a peaceful life of pious devotion. Thus, just as in his previous speeches, Eliphaz begins with a sarcastic comment about Job's alleged wisdom or righteousness and then proceeds to demonstrate his guilt with a series of arguments about the corrupt nature of man and the impartial justice of God. In his self-righteous impulse to prove his point and vindicate the justice of God, Eliphaz could find no room for Job's understanding of human integrity nor a corresponding appreciation for the grace of God.   ✲

JOB, THE COMPASSIONLESS SINNER

Then Eliphaz the Temanite answered: **22**

Can man be any benefit to God?   2
Can even a wise man benefit him?
Is it an asset to the Almighty if you are righteous?   3
Does he gain if your conduct is perfect?
Do not think that he reproves you because you are   4
    pious,
that on this count he brings you to trial.
No: it is because you are a very wicked man,   5
and your depravity passes all bounds.
Without due cause you take a brother in pledge,   6
you strip men of their clothes and leave them naked.
When a man is weary, you give him no water to drink 7
and you refuse bread to the hungry.
Is the earth, then, the preserve of the strong   8
and a domain for the favoured few?
Widows you have sent away empty-handed,   9
orphans you have struck defenceless.
No wonder that there are pitfalls in your path,   10
that scares are set to fill you with sudden fear.
The light*a* is turned into darkness, and you cannot see; 11
the flood-waters cover you.

☆ Eliphaz begins his final disputation with an axiom asserting
that man has neither the wisdom nor the capacity to benefit
God in any way. God is self-sufficient. Job's claim to superior
piety and knowledge suggests that he has something God
could use. According to Eliphaz, Job's attitude flies in the face
of that axiom. He should realize that his divine chastisement

[a] The light: *so Sept.; Heb.* Or.

is not due to excessive piety but excessive sinfulness. Job's crimes are no mere peccadilloes; they demonstrate a complete lack of moral fibre and compassion. Job is an unfeeling oppressor of the helpless in his society. That is why he is dwelling in the darkness of agony and death.

2. Eliphaz probably quotes this axiom in response to Job's frustration at not being able to 'teach God' anything (21: 22). Conceivably, the first man endowed with perfect wisdom could have assisted the Creator in planning the world (cp. on 15: 7–8). The average man, however, cannot (cp. 35: 7).

3–5. *conduct*: literally 'way' (cp. Prov. 4: 11). Even if Job has followed the 'way of wisdom' perfectly (cp. 1: 1), God would not stand to *gain*, or, as the Hebrew suggests, there is no 'profit motive' in it for him. Conversely, God does not benefit by chastising Job if he is pious. His motives are pure and his decisions impartial. The only conclusion that can be drawn, therefore, is that Job's suffering is a divine punishment for his excessive *depravity*. The verb *reprove* is translated 'rebuke' in 5: 17. In that context Eliphaz had left the door open for viewing Job's suffering as chastisement; here he stands condemned.

6–9. The ideal righteous man in the ancient Near East protected the rights of the less fortunate, especially in the law court. The rulers of Israel were expected to live up to that ideal (Jer. 22: 15–17; Ps. 72: 1–4).

6. Clothes taken from the poor as a *pledge* for a loan were to be returned by sundown so that they could be used as protection against the cold (Deut. 24: 10–13).

7. Job is accused of being more than unrighteous; he lacks compassion (cp. Matt. 25: 35, 42).

8. The oppressed are deprived of their rights while the powerful and *favoured few* appropriate the land (cp. Mic. 2: 1–2). Eliphaz probably includes Job among these greedy landlords.

9. *Widows* and *orphans* were supposed to be the objects of special protection (Exod. 22: 22, and often in prophetic teaching).

10–11. Job's terrors are the proof that he is guilty of the crimes cited above. Job fits the description of the wicked man in 18: 5–11. *darkness* is a recurring image for the destructive agony and depression arising from guilt (cp. 15: 22, 24, 29). ✻

GOD, THE HIDDEN OVERSEER

Surely God is at the zenith of the heavens   12
and looks down on all the stars, high as they are.
But you say, 'What does God know?   13
Can he see through thick darkness to judge?
His eyes cannot pierce the curtain of the clouds   14
as he walks to and fro on the vault of heaven.'
Consider the course of the wicked man,   15
the path the miscreant treads;
see how they are carried off before their time,   16
their very foundation flowing away like a river;
these men said to God, 'Leave us alone;   17
what can the Almighty do to us[a]?'
Yet it was he that filled their houses with good things,   18
although their purposes and his[b] were very different.
The righteous see their fate and exult,   19
the innocent make game of them;
for their riches[c] are swept away,   20
and the profusion of their wealth is destroyed by fire.

✻ 12. The teaching that God is 'afar off' *at the zenith of the heavens* is intended to highlight his capacity to scrutinize every detail of life on earth (Jer. 23: 23f.; Ps. 33: 13f.). He has a

[a] *So Sept.; Heb.* them.
[b] *So Sept.; Heb.* mine.
[c] *So Sept.; Heb. word unknown.*

perfect vantage point above *the stars*, the highest heavenly beings (cp. Isa. 14: 13).

13–14. The transcendence of God could also be introduced as an argument for the lack of divine involvement in the routine details of life. Job had previously maintained just the opposite; God the celestial 'Watcher' kept his insidious eagle eye on Job both day and night (7: 17–20). Eliphaz suggests that Job, despite his allegations to the contrary, secretly believes that God does not detect his sins. The verb *judge* involves ruling according to the dictates of cosmic justice. *vault* is rendered 'horizon' in 26: 10. God rules from high above the horizon of heaven (cp. Isa. 40: 22).

15–16. Following the ways of the wicked means premature death (15: 32f.; 20: 28).

17. Some claim that this cosmic overlord does not intervene directly in human affairs. Men know from experience that the wicked are not struck down dead when they perpetrate crimes. Job used the same quotation in his description of the wicked as comfortable and prosperous citizens (21: 14).

18. The *purposes* of the wicked are prosperity by any devious means. Despite this their homes are blessed with *good things* (cp. 21: 7–11; Hos. 2: 7–8). This allusion to the universal providence of God seems out of place in the mouth of Eliphaz.

19–20. The exultation of the righteous over the fate of the wicked is considered a legitimate response to the vindication of God's name and the confirmation of their faith in the justice of God (Pss. 52: 5–9; 107: 39–43). On *fire* as the agent of divine judgement see 1: 16 and 15: 34. ✳

AN APPEAL FOR RECONCILIATION

21 Come to terms with God and you will prosper;
    that is the way to mend your fortune.

22 Take instruction from his mouth
    and store his words in your heart.

If you come back to the Almighty in true sincerity,   23
if you banish wrongdoing from your home,
if you treat your precious metal as dust[a]   24
and the gold of Ophir as stones from the river-bed,
then the Almighty himself will be your precious metal;   25
he will be your silver in double measure.

Then, with sure trust in[b] the Almighty,   26
you will raise your face to God;
you will pray to him, and he will hear you,   27
and you will have cause to fulfil your vows.

In all your designs you will succeed,   28
and light will shine on your path;
but God brings down the pride of the haughty[c]   29
and keeps safe the man of modest looks.

He will deliver the innocent,[d]   30
and you will be delivered, because your hands are clean.

✻ After diverse arguments, bitter accusations and sarcastic
denunciations, Eliphaz confronts Job with the necessity of
making peace with God as the only solution. If he does God
will rescue him from his plight and shower him with blessings. In the mind of Eliphaz, however, Job seems to have
passed the point of no return.

21. The verb translated 'benefit' in verse 2 is here rendered
Come to terms with. It seems to be Eliphaz' contention that Job,
instead of trying to dictate terms, should submit to God's will.
In so doing Job will benefit immeasurably from the deal. *you
will prosper* should perhaps be 'make your peace'. *fortune* is a
happy translation; if Job makes a deal with God and submits
to his scheme of things, Job's 'fortune' will be made. Eliphaz,

[a] *Prob. rdg.; Heb.* if you put your precious metal on dust.
[b] with. . .in: *or* delighting in.
[c] but. . .haughty: *prob. rdg.; Heb. obscure.*
[d] *Prob. rdg.; Heb.* the not innocent.

who discounted any profit motive on God's part (verses 2–3), seems to be proposing just such a motive for inducing Job to capitulate.

22. A traditional appeal to take the *instruction* of the wisdom school to *heart* (cp. Prov. 4: 10, 20–1). Eliphaz presumes to be the orthodox spokesman for that school.

23. *come back* in the Hebrew expresses a radical reversal of attitude and conduct; it implies total repentance (Jer. 4: 1–4). *in true sincerity* is a translation based on a conjectured reading.

24–5. *Ophir* was a region to which Solomon sent for his gold (1 Kings 9: 26–8). It was most probably located in southern Arabia, though Africa and India have been proposed. Reversal of attitude means a reversal of values. Such a reversal is like trading *precious metal* for *dust* and *gold* for *stones*. The result of the trade will be a greater treasure, God himself. Elsewhere wisdom is portrayed as the ultimate treasure (cp. 28: 15–19; Prov. 3: 13–15).

26–7. Piety and acts of religious devotion are seen as the natural consequence of Job's repentance. The N.E.B. footnote, 'delighting in', is consistent with the theme of devout worship which Eliphaz is proposing as the outcome of Job's projected change.

28. To the profit motive is added the power motive. Verse 28*a* can be rendered, 'You will pass a decree and it will happen for you.' If Job is truly righteous like Abraham (Gen. 18: 21–3) or Noah or Danel (Ezek. 14: 14), he could expect to change the will of God by personal decree or prayer.

29. The Hebrew is obscure. An alternative translation consistent with the above interpretation of verse 28 would be, 'When others abase, you will have the authority to exalt, and God will save the lowly man!'

30. The original of verse 30*a* is apparently corrupt (see N.E.B. footnote). ✳

Job's Third Response to Eliphaz

✻ Job turns from the specific arguments espoused by his friends to the gnawing frustration of his own unresolved case. He had announced his readiness to argue his case before God's court, in spite of the biased character of his judge and the inequity of the situation. He had laid down conditions that would permit a fair hearing. God was to restrain his terrifying presence while Job testified free of intimidation (13: 15-22). But God remained mysterious and elusive. Job dreamed of an arbiter who could force God to appear in court and guarantee an honest trial (9: 32-5). He confessed his faith in a heroic redeemer who would vindicate him in court at the very end (19: 23-7). However, no arbiter or redeemer had yet arisen. There were no signs that Job could expect his case to be heard. Yet he refuses to relinquish his efforts for a showdown with God. God is still inaccessible and silent, but Job keeps summoning him. God is still terrifying and arbitrary, but Job continues to believe that if his case ever reached the floor of the courtroom he would be acquitted. Job's faith in his own integrity is unassailable. ✻

TAKE ME TO COURT

Then Job answered: **23**

My thoughts today are resentful,   2
for God's[a] hand is heavy on me in my trouble.
If only I knew how to find him,   3
how to enter his court,
I would state my case before him   4
and set out my arguments in full;
then I should learn what answer he would give   5
and find out what he had to say.

[a] *So Sept.; Heb.* my.

6   Would he exert his great power to browbeat me?
No; God himself would never bring a charge against
    me.

7   There the upright are vindicated before him,
and I shall win from my judge an absolute discharge.

8   If I go forward,[a] he is not there;
if backward,[b] I cannot find him;

9   when I turn[c] left,[d] I do not descry him;
I face[e] right,[f] but I see him not.

10   But he knows me in action or at rest;[g]
when he tests me, I prove to be gold.

11   My feet have kept to the path he has set me,
I have followed his way and not turned from it.

12   I do not ignore the commands that come from his lips,
I have stored in my heart[h] what he says.

13   He decides,[i] and who can turn him from his purpose?
He does what his own heart desires.

14   What he determines,[j] that he carries out;
his mind is full of plans like these.

15   Therefore I am fearful of meeting him;
when I think about him,[k] I am afraid;

16   it is God who makes me faint-hearted
and the Almighty who fills me with fear,

17   yet I am not reduced to silence by the darkness
nor[l] by the mystery which hides him.

[a] *Or* east.   [b] *Or* west.   [c] *Prob. rdg.; Heb.* he turns.
[d] *Or* north.   [e] *So Pesh.; Heb.* he faces.   [f] *Or* south.
[g] me. . .rest: *so Pesh.; Heb.* a way with me.
[h] in my heart: *so Sept.; Heb.* from my allotted portion.
[i] He decides: *prob. rdg.; Heb.* He in one.
[j] *So Pesh.; Heb.* What I determine.
[k] when. . .him: *or* I stand aloof.
[l] yet I am not. . .nor: *or* indeed I am. . .and. . .

124

☩ 2. This verse sets the tone of Job's latest lament. In spite of his great profession of hope (ch. 19) and the forceful rebuttal of his opponents' arguments (ch. 21), he is bitter, oppressed and overwhelmed. He lives in abject misery without hope or compassion. The punitive *hand* of God is still his constant torment (cp. on 19: 21). He is back where he was before his vision of a heroic redeemer (19: 23–7).

3–5. If Job could only bring God into court, present his case and hear God's answers, the situation would be much clearer. Earlier Job had challenged the justice of any trial with God and questioned whether God's response would be trustworthy (9: 2–3, 11–20). Perhaps Job's greatest frustration grows out of God's refusal to answer one way or the other. A silent God is distant, unfeeling and false.

6. This verse can be rendered, 'Would he employ an attorney to contend with me? He could not prove any charge against me!' Job is convinced that his case is completely watertight and that once his court is convened the evidence in his favour will be overwhelming, no matter what tactics God employs against him (cp. on 13: 18).

7. Significantly Job does not look to any outside arbiter, witness or vindicator to handle his case. Once in court, Job is confident he can convince the judge of his innocence and receive a favourable verdict (cp. 13: 13–19).

8–9. The futility of ever finding God to appear in court is still a reality for Job (as in verse 3). The uncertainty of the translation of these verses is evident from the several footnotes in the N.E.B.

10–12. *action*: literally 'way' (see on 3: 23; 21: 14). Job's conduct in following the way of wisdom is beyond reproach. Even under the severe testing of the current crisis he has faithfully kept the teachings of the wise. Similar protestations of innocence are found in the Psalms (Pss. 7: 3–4; 17: 3–5).

13–14. The reading *He decides* is a conjecture based on a related passage, Ps. 132: 13. God has the sovereign power to execute whatever he wills. If he chose, God could convene a

court for Job and execute whatever judgement God deemed
fitting.

15–16. God's almighty power and sovereign will terrify
Job and prevent him from being himself when they meet in
court. Earlier Job had requested God to restrain his mighty
terror to enable Job to appear before him unafraid (see on 13:
20–1). Not only is God elusive, all-powerful and silent, he is
fearful and unapproachable. Despite his bold protest of innocence Job is a weak, intimidated creature who falters in the
face of his accuser.

17. The rendering of this text is uncertain. Job seems to be
doggedly flinging his last gasping cries of injustice into the
great and mysterious void which surrounds his God.   *

An Anonymous Discourse

* Lacking an introduction, this speech (ch. 24) has been
attached to Job's preceding reply to Eliphaz (ch. 23). There
are several reasons to believe, however, that this discourse does
not belong to Job's cycle of speeches. Though it begins by
raising the question of why God keeps his day of reckoning
for the wicked a secret, it concludes (in verses 18–25) by in-
sisting that the despot of the earth can never escape his delayed
day of wrath. Job had complained bitterly that the opposite
was the case (21: 28–33). Even if this conclusion (verses 18–25)
is transposed to a point after 27: 13 as some scholars propose,
the bulk of the chapter offers general portraits of the wicked
and the poor which have the marks of a sensitive wisdom
teacher, but which lack the claims typical of Job that his
insidious and arbitrary God lets this injustice prevail. The portrait of the disenfranchised poor struggling to survive in their
isolated ghettos is one of the most touching descriptions of
human need in the Bible. One is reminded of the sensitive
portrait of the alcoholic in Prov. 23: 29–35. The description
of the evil ones as those who identify with the darkness is
typical of wisdom traditions (Prov. 2: 13; 4: 19), as are the

examples of the wicked people from the night. Whoever
wrote this chapter seems to reflect the general categories and
evaluation of humanity found in the wisdom school. No fist,
like Job's, is shaken at God in protest.   ✶

OUTCASTS OF THE EARTH

*a*The day of reckoning is no secret to the Almighty,   **24**
though those who know him have no hint of its date.
Wicked men*b* move boundary-stones   2
and carry away flocks and their shepherds.*c*
In the field they reap what is not theirs,*d*   6*e*
and filch the late grapes from the rich*f* man's vineyard.
·They drive off the orphan's ass   3
and lead away the widow's ox with a rope.
They snatch the fatherless infant from the breast   9
and take the poor man's child in pledge.
They jostle the poor out of the way;   4
the destitute huddle together, hiding from them.
The poor rise early like the wild ass,   5
when it scours the wilderness for food;
but though they work till nightfall,*g*
their children go hungry.*h*
Naked and bare they pass the night;   7
in the cold they have nothing to cover them.
They are drenched by rain-storms from the hills   8

[*a*] *Prob. rdg.; Heb. prefixes* Why.
[*b*] Wicked men: *prob. rdg., cp. Sept.; Heb. obscure.*
[*c*] and their shepherds: *so Sept.; Heb.* and feed them.
[*d*] *Lit.* his.
[*e*] *Verses 3–9 re-arranged to restore the natural order.*
[*f*] *Or* wicked.
[*g*] *Prob. rdg.; Heb.* Arabah.
[*h*] go hungry: *prob. rdg.; Heb.* to it food.

and hug the rock, their only shelter.

10   Naked and bare they go about their work,
      and hungry they carry the sheaves;

11   they press the oil in the shade where two walls meet,
      they tread the winepress but themselves go thirsty.

12   Far from the city, they groan like dying men,
      and like wounded men they cry out;
      but God pays no heed to their prayer.

✻   1. This verse should probably be prefaced by 'why' as the
N.E.B. footnote indicates. Why does God hide his *day of
reckoning* from his followers? This day of judgement is obviously intended for the catalogue of sinners which follows.
Those who suffer at the hands of the wicked are apparently
those who long for the advent of this day.

2–9. As the N.E.B. footnote states, these verses have been
re-arranged to restore the conjectural natural order. It does
not necessarily follow that we should expect a Hebrew poet
to arrange ideas as we might wish to do.

2. Removing *boundary-stones* to extend one's property is
frequently condemned in the Old Testament (Deut. 19: 14;
Prov. 22: 28; 23: 10).

3, 9. Widows and orphans were to be protected by special
ordinances (Deut. 14: 29). God himself is their special guardian (Deut. 10: 18) and any crime against them is considered
especially grievous (Isa. 1: 23). Deut. 24: 17 forbids taking a
widow's garment as a pledge. To take her child is doubly evil.

4. The poor are ejected from the mainstream of society and
forced to hide together, destitute and dehumanized.

5. The original text is obscure in places, but the general
image of the poor as starving human scavengers is quite clear.
They are like *the wild ass*, frantic and humiliated in their search
for food. They are reduced to living like animals, not human
beings.

7. Their hunger-pangs are coupled with the discomfort of their nakedness, whether working or sleeping.

8. Homeless, they are exposed to the elements like beasts crowded against a rock.

10–11. Their misery is intensified when they do find work, for they *carry the sheaves* but cannot enjoy the grain, they *tread* grapes but cannot drink the wine.

12. The poor are outcasts, forced to live and die outside the confines of civilization. Their agony grows with the realization that God, the protector of the poor and the father of the fatherless (Pss. 68: 4–5; 146: 5–9), is deaf to their cries of misery and hunger. ✳

LOVERS OF THE DARKNESS

Some there are who rebel against the light of day,	13
who know nothing of its ways	
and do not linger in the paths of light.	
The murderer rises before daylight	14
to kill some miserable wretch.*ᵃ*	
The seducer watches eagerly for twilight,	15
thinking, 'No eye will catch sight of me.'	
The thief prowls*ᵇ* by night,*ᶜ*	
his face covered with a mask,	
and in the darkness breaks into houses	16
which he has*ᵈ* marked down in the day.	
One and all,*ᵉ* they are strangers to the daylight,	
but dark night is morning to them;	17
and in the welter of night they are at home.	

[a] *See note on verse 15.*
[b] The thief prowls: *prob. rdg.; Heb.* Let him be like a thief.
[c] *Line transposed from end of verse 14.*
[d] *So Pesh.; Heb.* they have.
[e] One and all: *transposed from after* but *in next verse.*

✻ 13. *light* is probably used in two senses here, daylight and life. According to Proverbs 'the course of the righteous' who follow the way of wisdom leads to life 'like morning light' but 'the ways of the wicked are like darkness at night' (4: 10–19; cp. 5: 5–6; 6: 23). Verse 17 makes it clear that the wicked are at home in the darkness of evil and identify with the night.

14–16. *The murderer*, the adulterer and the *thief* all commit their crimes in the darkness. A portion of verse 14 has been transposed to the end of verse 15 where it fits better.   ✻

THE FALL OF THE MIGHTY

18 Such men are scum on the surface of the water;
    their fields have a bad name throughout the land,
    and no labourer will go near their*a* vineyards.

19 As drought and heat make away with snow,
    so the waters of Sheol*b* make away with the sinner.

20 The womb forgets him, the worm sucks him dry;
    he will not be remembered ever after.*c*

21 He may have wronged*d* the barren childless woman
    and been no help to the widow;

22 yet God in his strength carries off even the mighty;
    they may rise, but they have no firm hope of life.

23 He lulls them into security and confidence;
    but his eyes are fixed on their ways.

24 For a moment they rise to the heights, but are soon gone;
    iniquity is snapped like a stick.*e*

[a] *Lit.* the.
[b] snow...Sheol: *prob. rdg.; Heb.* snow-water, Sheol.
[c] *Prob. rdg.; Heb. here adds* iniquity is snapped like a stick (*see note on verse 24*).   [d] He...wronged: *so Targ.; Heb.* shepherd.
[e] *Line transposed from end of verse 20.*

They are laid low and wilt like a mallow-flower;
they droop like an ear of corn on the stalk.
If this is not so, who will prove me wrong   25
and make nonsense of my argument?

✴ 18. N.E.B. translates this verse as an additional description
of the wicked depicted in the preceding verses. Other scholars
consider verses 18–25 a unit which may belong after 27: 13
where the lot of wicked rulers is described.

19. The sinner is destined to enter *Sheol* as surely as the sun
melts the winter snow. On Sheol see at 7: 9 and 10: 21. The
translation of this verse remains uncertain, however (see
N.E.B. footnote).

20. In the grave the wicked man is gladly forgotten. The
line from this verse quoted in the N.E.B. footnote is transposed to verse 24, although it could be retained at this point.

21. Some scholars feel that verse 21 belongs earlier with the
discussion of the oppressed widows (verses 3, 9). Included here
it provides the ground for divine retribution against the mighty
ruler.

22. As in earlier references attention is fixed on monarchs
who have reached great heights of power and glory through
devious means. They are god-like heroes with clay feet. See
the comments on 20: 6–11; 21: 28.

22–4. These verses attempt to explain why tyrants rise to
such great power before they are destroyed (see on verse 1).
God holds a close watch on their evil 'ways', but he permits
them to be deluded into assuming their triumphs are the result
of their own inner resources. Their reign at the pinnacle of
success, however, is short-lived. The implication seems to be
that God allows evil to have free rein among some rulers so
as to demonstrate the potential destructive forces inherent in
all evil.

25. A concluding challenge for the opponent to gainsay the
speaker. ✴

The Third Discourse of Bildad

* The text has 25: 2–6 as Bildad's speech, but the form and central themes of 26: 5–14 suggest that these verses are not a speech of Job but belong to that truncated speech of Bildad. The arguments presented in 26: 5–14 are inconsistent with Job's earlier assertions that God uses his wisdom and might to create disorder (12: 13–22). Thus 26: 1–4 breaks the progression of a hymnic discourse that consists of 25: 2–6; 26: 5–14. 26: 1–4 should probably be transposed to replace 27: 1.

The key to Bildad's speech lies in the interpretative comment of 26: 14 which literally translated reads 'these are the extremities of his way'. When the term 'way' occurs in wisdom contexts it often involves the idea of governing principles and cosmic design rather than of sheer creative 'power' (28: 13, 23; Prov. 3: 17; 4: 11; 8: 22, 32). According to one rendering of Prov. 8: 22, Wisdom claims that 'Yahweh begat me first, his way before his works'. 'The extremities of his way' are apparently the structural outlines of his cosmic design, the ordering of creation by the Lord of Wisdom. These outlines are veiled in mystery according to Bildad (in 26: 14). Man strains to comprehend them but only hears of rumour about them (cp. Isa. 40: 21); the full impact of their mysterious power would be an incomprehensible thunder to the human ear.

The catalogue of creative acts in this cosmic plan is similar to the listing of Prov. 8: 22–9 and the longer enumeration of Job 38. In each case attention is given to the structural components of the cosmos. The terminology of Bildad's creation hymn has a strong affinity with the wisdom materials in ch. 28 and Prov. 8: 22–9. In the subsequent treatment of God's unfathomable wisdom (ch. 28) man is considered incapable of grasping the cosmic 'way' of wisdom (verse 13). God, however, 'understands the way' because he oversees 'the ends of the earth' (verses 23–4). These mysterious 'extremities of his way' are the concern of Bildad's discourse. His description of this cosmic design ranges from the celestial 'peace' established in the highest heaven to the turmoil evoked by God's un-veiling of the underworld, from the vast superstructures of heaven and earth to the horizons and boundaries of the visible world, and from the quaking emergence of the pillars of heaven to the ordering of chaos by violent conquest. In com-parison to this incomprehensible universe man is nothing. The implication is that Job's presumption exceeds all bounds when he, a mere worm, dares to challenge the justice of the inscrutable designer of the universe. Thus, instead of reciting this wisdom-oriented hymn as a vehicle for glorifying the creator, Bildad uses it to humiliate and dehumanize his fellow man. (Contrast the speeches of God, see pp. 199–201.) *

THE INSIGNIFICANCE OF MAN

Then Bildad the Shuhite answered: **25**

Authority and awe rest with him 2
who has established peace in his realm on high.
His squadrons are without number; 3
at whom will they not spring from ambush[a]?
How then can a man be justified in God's sight, 4
or one born of woman be innocent?
If the circling moon is found wanting, 5
and the stars are not innocent in his eyes,
much more so man who is but a maggot, 6
mortal man who is only a worm.

* 2. A similar formal hymnic opening appears in 12: 13*a*. God has complete control of the cosmos, including the celes-tial realms. The *peace* established on high may reflect a prior conflict with heavenly forces (cp. Ps. 82; Isa. 14: 12–14; 24:

[a] from ambush: *so Sept.; Heb.* his light.

21–2), but that theme is not developed here. Order, control and well-being in the celestial realm normally mean a corresponding order and peace on earth.

3. For God's celestial *squadrons* or host see 19: 12; Judg. 5: 20; Isa. 40: 26; Joel 2: 11. He is indeed the Lord of hosts. In Ps. 104: 1–4 the Creator makes his entry in cosmic splendour with an entourage of heavenly forces. He himself is clothed in 'light' (verse 2). This analogous creation psalm suggests that we retain the Hebrew text of Job 25: 3*b* and read 'on whom does his light not rise'. In 25: 3–5 we would then have a complete listing of sun, moon and stars. This creation plan begins, therefore, with an affirmation of the cosmic control and self-disclosure by the Creator.

4. See the comments on the axioms about man in 4: 17; 9: 2 and 15: 14.

5. Here the stars and the moon are singled out for their imperfections. In 4: 18 God's heavenly messengers are considered untrustworthy while in 15: 15 the very heavens are considered guilty in his eyes. For myths involving celestial revolt see the comment on 4: 18 above.

6. Bildad uses the argument from cosmic imperfection to dehumanize man, or more specifically Job.   ✳

Job's Third Response to Bildad

✳ This typical sarcastic retort of Job interrupts the sequence of Bildad's hymn to the inscrutable power of God (25: 2–6; 26: 5–14), and should probably be transposed to precede 27: 2–7. Job's biting comments belittle the capacity of his friends to function as genuine wisdom teachers when confronted with a case as drastic as Job's.   ✳

YOU PATHETIC TEACHERS!

Then Job answered: **26**

What help you have given to the man without resource,   2
what deliverance you have brought to the powerless!
What counsel you offer to a man at his wit's end,   3
what sound advice to the foolish!
Who has prompted you to say such things,   4
and whose spirit is expressed in your speech?

* 2. Job is indeed *without resource*, deserted by family, friends
and God. His search for a deliverer or vindicator has proved
futile.

3. The terminology of this verse reflects the language of the
wisdom school. Job derides his friends, who claimed to be
wisdom teachers, as weak and worthless.

4. On *spirit* or 'breath' see the note on 27: 3.   *

The Third Discourse of Bildad (continued)

* The third discourse of Bildad, begun in 25: 2-6, is continued at this point. For a general analysis of Bildad's hymn see
pp. 132-3.   *

.

THE EXTREMITIES OF HIS WAY

In the underworld the shades writhe in fear,   5
the waters and all that live in them are struck with
terror.[a]
Sheol is laid bare,   6
and Abaddon uncovered before him.
God spreads the canopy of the sky over chaos   7
and suspends earth in the void.

[a] are struck with terror: *prob. rdg.; Heb. om.*

8   He keeps the waters penned in dense cloud-masses,
       and the clouds do not burst open under their weight.

9   He covers the face of the full moon,[a]
       unrolling his clouds across it.

10   He has fixed the horizon on the surface of the waters
       at the farthest limit of light and darkness.

11   The pillars of heaven quake
       and are aghast at his rebuke.

12   With his strong arm he cleft the sea-monster,
       and struck down the Rahab by his skill.

13   At his breath the skies are clear,
       and his hand breaks the twisting[b] sea-serpent.

14   These are but the fringe of his power;
       and how faint the whisper that we hear of him!
       [Who could fathom the thunder of his might?]

✵ 5. The agony and exposure of *the underworld* results from a theophany of the Creator. The light of his appearance (25: 3) penetrates the watery abyss of Sheol, the land of the dead (cp. Ps. 18: 13-15). All the extremities of the created universe are under his jurisdiction (Amos 9: 2-3; Ps. 139: 7-9). The realms under the earth, however, are enclosed in water (cp. Pss. 24: 2; 136: 6; Jonah 2) where shades and monsters dwell. The Hebrew name for the *shades* is Rephaim, a term which may refer to lesser deities in Canaanite texts. In the Old Testament the expression can apply to aboriginal giants of the Transjordan area (Deut. 2: 10-11, 20-1; 3: 11; Josh. 12: 4) or to the inhabitants of the underworld. Whether it was thought that all who died became shades (Ps. 88: 10), or only the great on earth whose souls had the lasting power to survive as a shadow after death (Isa. 14: 9; 26: 14), is not entirely clear. Prov.

[a] *Or* He overlays the surface of his throne.
[b] *Or* primeval.

136

2: 18 and 9: 18 indicate that being among the shades is the undesirable result of leaving the way of wisdom that leads to life.

6. *Abaddon* derives from a Hebrew word meaning 'perish' or 'destroy' and serves as another name for *Sheol*, the nether-world of perdition and death (cp. Ps. 88: 11; Rev. 9: 11). Earlier Job had expressed a desire to be hidden among the dead in Sheol and thereby avoid God's persistent torments (14: 13). The 'uncovering' of the underworld before God's penetrating presence recalls the original removal of the chaotic deep that once formed a 'cover' over the earth (Ps. 104: 6–9).

7. *canopy of the sky* translates a Hebrew term meaning 'North' in its cosmic sense. The 'spreading' out of the 'North' is equivalent to pitching the heavens as a cosmic tent in which God reigns and appears in celestial splendour (cp. on 9: 8; Pss. 104: 2; 144: 5; Isa. 40: 22). Elsewhere the 'North' is associated with the cosmic mountain, Mount Zaphon, where the gods assemble (Isa. 14: 13–14). The earthly counterpart of the cosmic North among the Canaanites has been identified by some scholars with Jebel el 'Aqra, the ancient Mons Cassius on the Syrian coast. For many Israelites the cosmic mountain was 'Mount Zion in the far North' where Yahweh had made his abode (Ps. 48: 1–2). The cosmic tent or *canopy* of heaven is pitched over the primordial *chaos* upon which the earth is founded. The pitching of heaven and the founding of earth are recurring traditions which are coupled to express the establishment of the basic structures of the universe (Isa. 42: 5; 45: 11–12; 48: 12–13; 51: 13, 16). The earth is usually por-trayed as having its foundations fixed in the chaos water. This verse describes that act as 'suspending earth' in a formless *void* (cp. Gen. 1: 2). There is no reason to believe that the author of Job espoused a modern cosmology which viewed the earth as floating in space (cp. verse 11 and 38: 4–7).

8. The author apparently does not consider the *clouds* water vapour but vast sacks like wine skins which hold heavy masses of water but do not *burst open under their weight* (cp. 38: 37;

Prov. 30: 4). These cloud structures are another of the mysteries of God's cosmic design that challenge human wisdom (cp. 38: 37).

9. Not only do the clouds serve as vessels for water, but they can also be employed as chariots for God to ride across the *face of the full moon* (cp. Ps. 104: 3). Elsewhere Yahweh assumes the title Rider of the Clouds which once belonged to Baal, the Canaanite storm god (cp. Ps. 68: 33). The clouds in this verse are specifically *his clouds*, and perhaps the chariots or charioteers at his disposal.

10. This verse refers to two extremities of the cosmic superstructure, the *horizon* or circle drawn at the limits of the primeval deep (Prov. 8: 27) and the distant boundary between *light and darkness*, i.e. day and night (cp. Gen. 1: 3–5, 7–9). Neither the deep nor the darkness can transgress their established *limit* (Ps. 104: 9, 19, 20). Some passages suggest that this horizon was thought to extend from the earth's surface across the heavens like an enormous vault where God reigns (22: 14; Isa. 40: 22).

11. In Ps. 104: 6–8 the *rebuke* of the Creator puts the chaos waters to flight and exposes the peaks of the primeval mountains beneath. These mountains were apparently considered pillars supporting the vault of heaven (cp. Ps. 18: 7 and 2 Sam. 22: 8). Here earthquakes seem to accompany the emergence of the mountains from beneath the primordial deep.

12. The control of primordial chaos could also be depicted in terms of the widespread Near Eastern myth of conquest over a chaos dragon. In this text chaos is designated Yam, the sea, or *sea-monster*. The same figure appears in a Canaanite myth in which the forces of chaos who threaten to overwhelm the ordered universe are conquered by the storm God Baal. *Rahab*, a second name for this chaos figure, is so far attested only in the Old Testament (9: 13; Ps. 89: 10; Isa. 51: 9). The same myth is alluded to in Ps. 74: 12–14; Isa. 27: 1; Hab. 3: 8, 15). The *skill* involved in the control of chaos is the same ingenuity which, according to other wisdom traditions, the

LORD employed in ordering the universe according to his cosmic design (Prov. 3: 19–20; Job 12: 13; Jer. 10: 12).

13. The expression *twisting sea-serpent* is virtually identical with a designation for Leviathan (cp. Isa. 27: 1), an alternate name for the chaos dragon, found in the Canaanite myth mentioned above. The verb used for the striking and slaughter of this monster in the Canaanite myth is identical with the verb found in the previous verse. Verse 13*a*, however, seems to introduce elements from a Babylonian chaos-conquest myth according to which Tiamat, the chaos monster, representing the primordial sea waters, is defeated by the storm god Marduk and split 'like a shellfish' into two parts which become the earth and the sky. Marduk's battle techniques involve the use of violent winds and a huge net (cp. 19: 6). A number of scholars therefore read verse 13*a* 'By his wind he caught Yam in a net.'

14. For similar interpretative summaries or conclusions see 5: 27; 8: 19; 18: 21; 20: 29; 27: 13. The *fringe of his power* is literally the 'extremities of his way', or the structural outlines of his cosmic design. See the introduction to Bildad's third discourse on p. 132. The outer limits of God's creation plan are so distant that man can only catch a whisper of the mysteries involved in their origin. Before them man is reduced to total insignificance and utter amazement. Such is the effect Bildad hoped to achieve in the case of Job. ✳

Job's Third Response to Bildad (continued)

✳ Only the first seven verses of this chapter belong to Job; the remainder are an anonymous discourse similar to ch. 24. No doubt this speech of Job was originally much longer. What remains is a vehement oath in which Job swears to protest his innocence and demand justice from God until he dies. Job's longer oath of clearance is found in ch. 31. ✳

I SWEAR I AM INNOCENT

27 Then Job resumed his discourse:

2   I swear by God, who has denied me justice,
       and by the Almighty, who has filled me with bitter-
           ness:
3   so long as there is any life left in me
       and God's breath is in my nostrils,
4   no untrue word shall pass my lips
       and my tongue shall utter no falsehood.
5   God forbid that I should allow you to be right;
       till death, I will not abandon my claim to innocence.
6   I will maintain the rightness of my cause, I will never
           give up;
       so long as I live, I will not change.
7   May my enemy meet the fate of the wicked,
       and my antagonist the doom of the wrongdoer!

✵ 1. This verse should perhaps be deleted as a late addition,
since the original speeches of Job normally begin 'Then Job
answered'. An appropriate opening for this speech would be
the misplaced verses of 26: 1–4. See the comment there.

2. Job swears a solemn oath by the God of the patriarchs,
here designated El (*God*) and Shaddai (*Almighty*, see at 5: 17).
Job has repeatedly claimed that God is the real source of his
agony (e.g. 19: 6–12) and the ultimate roadblock in his pursuit of justice (e.g. 9: 2–31). God has denied Job a hearing of
any kind.

3–4. In Job the *breath* of God is not only the animating life-
force but also the faculty of understanding (cp. on 12: 10;
20: 3; 26: 4; 32: 8). While Job is alive and of sound mind he
will maintain his integrity and speak no deceit.

5–6. As repulsive as contemplating hypocrisy on his own

part is the thought that Job should concede the case to his friends and, in effect, vindicate them rather than himself. Job will protest his *innocence* (as in 1: 1; 9: 20–1), and prosecute his case against God until he dies.

7. This verse is awkward in the mouth of Job. He may be merely using a formal imprecation as the conclusion of his preceding oath. Elsewhere the friends and God himself are Job's enemies (e.g. 16: 7–14). Job, it would seem, comes very close to cursing God at this point (cp. 1: 11; 2: 9).   ✻

A Second Anonymous Discourse

✻ This anonymous speech (cp. ch. 24) has no introduction typical of earlier speeches by the friends. The position it espouses, however, is identical with theirs. It seems to be a random collection of materials about the futile hope of the godless and the ultimate fate of the wicked (cp. 18: 5–20). Some scholars consider these materials part of Zophar's final speech since he alone of all the friends has no recorded third discourse. The only new theme in this portrayal of the wicked is the idea that the righteous will enjoy the wealth left by the departed wicked.   ✻

AN EAST WIND FOR THE WICKED

What hope has a godless man, when he is cut off,[a]	8[b]
when God takes away his life?	
Will God listen to his cry	9
when trouble overtakes him?	
Will he trust himself to the Almighty	10
and call upon God at all times?	
I will teach you what is in God's power,	11

[a] *Or* What is a godless man's thread of life when it is cut. . .
[b] *It is possible that verses 8–23 are part of a speech by Zophar otherwise lost from the third cycle of speeches.*

I will not conceal the purpose of the Almighty.

12 If all of you have seen these things,
why then do you talk such empty nonsense?

13 This is the lot prescribed by God for the wicked,
and the ruthless man's reward from the Almighty.

14 He may have many sons, but they will fall by the
sword,
and his offspring will go hungry;

15 the survivors will be brought to the grave by pestilence,
and no widows will weep for them.

16 He may heap up silver like dirt
and get himself piles of clothes;

17 he may get them, but the righteous will wear them,
and his silver will be shared among the innocent.

18 The house he builds is flimsy as a bird's nest
or a shelter put up by a watchman.

19 He may lie down rich one day, but never again;[a]
he opens his eyes and all is gone.

20 Disaster overtakes him like a flood,
and a storm snatches him away in the night;

21 the east wind lifts him up and he is gone;
it whirls him far from home;

22 it flings itself on him without mercy,
and he is battered and buffeted by its force;

23 it snaps its fingers at him
and whistles over him wherever he may be.

✻ 8–10. The *hope* of the *godless* was introduced by Bildad in
8: 13. On the rendering 'thread of life' in the N.E.B. footnote
see the comment on 7: 6. The godless live in defiance of God's

[a] but. . .again: *so* Sept.; *Heb.* but he is not gathered in.

will and never expect deliverance when they meet disaster. No room seems to be left for repentance and no hint is given of Paul's theme that God will 'justify the godless' who turn to him (Rom. 5: 6-11).

11-12. These verses may be a misplaced introduction for this or another speech. The spokesman claims to be a wisdom teacher whose insight into God's power and purpose can be verified by public evidence. *power*, or literally 'hand', was understood negatively by Job (12: 9; 19: 21).

13. A modified version of 20: 13 which seems to have provided the springboard for the following portrait of the lot prescribed *for the wicked*.

14-15. The wicked can find no joy in a progeny doomed to reap the reward of the evil sown by their ruthless fathers. See the note on 21: 19-21.

16-17. These verses introduce a theme not stressed earlier in the portraits of the wicked, namely, the equitable distribution of the wicked man's wealth to the righteous and innocent. Not only are the wicked to be punished but the faithful are to be rewarded with spoils from the fall of their oppressors (cp. Prov. 13: 22).

18-19. Neither his abode nor his riches provide the wicked man with any real security. His possessions are as transitory as his life (cp. 15: 27-35).

20-3. The *Disaster* sent by God against the wicked is described as an east wind which *whirls* them away in a tempest. An act of God is appointed to terminate their lives. The verb 'whirl' is related to the noun for 'tempest' used in 38: 1 where God speaks to Job (see also on 9: 17). On God's use of the *east wind* to punish see Jer. 18: 17; Hos. 13: 15. Job's household was struck by a similar wind (1: 19).   ✻

God's unfathomable wisdom

✲ This chapter is an independent poem about the hidden
wisdom of the cosmos. Although wisdom is a concern of Job
(12: 2, 12, 13) and his friends (8: 8–10; 11: 6–11; 15: 7–8), no
attempt is made in this poem to relate the inaccessibility of
divine wisdom to the dilemma Job is facing. No direct connection is made with any of the major arguments of the
preceding discourses where probing the justice and wisdom of
God is a legitimate facet of the debate. Here the unfathomable
nature of divine wisdom is the single consideration of the poet.
Wisdom lies far beyond the most penetrating investigation of
man (cp. Prov. 30: 1–4).

Man is a natural explorer, according to this poet. He is
driven to probe the limits of his world and search for the
precious in hidden realms of the universe. His efforts at mining
ores from the earth are spectacular examples of this characteristic in man. Like all natural phenomena, the ores have their
appointed 'place' in the order of the universe, a hidden 'place'
which man in his ingenuity has discovered. In his exploration
man is willing to risk great dangers and undergo extreme
hardships to unearth what is hidden. This characteristic of man
sets the stage for the ultimate quest, the search for the 'place'
of wisdom. The word 'place' (Hebrew *māqōm*) is a key word
in this chapter, though rendered in various ways.

Wisdom is a mysterious figure operating throughout the
universe as she has since the beginning of the world. She is the
governing principle of the universe, the mind which determines the order and splendour of the cosmos. Her veiled
presence fascinates the curious and lures human beings in a
quest for the most precious treasure of all, wisdom herself (cp.
Prov. 3: 13–15). To discover wisdom means discovering the
tree of life at the centre of the world, and perhaps life eternal
(cp. Prov. 3: 16–18; Gen. 3: 22). The inaccessibility of wisdom

is symbolized by her hidden abode. She too has a 'place', an appointed locale with a fixed 'way' of access. But God alone knows the secret path to her house. From the creation of the world he has known and cherished her, for it was he who first discovered her and learned of her importance in regulating the universe (cp. Prov. 8: 22–31). Man may be a natural explorer, but he will never be able to match the original discovery of God and find the very source of world wisdom. ✳

MAN'S QUEST FOR TREASURE

There are mines for silver **28**
and places where men refine gold;
where iron is won from the earth 2
and copper smelted from the ore;
the end of the seam lies in darkness, 3
and it is followed to its farthest limit.[a]
Strangers cut the galleries;[b] 4
they are forgotten as they drive forward far from men.[c]
While corn is springing from the earth above, 5
what lies beneath is raked over like a fire,
and out of its rocks comes lapis lazuli, 6
dusted with flecks of gold.
No bird of prey knows the way there, 7
and the falcon's keen eye cannot descry it;
proud beasts do not set foot on it, 8
and no serpent comes that way.
Man sets his hand to the granite rock 9
and lays bare the roots of the mountains;
he cuts galleries in the rocks, 10

[a] *Prob. rdg.; Heb. adds* stones of darkness and deep darkness.
[b] Strangers. . .galleries: *prob. rdg.; Heb. obscure.*
[c] *Prob. rdg.; Heb. adds* languishing without foothold.

and gems of every kind meet his eye;
11   he dams up the sources of the streams
       and brings the hidden riches of the earth to light.

✻ 1. *silver* was imported into Israel from Tarshish (Jer. 10: 9) and *gold* from Ophir and Sheba (1 Kings 10: 2, 11). The mining and refining process, however, was well known to the Israelites. The word translated *mines* literally means 'place of origin' or 'source', and stands in parallelism to *place (māqōm)*. In verse 23 the N.E.B. translates *māqōm* as 'source'. The hidden source of silver and gold is comparable to the secret source of wisdom.

2. The promised land is described as 'a land whose stones are iron ore and from whose hills you will dig copper' (Deut. 8: 9). There is something of a mystery in the mining process; iron is extracted from the *earth* or, literally, 'the dust'.

3–4. In the interests of poetic uniformity the N.E.B. has relegated the ending of each of these two verses to footnotes. The thoughts they express, however, are consistent with the context.

3. The translation *seam* is based on a conjecture, designed to preserve the mining imagery. The focus of the verse, however, is on the *limit* and the *end* of things where man is willing to penetrate, even if these extremities lie deep in darkness. In contrast to these limits set by God in his universe (cp. 26: 10), the 'limit of the Almighty' himself is impossible for man to fathom (see note on 11: 7).

4. In their search for the precious metals men are willing to labour far from civilization and risk great dangers. The N.E.B. footnote can be translated 'they are suspended, they waver far from men'. The allusion is to the ancient practice of suspending miners by ropes into the mine shafts.

5. In contrast to the quiet growth of crops which also originate from the earth, great upheavals are happening below the surface. *raked over*: more properly 'turned upside down' or

'overthrown'. The word is used of the overthrow of mountains (cp. 9: 5), or of Sodom (Gen. 19: 25). While some scholars suggest a kind of underground smelting here, the reference is probably to a mysterious subterranean fire which transforms rock into precious metal. Such an idea was no doubt fostered by the eruption of volcanos. Into that strange and dangerous place of fire the miners descend.

6. *out of. . .comes* renders the word *māqōm*, 'place'. *lapis lazuli* or perhaps 'sapphires' and similar precious gems each have their hidden 'place' deep in the rocks of earth.

7–8. These precious stones are invisible to the *keen eye* of birds soaring above, to *proud beasts* who roam the earth (cp. 41: 34) and to the *serpent* who lives among the rocks. These creatures do not possess the capacity of man to penetrate the mysteries of the earth. The allusion to *serpent* here is uncertain; the Hebrew word is usually rendered 'lion' (cp. 4: 10; 10: 16). The term *way* in verse 7 introduces another of the terms connected with the search for wisdom; each mystery of the universe has its divinely ordained 'place', and the appropriate 'way' to discover or grasp it.

9–10. Man has the ability to extract gems from rocks and disturb the very *roots of the mountains*. In this he is god-like. *lays bare*: 'turned over' so that the hidden base of the mountains is exposed. The same word is used in verse 5. Man's ingenuity is matched by his great power. Exposing the 'roots of the mountains' indicates man's ability to penetrate to the very foundations of the earth.

11. *the sources of the streams* seems to be a reference to the abode of the Canaanite father god El, where the cosmic waters meet. The implication is that man even strives to control these hidden cosmic waters. From the dark and hidden places he can bring mysteries to light. *hidden riches* may refer to hidden things or mysteries in general (as in 11: 6) rather than precious items from the earth. After the first eleven verses of this chapter the reader is left with the question, 'Is there any hidden secret man cannot probe?' ✳

MAN'S QUEST FOR WISDOM

12   But where can wisdom be found?
     And where is the source of understanding?
13   No man knows the way to it;[a]
     it is not found in the land of living men.
14   The depths of ocean say, 'It is not in us',
     and the sea says, 'It is not with me.'
15   Red gold cannot buy it,
     nor can its price be weighed out in silver;
16   it cannot be set in the scales against gold of Ophir,
     against precious cornelian or lapis lazuli;
17   gold and crystal[b] are not to be matched with it,
     no work in fine gold can be bartered for it;
18   black coral and alabaster are not worth mention,
     and a parcel of wisdom fetches more than red coral;
19   topaz[c] from Ethiopia is not to be matched with it,
     it cannot be set in the scales against pure gold.
20   Where then does wisdom come from,
     and where is the source of understanding?
21   No creature on earth can see it,
     and it is hidden from the birds of the air.
22   Destruction[d] and death say,
     'We know of it only by report.'

✶ 12–14. *source* renders the Hebrew *māqōm*, 'place', and *way*
the probable reading *derek* (as in verse 23). Wisdom is here
portrayed as a mysterious figure whose abode or 'place of
origin' remains unknown and inaccessible. The 'way' to this

[a] So Sept.; Heb. knows its value.
[b] Lit. glass.
[c] Or chrysolite.
[d] Heb. Abaddon, cp. 26: 6.

hidden place cannot be found on earth among men or in the
cosmic deeps where gods were thought to dwell (see on verse
11). The home of wisdom is beyond any point man can penetrate with his skill or his mind. Wisdom is a distant, strange
and alluring force whose origins can never be traced by man,
but who remains the ultimate goal of every human being's
quest in life. In Proverbs, however, wisdom is far from inaccessible; she invites the unlearned to her abode (4: 7–12;
9: 1–6). Her truths may not all be fathomed, but she challenges
man to try.

15–19. Wisdom is no ordinary commodity. It cannot be
purchased on the open market, no matter how good the gold
offered in exchange. No treasure extracted by man at great cost
can procure wisdom; she is more precious than all the jewels
in the world (Prov. 2: 2–4; 3: 13–20). She is the mystery that
gives meaning to life itself. On *silver* and *gold of Ophir* see verse 1.

20. A virtual repetition of verse 12, as a kind of refrain.

21. The world of nature cannot discern the 'place' of wisdom any more than man (cp. Job's claims in 12: 7–12). If the
piercing eye of the falcon cannot discover treasures beneath
the earth, the location of wisdom is far beyond his vision (cp.
verse 7).

22. *death* and *Destruction* ('Abaddon' as in 26: 6) are again
personified (cp. 18: 11–14). As a last resort the searcher may
go to the underworld to visit God's enemy, Death. As formidable as he is, he can only share vague rumours about the
abode of wisdom.   *

GOD'S DISCOVERY OF WISDOM

But God understands the way to it,   23
he alone knows its source;
for he can see to the ends of the earth   24
and he surveys everything under heaven.
When he made a counterpoise for the wind   25

and measured out the waters in proportion,

26 when he laid down a limit for the rain
and a path for the thunderstorm,

27 even then he saw wisdom and took stock of it,
he considered[a] it and fathomed its very depths.

28 And he said to man:
The fear of the Lord is wisdom,
and to turn from evil is understanding.

✻ 23. God alone knows the *source* (*māqōm*) or 'place' of wisdom and the *way* (*derek*) of access to it. Wisdom seems to be portrayed here as a feminine figure independent from God, whose abode is familiar to him. In Prov. 8: 22–31 wisdom was God's companion before creation and 'played' in his presence.

24. Regardless of where wisdom chose to hide herself in the universe, God could discern her presence. He is the distant God who encompasses the universe in his vision (Jer. 23: 23–4) from the very heavens he once made by wisdom (Prov. 3: 19–20). Later traditions outside the Bible speak of wisdom searching in vain for a dwelling place among men and finally returning to her 'place' among the angels. Such an idea is found in the book of Enoch (42: 1–2), a Jewish writing or collection of writings belonging mainly to the last two centuries B.C. (See *The Making of the Old Testament* in this series, pp. 78–80.)

25–6. The weather is governed by the wisdom of God (cp. 5: 10; 38: 22–7, 33–8; Isa. 40: 12–14). Under the guidance of wisdom, the various 'limits', boundaries, courses and places for the components of the universe were established (cp. Prov. 8: 27–9). These structural orders of the universe are evidence of the great mind of wisdom working behind the scenes. How she operates, however, is a mystery known only to God.

27. This verse is unique among biblical affirmations about

[a] *So some MSS.; others* established.

wisdom. In Proverbs wisdom is God's counsellor and companion, begotten before the world began (8: 22–31). Wisdom is also his governing principle in creation (Prov. 3: 19–20). Here, however, wisdom is neither created nor born; she is discovered in the very process of constructing the universe. God• alone found wisdom, like a previously undiscerned mystery at work in the very world he was making. Just as man explores the depths of the earth for treasure, so God probed his newly discovered ally to test her worth. Man, however, remains fascinated by the powerful presence of wisdom hidden in the universe and strives to grasp the mystery of her ways.

28. This verse appears to be a later comment by a pious editor who attempted to soften the assertion of the preceding verses that the wisdom by which God operates the universe is totally inaccessible to human beings. According to this comment a practical wisdom is made available for the devout who, like Job, avoid wrongdoing (1: 1). *The fear of the Lord* represents the traditional way of life of the pious wisdom school whose theology is reflected in Prov. 1–9 (cp. 4: 6; Prov. 1: 7, 29; 2: 5). ✶

Job's final survey of his case

✶ In his closing soliloquy (chs. 29–31) Job surveys his case as if it were a summing up in court. He begins with a nostalgic rehearsal of the good life he once knew. He recalls his activities as a wise leader whose name was revered by all and whose counsel was supreme. He could boast a long record of righteousness and justice for all, especially the unfortunate. He lived with the traditional expectation of rich rewards for his noble life of good works (ch. 29). This recital of past experiences is more than an exercise in sentimentality; Job is confronting God with the reality of his former mercy and goodness so that he might be moved to compassion before it is too late. Job follows his rehearsal of past events with a vivid portrayal of his current agonies and anxieties. The joys of yesterday have turned into a nightmare of terrors. In this lament Job focuses on the ignominy and torment of public derision by the scum and rabble of his community. His abuse by the mob is matched by the violent humiliation he suffers at the hands of his ultimate enemy, God himself. Job's plight is worse than that of the wild beasts who are, in the end, his only friends (ch. 30). This complaint is Job's final attempt to rouse the justice of God so that he might get a fair trial before he dies, even though his heroic vindicator had not stepped forward to rescue him at the last minute (cp. on 19: 23–7). Job has completed his case and made his demands. All that remains is the final ominous oath of innocence which he swears before God (see the discussion at ch. 31). The last move is then up to God. ✷

MY COUNSEL WAS SUPREME

29 Then Job resumed his discourse:

2   If I could only go back to the old days,
      to the time when God was watching over me,
3   when his lamp shone above my head,
      and by its light I walked through the darkness!
4   If I could be as in the days of my prime,
      when God protected my home,[a]
5   while the Almighty was still there at my side,
      and my servants stood round me,
6   while my path flowed with milk,
      and the rocks streamed oil!
7   If I went through the gate out of the town
      to take my seat in the public square,

[a] when...home: *so Sept.; Heb.* in the secret council of God upon my home.

young men saw me and kept out of sight;   8
old men rose to their feet,
men in authority broke off their talk   9
and put their hands to their lips;
the voices of the nobles died away,   10
and every man held his tongue.
They listened to me expectantly   21[a]
and waited in silence for my opinion.
When I had spoken, no one spoke again;   22
my words fell gently on them;
they waited for them as for rain   23
and drank them in like showers in spring.
When I smiled on them, they took heart;   24
when my face lit up, they lost their gloomy looks.
I presided over them, planning their course,   25
like a king encamped with his troops.[b]

* 2–3. Job looks back with nostalgia to the good old days
when he was blessed by his God *watching over* him and causing
his face to shine upon him (cp. Num. 6: 24–6). Job had previously recalled God's providential 'watching' in an effort to
arouse a genuine compassion for his personal creation (10:
8–12). Job's wish, therefore, is more than a withdrawing into
the comfortable memories of the past. He is forcing God to
remember his goodness to Job and to act with sympathetic justice. The *light* of God is a life-giving power emanating from his presence or wisdom (Ps. 18: 29; Isa. 60: 3;
Prov. 6: 23).

4–6. Job recalls days of ease and prosperity under the bene-
ficent protection of the Almighty. *milk* and *oil* are symbols of

[a] *Verses 21–5 transposed to this point.*
[b] *Prob. rdg.; Heb. adds* as when one comforts mourners.

plenty (cp. on 20: 17). These verses may reflect the tradition of Job as a rich patriarchal hero (1: 2–3).

7–10. Job remembers the day when he was a respected wise man and elder whose authority was evident in his counsel as well as his position. Job is here a distinguished city leader rather than a rich sheikh (as in 1: 1–3).

7. The city *gate* was the arena for commercial and judicial activities in the ancient Near East (e.g. Ruth 4: 1).

8. Job reflects on his position as a revered and powerful figure in his community.

9. *men in authority*: literally 'princes'. Job was honoured by royalty and may himself have been a ruler.

21–5. These verses have been transposed to this point where they seem to belong in the sequence of ideas. As an ideal wisdom teacher and leader Job's presence was honoured and his counsel effective.

21. Job's *opinion* is more precisely his 'counsel', his 'effective advice' as a wisdom teacher (cp. 26: 3; 2 Sam. 17: 7; Prov. 20: 5). What Job once said was hailed as the truth; now his friends ridicule him as an irreligious fool.

22–3. Job had the last word; his advice had the weight of authority and the capacity to revive the weak. His presence, like that of a king, was as refreshing as spring showers (cp. Prov. 16: 15; Ps. 72: 6).

25. *planning their course* is literally 'choosing their way'. Job selected the course of action and determined the destiny of those over whom he presided as counsellor and leader. He functioned with all the authority of a king directing his troops. On 'way' see on 3: 23; 12: 24; 23: 10–11; 26: 14. Verse 25c (see N.E.B. footnote) is a late addition that seems inconsistent with the preceding verses.   ✳

MY CONCERNS WERE RIGHTEOUS

Whoever heard of me spoke in my favour,   11
and those who saw me bore witness to my merit,
how I saved the poor man when he called for help   12
and the orphan who had no protector.
The man threatened with ruin blessed me,   13
and I made the widow's heart sing for joy.
I put on righteousness as a garment and it clothed me;   14
justice, like a cloak or a turban, wrapped me round.
I was eyes to the blind   15
and feet to the lame;
I was a father to the needy,   16
and I took up the stranger's cause.
I broke the fangs of the miscreant   17
and rescued the prey from his teeth.
I thought, 'I shall die with my powers unimpaired   18
and my days uncounted as the grains of sand,*a*
with my roots spreading out to the water   19
and the dew lying on my branches,
with the bow always new in my grasp   20
and the arrow ever ready to my hand.'*b*

✻ 11. Job's record as a leader was hailed by a public ready to testify to his compassion and justice. Now his own friends condemn him for neglect of those very duties he executed so faithfully (22: 5–9).

12–13. Job was a champion of the underdog, a liberator and redeemer for the oppressed. As such he was a perfect example of a righteous ruler whose chief task was to protect the weak (Ps. 72: 1–12; Isa. 11: 3–4). When Job was crushed, however,

[a] *Or* as those of the phoenix.
[b] *Verses 21–5 transposed to follow verse 10.*

he had no liberator or vindicator to espouse his cause (10: 7; 9: 33-4).

14. *righteousness*, like other qualities, is often represented in terms of clothing (19: 9; 40: 10; Ps. 132: 9); in this context it is not primarily piety or sinless behaviour, but a way of life which involves continuous intervention and compassion for the weak and oppressed so that *justice* is achieved in their lives. Righteousness imparts new life and hope to the disenfranchised or the depressed.

15-16. As a righteous counsellor Job took the case of help-less suppliants in court. He overcame their deficiencies for them, even playing the role of father to redeem the poor (on 'redeemer' see at 19: 25).

17. Job's justice extended to the punishment of the wicked, a phenomenon he cannot now discern in his life. His God has become a promoter of chaos and injustice (12: 16-25). He is God's prey (19: 6-12).

18-20. In the light of the wisdom teaching he had endorsed, Job expected to be rewarded for his righteousness, live a blessed life full of vitality and die healthy at a ripe old age. The N.E.B. footnote for 18*b* mentions the 'phoenix', a mythological bird which returns to life periodically. Accord-ing to one later Jewish legend this bird alone refused to eat of the forbidden fruit of Eden and was therefore immortal. ✻

SCORNED BY SCUM

30   But now I am laughed to scorn
       by men of a younger generation,
       men whose fathers I would have disdained
       to put with the dogs who kept my flock.
2   What use were their strong arms to me,
       since their sturdy vigour had wasted away?
3   They gnawed roots*a* in the desert,

[a] roots: *prob. rdg.; Heb. om.*

gaunt with want and hunger,[a]
they plucked saltwort and wormwood
and root of broom[b] for their food.   4

Driven out from the society of men,[c]   5
pursued like thieves with hue and cry,
they lived in gullies and ravines,   6
holes in the earth and rocky clefts;
they howled like beasts among the bushes,   7
huddled together beneath the scrub,
vile base-born wretches,   8
hounded from the haunts of men.

Now I have become the target of their taunts,   9
my name is a byword among them.
They loathe me, they shrink from me,   10
they dare to spit in my face.
They run wild and savage[d] me;   11
at sight of me they throw off all restraint.
On my right flank they attack in a mob;[e]   12
they raise their siege-ramps against me,
they tear down my crumbling defences to my   13
    undoing,
and scramble up against me unhindered;
they burst in through the gaping breach;   14
at the moment of the crash they come rolling in.
Terror upon terror overwhelms me,   15
it sweeps away my resolution like the wind,
and my hope of victory vanishes like a cloud.

[a] *Prob. rdg.; Heb. adds* yesterday waste and derelict land.
[b] root of broom: *probably* fungus on broom root.
[c] the society of men: *prob. rdg.; Heb. obscure.*
[d] They run. . .savage: *prob. rdg.; Heb.* He runs. . .savages.
[e] *Prob. rdg.; Heb. adds* they let loose my feet.

16 So now my soul is in turmoil within me,[a]
    and misery has me daily in its grip.
17 By night pain pierces my very bones,
    and there is ceaseless throbbing in my veins;
18 my garments are all bespattered with my phlegm,
    which chokes me like the collar of a shirt.

* 1. Job, who had once been revered by young and old alike
(29: 2–9), is now scorned by the scum of the earth, the obnoxious children of men whom Job considered *dogs*. Dogs
were considered vile scavengers in the ancient Near East (cp.
Prov. 26: 11; Exod. 22: 31).

2–8. Job indulges in a lengthy description of his disgusting
persecutors. They are brutish and wretched outcasts of society.

3. The rendering of this verse is uncertain (see N.E.B. footnotes).

4. These scavengers are often forced to eat unsavoury shrubs
for their survival. *the root of broom* (cp. 1 Kings 19: 4) is probably not edible; the N.E.B. footnote therefore suggests that
a fungus on the broom is intended. According to Jewish
tradition *saltwort* is a sour plant eaten by the very poor.

5–7. These outcasts, who are the object of abuse by the
good people of the community, are forced to find shelter in
caves or *scrub*.

8. *base-born* is literally 'sons of the nameless'. As such this
rabble has no identity or place in society.

9–10. Job has now become the object of public ridicule to
those base members of the community who enjoy the ugly
sport of abusing their fellow human beings.

11–14. Despite some obscurities in these verses (see N.E.B.
footnotes), the general theme is that of an attack on Job by
a savage horde of outcasts. According to the N.E.B. translation Job is like a fortress that is breached by their persistent

[a] *Lit.* is poured out upon me.

onslaughts. They invade *unhindered*; Job is still destitute of any support from heaven or earth (10: 7; 9: 33–4).

15. *hope of victory* is literally 'salvation'. With no chance of deliverance Job experiences his suffering in terms of terrors that consume all the resources within him.

16–18. Like many Psalmists Job portrays his suffering as a rending of various parts of his body with cruel pain and extreme discomfort (cp. Ps. 22: 14–18). The cause of this agony is as much mental and spiritual as it is physical. ✳

HUMILIATED BY GOD

God himself*a* has flung me down in the mud,   19
no better than dust or ashes.

I call for thy help, but thou dost not answer;   20
I stand up to plead, but thou sittest aloof;
thou hast turned cruelly against me   21
and with thy strong hand pursuest me in hatred;
thou dost snatch me up and set me astride the wind,   22
and the tempest*b* tosses me up and down.
I know that thou wilt hand me over to death,   23
to the place appointed for all mortal men.

Yet no beggar held out his hand   24
but was relieved*c* by me in his distress.
Did I not weep for the man whose life was hard?   25
Did not my heart grieve for the poor?
Evil has come though I expected good;   26
I looked for light but there came darkness.
My bowels are in ferment and know no peace;   27
days of misery stretch out before me.

[a] God himself: *prob. rdg.; Heb. om.*
[b] the tempest: *prob. rdg.; Heb. unintelligible.*
[c] was relieved: *prob. rdg.; Heb. unintelligible.*

28 I go about dejected and friendless;
    I rise in the assembly, only to appeal for help.
29 The wolf is now my brother,
    the owls of the desert have become my companions.
30 My blackened skin peels off,
    and my body is scorched by the heat.
31 My harp has been tuned for a dirge,
    my flute to the voice of those who weep.

✶ 19. The context shifts from the scene of Job's public persecutors to the vicious torment of a key assailant, who is
obviously God, even though his name is omitted from the
Hebrew text (see N.E.B. footnote). Job is reduced to the *dust*
even before he is dead. His God flings him in the mire as if he
were trash (cp. 9: 31).

20. Job repeats his accusation that God refused to bring his
case to court and give him a just hearing (cp. 9: 2-4, 11-20).

21. God has been transformed into a ferocious enemy
attacking Job like some wild beast (cp. 16: 9). God's character
is now different from that which Job had previously known;
his God seems to have a dark side that now controls his actions
toward Job.

22. Like an angry storm deity, God employs his celestial
forces to buffet and torment Job (cp. on the note on 9: 17).
On the proposed rendering *tempest* compare on 9: 17.

23. *death* is here personified as in 18: 11-14. Death's abode
is the final meeting-place for all men, the house to which the
oppressed look for freedom and peace (cp. on 3: 13-19).

24-5. Job cites additional examples from his righteous
record to reaffirm his innocence (cp. 29: 11-20). He testifies
again to his compassion for the poor and distressed, a compassion that was not reciprocated when he experienced hard
times.

26. Job expected peace, a full life and prosperity as a reward
for his life of righteous deeds and liberality (cp. on 29: 18-20).

But instead of all those joys symbolized by *light* Job met *darkness*, the world of evil, death and destruction (cp. on 3: 4; 10: 21–2; 29: 3; Amos 5: 18–20). This unexpected turn of events cannot be credited to Job's misdeeds but God's 'dark' ways.

27–31. Job describes again the physical, emotional and social misery of his existence (cp. 3: 24–6; 7: 3–6; 19: 13–20). All the honour and prestige of his past life (29: 2–10) has now been transformed into ignominy and rejection. He is a social outcast who hears the imminent dirge for his own funeral.

29. Job has been reduced to brute nature. The only true friends he knows are the wild animals who seem to understand his plight (cp. 12: 7–9). All human and heavenly friends have deserted him (cp. on 6: 14–17; 16: 20; 19: 13). ✳

JOB'S OATH OF INNOCENCE

What is the lot prescribed by God above,   **31** 2[a]
the reward from the Almighty on high?
Is not ruin prescribed for the miscreant   3
and calamity for the wrongdoer?
Yet does not God himself see my ways   4
and count my every step?

I swear I have had no dealings with falsehood   5
and have not embarked on a course of deceit.
I have come to terms with my eyes,   1
never to take notice of a girl.
Let God weigh me in the scales of justice,   6
and he will know that I am innocent!
If my steps have wandered from the way,   7
if my heart has followed my eyes,
or any dirt stuck to my hands,

[a] *Verse 1 transposed to follow verse 5.*

8   may another eat what I sow,
    and may my crops be pulled up by the roots!
9   If my heart has been enticed by a woman
    or I have lain in wait at my neighbour's door,
10 may my wife be another man's slave,*a*
    and may other men enjoy her.
11 [But that is a wicked act, an offence before the law;
12 it would be a consuming and destructive fire,
    raging*b* among my crops.]
13 If I have ever rejected the plea of my slave
    or of my slave-girl, when they brought their complaint
        to me,
14 what shall I do if God appears?
    What shall I answer if he intervenes?
15 Did not he who made me in the womb make them?
    Did not the same God create us in the belly?
16 If I have withheld their needs from the poor
    or let the widow's eye grow dim with tears,
17 if I have eaten my crust alone,
    and the orphan has not shared it with me –
18 the orphan who from boyhood honoured me like a
        father,
    whom I guided from the day of his*c* birth –
19 if I have seen anyone perish for lack of clothing,
    or a poor man with nothing to cover him,
20 if his body had no cause to bless me,
    because he was not kept warm with a fleece from my
        flock,

[*a*] be. . .slave: *lit.* grind corn for another.
[*b*] *Prob. rdg.; Heb.* uprooting.
[*c*] *Prob. rdg.; Heb.* my.

if I have raised[a] my hand against the innocent,[b]   21
knowing that men would side with me in court,[c]
then may my shoulder-blade be torn from my shoulder,   22
my arm be wrenched out of its socket!
But the terror of God was heavy upon me,[d]   23
and for fear of his majesty I could do none of these
   things.

If I have put my faith in gold   24
and my trust in the gold of Nubia,
if I have rejoiced in my great wealth   25
and in the increase of riches;
if I ever looked on the sun in splendour   26
or the moon moving in her glory,
and was led astray in my secret heart   27
and raised my hand in homage;
this would have been an offence before the law,   28
for I should have been unfaithful to God on high.

If my land has cried out in reproach at me,   38[e]
and its furrows have joined in weeping,
if I have eaten its produce without payment   39
and have disappointed my creditors,
may thistles spring up instead of wheat,   40
and weeds instead of barley!

Have I rejoiced at the ruin of the man that hated me   29
or been filled with malice when trouble overtook him,
even though I did not allow my tongue[f] to sin   30
by demanding his life with a curse?
Have the men of my household[g] never said,   31

[a] *Or* waved.   [b] *Or* orphan.   [c] *Lit.* in the gate.
[d] *Prob. rdg.; Heb.* A fear towards me is a disaster from God.
[e] *Verses 38–40 transposed (but see note c, page 168).*
[f] *Lit.* palate.   [g] *Lit.* tent.

'Let none of us speak ill of him!

32   No stranger has spent the night in the street'?
     For I have kept open house for the traveller.

33   Have I ever concealed my misdeeds as men do,
     keeping my guilt to myself,

34   because I feared the gossip of the town
     or dreaded the scorn of my fellow-citizens?

✻ Job concludes the survey of his case with a lengthy oath of innocence which he appends to his arguments, testimony and charges. He is no longer interested in disputing with his friends or lamenting his condition before God. He wants a resolution of his case. He could either curse God and die as his wife had proposed (2: 9), or supplement his testimony by swearing before heaven that he had lived a life free from blame and then wait for the consequences. Formal oaths of this nature involved the imposing of curses that were expected to strike anyone who lied under oath. If Job were innocent God's continued silence would clear his name and vindicate his integrity. If Job had sworn falsely God would be forced to intervene and impose the sanctions Job had designated. Job has taken a final stand. He does not entertain the possibility that God might intervene and enter the dispute, rather than clear or condemn Job outright (see on ch. 38). The dilemma of innocent suffering and the experience of divine injustice cannot be resolved by a dramatic declaration of innocence, even though Job attempts to do so. With careful deliberation he outlines a life of piety, concern for justice, and compassion for the oppressed that go beyond the expected norms of his days. He has been a paragon of virtue, benevolence, hospitality and faithfulness. The sanctions Job imposes on himself in his oath are similar to curses found throughout the ancient world and frequently intended as fitting punishment for the crime involved. Job's motives for his life style are an unswerving devotion to God and his common humanity with all men as created in the womb by the same God.

Verse 1 is transposed to follow verse 5 since it belongs to the catalogue of misdeeds Job has avoided rather than the introductory comments of verses 2-4. Job claims to have acted modestly toward all women. Some scholars look for a more general item to begin this oath of innocence and so propose the emendation 'folly' for *girl*.

2–4. Job seems to be repeating a traditional formula about the lot of the wicked (20: 29; 27: 13) which he himself had challenged earlier (21: 7-15). Job who has previously accused God of watching him with a merciless eye (7: 17-20; 10: 13–14), and branding his feet with slave-marks to trace all his steps (13: 27), boldly turns the situation to his own advantage. God 'the watcher of men' could be the perfect witness to the truth of Job's oath of innocence (cp. Ps. 7: 9; Jer. 12: 3). The life-history of Job which follows is his own analysis of his 'way' (see on 3: 23; 23: 11).

5–6. Job's initial oath is a repudiation of all dishonesty and deceit. His forthcoming testimony is therefore true and God is challenged to test the veracity of Job's evidence in the scales of divine justice. Job's previous claims to innocence were usually coupled with an attack on the fairness of God's justice (9: 2-4, 14-21; 16: 15- 22). For verse 1 see note above.

7. *If* introduces a formal oath. The implied preamble to this oath is probably, 'I swear to God that if. . .' Job contends that his entire life, his motives and his conduct, have been faithful to *the way* of wisdom to which he is committed (see verse 4; Prov. 4: 7-27).

8. A self-condemnation normally completes the oath. Job calls for the destruction or raiding of his *crops*, if his testimony is not true. The implication is that God, who witnesses the swearing of an oath, would bring these sanctions against anyone who lied under oath.

9–10. In wisdom thinking the wicked woman was considered a powerful temptation (cp. Prov. 6: 27-35; 7: 6-23).

Here the punishment is intended to fit the crime (Exod. 20: 17).

11–12. These verses are a comment by Job or a later editor (as the N.E.B. brackets propose) expressing disgust over the preceding crime and its inevitable consequences. *wicked act* can be rendered 'lewd deed' and *a consuming and destructive fire* can be translated 'a fire that consumes into Abaddon' (see on 26: 6; cp. Prov. 6: 27–9). All hell breaks loose when this crime is committed and its sanctions are imposed.

13–15. In the ancient world slaves were usually considered property and therefore outside the confines of human justice. Job's compassion for his slaves is based on his common humanity with them; both slave and free are created in a human womb by the same Creator. The doctrine of the common fatherhood of God for all men is integral to wisdom theology. 'Rich and poor have this in common: the LORD made them both' (Prov. 22: 2; cp. 14: 31; 17: 5). Job extends this doctrine to his slaves, and makes it the basis for universal justice (cp. Eph. 6: 9).

16–18. Concern for the widow, the orphan and the poor was a basic pillar of Israelite justice (see on 22: 6–9; 24: 2–4). Job's sympathy for the unfortunate, which was portrayed earlier (29: 11–17), is here broadened to include the idea that Job actually accepted orphans into his household and raised them as a father.

19–20. Those whom Job provided with clothing had a reason to bless Job for his generosity.

21–3. The reading of this passage is uncertain at several points (see N.E.B. footnotes). Job claims that he never took action against the innocent in court, counting on men's support for him as a prominent citizen; he lived rather with an acute awareness of the fearsome presence of God and his punitive wrath. Despite his life of righteousness Job has now experienced the full impact of this divine terror without just cause (cp. on 9: 34; 13: 21).

24–5. Although rich, Job has never made his wealth an idol

or an obsession. God has been the sole object of his trust and worship.

26–8. Job has never worshipped heavenly bodies like *the sun* or *the moon*, a practice widespread in the ancient world (cp. Deut. 4: 19; 2 Kings 23: 5, 11). Idolatry is the epitome of unfaithfulness in Job's eyes.

38–40. This passage belongs to Job's series of oaths and has been transposed from after his concluding challenge (verses 35–7) to an appropriate point such as this. Nature was thought to be sympathetic to the suffering caused by human injustice and evil (cp. Jer. 12: 4; 14: 1–8). Job's land, however, need never cry to God for justice (cp. Gen. 4: 10), since his treatment of his peasant farmers has been scrupulously fair. The sanction Job imposes on himself (in verse 40) reflects the curses of God pronounced on the earth after the fall of the first man (Gen. 3: 17–18).

29–30. From verse 29 onwards, the 'if' style changes to a question style. Job has not called down vengeance upon his enemies or rejoiced over their downfall as many psalmists of Israel did (Job 8: 21–2; 27: 7; Pss. 69: 21–8; 109: 1–20).

31–2. Like Abraham, Job is a paragon of hospitality, one of the great virtues of the biblical world (cp. Gen. 18: 1–8). *No stranger* was turned from his door at nightfall, when the streets were no longer safe. Verse 31*b* literally reads, 'O that we might not sate ourselves with his flesh', an expression that implies sexual abuse. Strangers were safe from sexual assault within Job's household, regardless of what perversions were rampant on the street (cp. Gen. 19: 1–4).

33. *as men do* can be rendered 'as Adam'. Unlike Adam, Job has never concealed his guilt and pretended to be innocent. He is truly innocent! In this context the sexual dimension of the sin of the first human beings may be implied. Job is not guilty of some hidden sex-crimes.

34. The closing line from the Hebrew text of this verse, which the N.E.B. transposes after verse 35, can be translated, 'I brought no man through my door', and retained at this

point. *the gossip of the town* can be rendered 'the clamour of the crowd'. The implication of these renderings is that Job was not intimidated by the crowd and therefore forced to surrender his guests to the street rabble for their sport and abuse (cp. Gen. 19: 1–11; Judg. 19: 22–6). ✴

JOB'S FINAL CHALLENGE

35 Let me but call a witness in my defence!
    Let the Almighty state his case against me!
    If my accuser had written out his indictment,
    I would not keep silence and remain indoors.[a]
36 No! I would flaunt it on my shoulder
    and wear it like a crown on my head;
37 I would plead the whole record of my life
    and present that in court as my defence.[b]
    Job's speeches are finished.[c]

✴ Job closes his own defence with a challenge to God Almighty to answer Job's arguments. To this point Job has complained bitterly that God refuses to give him a fair hearing or even bring his case before the court of heaven. Job stands condemned by the very disasters and diseases inflicted on him by God. By making his own public oath of innocence, however, Job has taken matters into his own hands. If none of the curses he has invoked fall on his head, he is morally vindicated. Job is so sure of his own integrity that he summons his opponent to write a document of acquittal which Job will wear with pride.

35. Literally this verse reads,

O that I had a listener!

[a] *Line transposed from verse 34.*
[b] *Verses 38–40 transposed to follow verse 28 (but see note c).*
[c] *The last line of verse 40 retained here.*

Behold my signature! Let the Almighty answer me.
Let my opponent write a document.

Job has no court where he can get a hearing with a 'listener'.
N.E.B. considers this listener a *witness*. Job's case now rests and
he affixes his signature to his testimony. God himself must
make the next move and answer Job's assertions. God is Job's
opponent, his *accuser* and his judge. His verdict will be deci-
sive. Job, however, is so certain of his innocence that he wants
the verdict recorded in a document. He, of course, anticipates
that the verdict will be an acquittal. The N.E.B. interpretation
of this document as an *indictment* is not demanded by the
Hebrew text.

36. Job had previously felt himself stripped of the crown
and honour of his integrity as a true human being (see on
19: 9). He now intends to wear his inscription of acquittal as
the symbol of his new status as a vindicated human being.
Acquittal was sometimes symbolized by the change of
clothes (Zech. 3: 1-6). Job's new clothes are his inscription
worn on his shoulder and forehead (cp. Exod. 13: 16; Deut.
11: 18).

37. *as my defence* is literally 'as a prince'. Job's acquittal will
give him the prestige and confidence of a prince; his whole
life will be vindicated. ✻

Speeches of Elihu

✻ Elihu enters as an angry young man bent on refuting Job
where his three friends have failed. No mention is made of
Elihu in either the prologue or the epilogue; he is an intruder
who plays no part in the prose story of Job. Many scholars
therefore consider Elihu's speeches an interpolation by a pious
wisdom teacher who wanted to improve on the efforts of the
three friends to defend God's justice. His discourses, however,
are but a reworking of arguments from friends. Most of the

novel contributions he offers are ideas taken from God's speech (in ch. 38), and this in some measure anticipates the divine speech, perhaps deliberately. Elihu feels compelled to formulate two lengthy apologies for presuming to interfere in the debate (32: 6-22; 33: 1-7). Four discourses follow in which he argues that Job has no right to challenge God's justice because he is infinitely greater than human beings in wisdom, might and goodness. He has no need to appear in court to grant Job a hearing; the case has already been researched by a God who has watched every minute of the action from on high. He has, moreover, provided the vehicles for communicating his will to the impenitent. The pains and calamities he sends are disciplinary messages designed to bring the rebellious to their knees. The justice of God is confirmed by the majestic expression of his wisdom and power throughout the universe. The Lord who rules the universe with such inscrutable knowledge cannot be held accountable to insignificant complainers like Job. ✶

ELIHU, AN ANGRY YOUNG MAN

32 So these three men gave up answering Job; for he continued to think himself righteous. Then Elihu son of Barakel the Buzite, of the family of Ram, grew angry; angry because Job had made himself out more righteous than God,[a] and angry with the three friends because they had found no answer to Job and had let God appear wrong.[b] Now Elihu had hung back while they were talking with Job because they were older than he; but, when he saw that the three had no answer, he could no longer contain his anger.

[a] *Or* had justified himself with God.
[b] *Prob. original rdg., altered in Heb. to* and had not proved Job wrong.

✴ Elihu bursts on the scene like a tornado. He is angry, impetuous and ready to resolve a lengthy debate that has reached an impasse. Four times his anger is mentioned as the reason for his dramatic intrusion. He is angry against Job for his self-righteousness, against his friends for allowing Job to make them look like fools, and against the whole situation which seems to declare Job the winner. Elihu's righteous indignation had given way to violent emotion.

1. The *three men* were called 'friends' earlier (2: 11).

2. There is no reason to identify this Elihu with any other figure by that name in the Old Testament (e.g. 1 Sam. 1: 1). On the preferable footnote translation 'had justified himself with God' see the comment at 4: 17.

3. The N.E.B. footnote follows the tradition of ancient biblical scribes and suggests that the original reading was probably altered in the interests of piety so that Job rather than God would *appear wrong*.

4. Wisdom was associated with age; the young were expected to listen and learn (cp. 12: 12). ✴

ELIHU'S RIGHT TO SPEAK

So Elihu son of Barakel the Buzite began to speak: 6

I am young in years,
and you are old;
that is why I held back and shrank
from displaying my knowledge in front of you.
I said to myself, 'Let age speak, 7
and length of years expound wisdom.'
But the spirit of God himself[a] is in man, 8
and the breath of the Almighty gives him understanding;
it is not only the old who are wise 9

[a] the spirit. . .himself: *so Symm.; Heb.* a spirit.

or the aged who understand what is right.

10 Therefore I say: Listen to me;
    I too will display my knowledge.

11 Look, I have been waiting upon your words,
    listening for the conclusions of your thoughts,
    while you sought for phrases;

12 I have been giving thought to your conclusions,
    but not one of you refutes Job or answers his argu-
    ments.

13 Take care then not to claim that you have found
    wisdom;
    God will rebut him, not man.

14 I will not string*a* words together like you*b*
    or answer him as you have done.

15 If these men are confounded and no longer answer,
    if words fail them,

16 am I to wait because they do not speak,
    because they stand there and no longer answer?

17 I, too, have a furrow to plough;
    I will express my opinion;

18 for I am bursting with words,
    a bellyful of wind gripes me.

19 My stomach is distended as if with wine,
    bulging like a blacksmith's*c* bellows;

20 I must speak to find relief,
    I must open my mouth and answer;

21 I will show no favour to anyone,
    I will flatter no one, God or man;*d*

[a] *Prob. rdg.; Heb.* He has not strung.
[b] *Prob. rdg.; Heb.* towards me.
[c] *So Sept.; Heb.* like new.
[d] *Prob. rdg.; Heb.* I will not flatter man.

for I cannot use flattering titles,   22
or my Maker would soon do away with me.

* In this introductory speech Elihu justifies his bold intrusion
and defends his right to speak to his elders. He claims to have·
the wisdom and the arguments required to answer Job where
wise teachers had failed. In addition, he is bursting with ideas
which he can no longer restrain. Like the prophets, he is
compelled to speak.

6-7. Elihu confesses his youth and his respect for age. He
waited for the wisdom of his elders to be spent before he found
the courage to speak. He knew wisdom was supposed to be
the special gift of the hoary (12: 12; 15: 10).

8-9. Elihu contends that *the breath of the Almighty* not only
imparts life (Gen. 2: 7), but also the mental abilities of insight
and wisdom (cp. Isa. 11: 2). Job seems to have made a similar
claim when he was deriding the wisdom of his elders (see on
12: 10-12; cp. 27: 3). If wisdom is dependent upon the spirit
of God, age is no prerequisite for receiving it.

11-12. The man who speaks last has a great advantage. As
the final speaker Elihu assures his audience that his answers are
based on a meticulous analysis of all the preceding arguments
presented.

13. Elihu seems to be making an arrogant assertion that the
answers of the three friends were not an expression of *wisdom*
and that God would rebuke them for their poor efforts (cp.
42: 7). Elihu, in turn, presumes to do better.

14. As the footnotes indicate, verse 14*a* is based on a conjectured reading of the original. The N.E.B. translation has
Elihu claiming to be able to refute Job without lengthy
speeches.

15-17. Tactlessly, Elihu describes the friends as *confounded*
wisdom teachers with nothing more worth saying. In such a
situation Elihu feels justified in filling the void with his own
brilliant ideas.

18-20. Elihu is driven by an inner compulsion to speak his

173

mind; his thoughts are exploding within him. Much like the prophets who felt a fierce impulse to speak God's word pent up within them (Jer. 20: 8–9; cp. Amos 3: 8), Elihu can find no relief until the words of wisdom within him are given free expression. He is as tight as a wine skin about to burst.

21–2. *God or man* is a probable reading which heightens the claim of Elihu to be completely fair. Verse 22*a* can be rendered, 'for I do not know how to flatter'. Elihu speaks of himself as a man without guile, incapable of flattery. If his claim to be sincere were a lie, his Maker would destroy him.   ✳

Elihu's First Discourse

✳ Elihu begins by offering a second justification for speaking; he reiterates his claim to wisdom and sincerity. This apology is addressed to Job rather than the friends (verses 1–7). Elihu then attacks Job for boasting about his alleged innocence and calling God a tyrant. God, by his very nature, is far superior to human beings, especially a man like Job (verses 8–13). Job had complained forcefully that God in his distant heavens had refused to speak with him and answer his accusations. Elihu replies by contending that God has several ways of communicating with recalcitrant human beings like Job in order to discipline them. His frightening messages are pathways to repentance which lead the sinner back from the pit of death. They can be discerned in hideous dreams, intense suffering or the appearance of a mediator. The precise role of this figure is disputed by scholars. In all probability Elihu's mediator is viewed as winning redemption for a guilty sufferer by contending that his suffering is sufficient ransom for his guilt. Once redeemed, the sufferer would repent of his guilt. Job, however, sought a mediator who would vindicate his innocence and integrity.   ✳

GOD IS GREATER THAN MAN

Come now, Job, listen to my words   **33**
and attend carefully to everything I say.
Look, I am ready to answer;   2
the words are on the tip of my tongue.*ᵃ*
My heart assures me that I speak with knowledge,   3
and that my lips speak with sincerity.
For the spirit of God made me,   4
and the breath of the Almighty gave me life.
Answer me if you can,   5
marshal your arguments and confront me.
In God's sight*ᵇ* I am just what you are;   6
I too am only a handful of clay.
Fear of me need not abash you,   7
nor any pressure from me overawe you.
You have said your say and I heard you;   8
I have listened to the sound of your words:
'I am innocent', you said, 'and free from offence,   9
blameless and without guilt.
Yet God finds occasions to put me in the wrong*ᶜ*   10
and counts me his enemy;
he puts my feet in the stocks   11
and keeps a close watch on all I do.'

Well, this is my answer: You are wrong.   12
God is greater than man;
why then plead your case with him?   13
for no one can answer his arguments.

[a] *Lit.* my tongue speaks with my palate.
[b] In God's sight: *or* In strength.
[c] *So Pesh.; Heb.* finds ways of thwarting me.

14 Indeed, once God has spoken
he does not speak a second time to confirm it.

✻ 1. A summons for Job to listen, as if he were Elihu's pupil.
In the previous discourses the friends never address Job by
name as Elihu presumes to do.

3. *sincerity* can also be rendered 'purity'. Elihu not only
repeats his claim to sincerity (32: 21–2), but also tries to match
Job who insisted that his prayer was pure and his heart blameless (16: 17; 9: 20–1: cp. 11: 4). Elihu has no ulterior motive
in speaking; his insights rise from a righteous soul.

4. See the comment on 32: 8.

5. Elihu is so sure of himself he challenges Job to refute him.

6–7. *Fear of me* can be translated 'My terror'. Job as a mere
mortal had confessed his fear that the overwhelming 'terror'
of God would prevent him from speaking freely before God
(see on 9: 34; 13: 21). Elihu's sarcastic response is that he is a
mortal like Job who need never be intimidated by Elihu's
great 'terror'.

8–11. Elihu quotes two of Job's assertions: that he is free
from guilt (9: 20–1; 10: 7; 16: 17; 27: 5; 31) and that he is
God's enemy and victim (7: 12, 20; 10: 16–17; 13: 24–7). Job
claimed to be a slave thrown into chains by his taskmaster
(7: 1–2; 13: 27).

12–13. In the eyes of Elihu Job cannot possibly be right in
his assertion that God acts unjustly. *God is greater than man*; it
is therefore not possible or right to argue with him. Job was
well aware that God was superior to him in every way and
that taking God to court seemed a futile project for man
(9: 2–19), but that did not prevent Job from demanding justice and challenging God to answer his charges (23: 2–17;
31: 35–7). The force of Job's inner integrity was far more
powerful than any rational argument about God's sovereignty.

14. Elihu seems to be saying that Job missed God's answer
when he did speak, and that he may not speak again. God had

indeed sent Job ugly nightmares, but he had discovered no
answer to his cries in them – only added torment (cp. 7:
13–14). ✳

PATHWAYS TO REPENTANCE

In dreams, in visions of the night,	15
when deepest sleep falls upon men,	
while they sleep on their beds, God makes them listen,	16
and his correction strikes them with terror.	
To turn a man from reckless conduct,	17
to check the pride*[a]* of mortal man,	
at the edge of the pit he holds him back alive	18
and stops him from crossing the river of death.	
Or again, man learns his lesson on a bed of pain,	19
tormented by a ceaseless ague in his bones;	
he turns from his food with loathing	20
and has no relish for the choicest meats;	
his flesh hangs loose upon him,	21
his bones are loosened and out of joint,	
his soul draws near to the pit,	22
his life to the ministers of death.	
Yet if an angel, one of thousands, stands by him,	23
a mediator between him and God,	
to expound what he has done right	
and to secure mortal man his due;*[b]*	
if he speaks in the man's favour and says, 'Reprieve*[c]*	24
him,	
let him not go down to the pit, I have the price of his	
release';	

[a] the pride: *prob. rdg.; Heb. obscure.*
[b] *Line transposed from verse 26.*
[c] *So some MSS.; others have an unknown word.*

25 then that man will grow sturdier[a] than he was in youth,
    he will return to the days of his prime.

26 If he entreats God to show him favour,
    to let him see his face and shout for joy;[b]

27 if he declares before all men, 'I have sinned,
    turned right into wrong and thought nothing of it';

28 then he saves himself from going down to the pit,
    he lives and sees the light.

29 All these things God may do to a man,
    again and yet again,

30 bringing him back from the pit
    to enjoy the full light of life.

31 Listen, Job, and attend to me;
    be silent, and I myself will speak.

32 If you have any arguments, answer me;
    speak, and I would gladly find you proved right;

33 but if you have none, listen to me:
    keep silence, and I will teach you wisdom.

✷ 15–16. Elihu contends that dreams and nightmares are
vehicles of divine revelation (cp. Gen. 20: 3; 31: 24; 41: 25);
they strike terror in human hearts and lead men to repentance.
Eliphaz had claimed to hear God speaking through a similar
terrifying experience (4: 12–16).

17–18. The purpose of these dreams is to turn man from
his evil work and crush his *pride* (see N.E.B. footnote), a
divine task endorsed earlier by Eliphaz (22: 29). The penitent
and the innocent can expect to be rescued from the *pit*
of death, a fact which Job disputes (see on 9: 30–1 where
the word for 'pit' is rendered 'mud'). Earlier when Job had

[a] will grow sturdier: *prob. rdg.; Heb. unintelligible.*
[b] *See note on verse 23.*

contemplated death, he had called the 'pit' (translated 'grave') his father (17: 14).

18*b. the river of death*: literally 'the channel'. In some Greek and Mesopotamian myths, the dead had to cross a mighty river to enter the underworld.

19–22. When God brings human beings to the verge of death, he wants to teach them a *lesson*. Their misery is a message from God, whether they hear it or not. Suffering is intended to be disciplinary (cp. 5: 17) not destructive. Elihu is no compassionate friend; he only offers the cruel comfort of resignation and meaningless submission.

22*b. ministers of death* may refer to the destroying angels (cp. 2 Sam. 24: 16; Exod. 12: 23; 2 Kings 19: 35), or to the sons of Resheph who fly forth from the underworld to plague men (see on 5: 7).

23–8. Elihu addresses the question of a heavenly *mediator* (*mēlīts*) raised several times by Job (see on 9: 33; 16: 19–22; 19: 22–7). The specific term used here is found in 16: 20 but not elsewhere in Job. Elihu describes how a mediator could perhaps intervene in court and announce his willingness to pay the ransom for one in need (cp. on 19: 25). The mediator, according to Elihu, is also an interpreter of God's will to suffering men. The anticipated response of the informed sufferer to his redemption is a song of joy and a confession of guilt. Thus the redeemer leads men to repentance through a gracious act of intervention on their behalf. Job, however, had no crime to confess. He saw his heavenly interpreter as a vindicator of his integrity, not an angel who led him to confess sins he had never committed.

23. The same term for *mediator* appears in 16: 20. God's council consisted of innumerable holy ones who could be sent as messengers to men (cp. on 5: 1).

24. *the price of his release*: a gift offered in exchange for a person's life (Exod. 30: 12). Perhaps this angel mediator is proposing that Job's suffering and projected repentance be accepted as a ransom for his life. Job, however, was not willing

to accept any redemption price that was not at the same time a vindication of his innocence (cp. on 19: 23–7). Other scholars suggest that this ransom is the forgiving grace of God which moves men to contrition and hope.

27. A confession of sins is the expected outcome of Job's redemption by this hypothetical mediator. Job's integrity prevented him from making such a confession.

28. The *pit* means 'death' as in verses 18, 22.

29–30. A summary of God's salutary purposes in the process of the preceding verses (verses 12–28).

31–3. A pompous taunt by young Elihu who challenges Job to demonstrate his righteousness or keep silent while he regales the suffering Job with wisdom. ✻

Elihu's Second Discourse

✻ Elihu condemns Job for accusing God of arbitrary and unfair dispensation of justice, Job himself being a prime target. God, according to Elihu, can do no wrong since he is the epitome and example of righteousness. He is good, just and true. His sovereign rule on high, moreover, sets him far above all human weaknesses and distorted earthly vision. His celestial supervision of all activities on earth guarantees a perfect execution of justice according to the evidence without the necessity of an inquiry before the council of heaven. Job's claim to innocence is therefore intolerable presumption. ✻

GOD CAN DO NO WRONG

34 Then Elihu went on to say:

2   Mark my words, you wise men;
    you men of long experience, listen to me;
3   for the ear tests what is spoken
    as the palate savours food.
4   Let us then examine for ourselves what is right;

let us together establish the true good.

Job has said, 'I am innocent,   5
but God has deprived me of justice,
he has falsified*a* my case;   6
my state is desperate, yet I have done no wrong.'

Was there ever a man like Job   7
with his thirst for irreverent talk,
choosing bad company to share his journeys,   8
a fellow-traveller with wicked men?

For he says that it brings a man no profit   9
to find favour with God.

But listen to me, you men of good sense.   10
    Far be it from God to do evil
    or the Almighty to play false!

For he pays a man according to his work   11
and sees that he gets what his conduct deserves.

The truth is, God does no wrong,   12
the Almighty does not pervert justice.

Who committed the earth to his keeping?   13
Who but he established the whole world?

If he were to turn his thoughts inwards   14
and recall his life-giving spirit,

all that lives would perish on the instant,   15
and man return again to dust.

✵ 2–4. Elihu begins his second discourse with a taunt to his
learned companions to test the veracity of his arguments. The
proverb he cites (verse 3) in support of his challenge was used
with a different intent by Job (12: 11). Elihu believes that a
communal proving of his ideas will reveal what is best for Job.

[a] *So Sept.; Heb.* am I falsifying.

Elihu assumes the role of an arbiter whose handling of Job's case will result in a valid decision about *what is right*.

5-6. Elihu quotes Job's testimony before the court (cp. 27: 2; 33: 9–11; 9: 15). The arrogance of Job lies in his contention that God is anything but impartial in his dispensation of justice. Job maintains that he is the injured party and that God is guilty of gross injustice.

7-8. Job's testimony is met with derision. Instead of arguing the case, Elihu mocks Job as a blasphemous vagrant who enjoys the company of criminals.

9. A twisted quotation of Job taken out of context (cp. 10: 3; 22: 2). Job had thought his life of good deeds would mean prosperity (29: 18–20), but his hopes were proven illusory.

10. Fundamental to Elihu's argument is the unwavering good intentions of God. For God *to do evil* is a contradiction in terms for Elihu. God is the ultimate in good. Job's contentions are therefore blasphemous as well as illogical.

11-12. God's goodness is matched by his *justice*, dispensed rigidly according to the doctrine of reward and punishment (see the introduction to Eliphaz' first discourse, pp. 24–5). Wisdom theology endorsed the axiom that each man gets what he deserves. Elihu progressed no further than his friends in re-evaluating the truth of this axiom.

13-15. Elihu couples the righteous providence of God with his sovereign rule as Creator. The Almighty is not a lesser deity given the earth as his responsibility from a greater god (cp. Isa. 40: 13–14). He is the Creator of the universe who can destroy all life by merely withholding his breath (cp. Ps. 104: 29–30). His righteous rule, however, prevents that from transpiring. *

GOD NEEDS NO INQUIRY

Now Job, if you have the wit, consider this;	16
listen to the words I speak.	
Can it be that a hater of justice holds the reins?	17
Do you disparage a sovereign whose rule is so fair,	
who will say to a prince, 'You scoundrel',	18
and call his magnates blackguards to their faces;	
who does not show special favour to those in office	19
and thinks no more of rich than of poor?	
All alike are God's creatures,	
who may die in a moment, in the middle of the night;	20
at his touch the rich are no more,	
and the mighty vanish though no hand is laid on them.	
His eyes are on the ways of men,	21
and he sees every step they take;	
there is nowhere so dark, so deep in shadow,	22
that wrongdoers may hide from him.	
Therefore he repudiates all that they do;	25
he turns on them in the night, and they are crushed.	
There are no appointed days for men	23
to appear before God for judgement.	
He holds no inquiry, but breaks the powerful	24
and sets up others in their place.	
For their crimes he strikes them down[a]	26[b]
and makes them disgorge their bloated wealth,[c]	
because they have ceased to obey him	27
and pay no heed to his ways.	
Then the cry of the poor reaches his ears,	28

[a] he strikes them down: *prob. rdg.; Heb. om.*
[b] *Verse 25 transposed to follow verse 22.*
[c] *Or* and chastises them where people see.

and he hears the cry of the distressed.

9-30 [Even if he is silent, who can condemn him?
If he looks away, who can find fault?
What though he makes a godless man king
over a stubborn*a* nation and all its people?]

31 But suppose you were to say to God,
'I have overstepped the mark; I will do no more*b*
mischief.

32 Vile wretch that I am, be thou my guide;
whatever wrong I have done, I will do wrong no
more.'

33 Will he, at these words, condone your rejection of
him?
It is for you to decide, not me:
but what can you answer?

34 Men of good sense will say,
any intelligent hearer will tell me,

35 'Job talks with no knowledge,
and there is no sense in what he says.

36 If only Job could be put to the test once and for all
for answers that are meant to make mischief*c*!

37 He is a sinner and a rebel as well*d*
with his endless ranting against God.'

✻ 17-19. Elihu tries to argue that human rulers are just and
deserve respect. If insolence to earthly protectors of justice is
intolerable, how much more any disrespect for the Lord of
justice himself. Job had accused God of throwing all govern-
mental agencies into chaos (12: 17-25).

[*a*] a stubborn: *so Sept.; Heb.* the snares of a...
[*b*] more: *prob. rdg.; Heb. obscure.*
[*c*] that...mischief: *so some MSS.; others* among mischief-makers.
[*d*] *Prob. rdg.; Heb. adds* between us it is enough.

20. God has the power to expunge life in an instant, especially the life of leaders responsible to him for justice.

21-2. Job also recognized the penetrating surveillance of God, but found it oppressive (7: 12–20; cp. 31: 4). For Elihu it was the assurance that no unrighteous deeds would go unchecked. The spying of God in every corner of human life seemed acceptable if there was no question about the integrity of the celestial ruler. Job, however, argues that an arbitrary sovereign can use that kind of power to persecute and harass his creatures. That argument is beyond Elihu's frame of reference; he cannot sympathize with Job's personal experience of an unscrupulous divine detective.

25. This verse is transposed here to state the conclusion of Elihu's argument at the appropriate point. God punishes all whose evil deeds are exposed by his close scrutiny. He strikes *in the night* when the wicked think they are safe (cp. on 24: 13–17).

23-4. One of Job's major complaints was that he had been branded as guilty without a hearing. His overriding obsession was to face God in court and gain an acquittal (9: 32–5; 13: 3, 13–22; 23: 3–7). He dreamed of a fixed date when his case could be heard (14: 13). Elihu counters by proclaiming God judge, jury and executioner. He is also the detective who gleaned the evidence against Job (verses 21–2). An *inquiry* is therefore unnecessary; a day in court is pointless.

26-7. As the N.E.B. footnotes indicate, verse 26 is obscure. God punishes, without trial, those who have not followed in *his ways*. Elihu seems to imply that Job's calamities are proof that he has left 'the way', despite Job's oath to the contrary (31: 7). On 'way' see on 3: 23.

28. Judgement on the wicked was considered synonymous with the vindication and liberation of the oppressed.

29-30. There is some question about the authenticity of these verses as the brackets indicate. The N.E.B. rendering of this obscure text suggests that an editor has softened Elihu's hard line and allowed for the possibility that God sometimes tolerates certain injustices for his own purposes, but that man has no right to find fault with him.

31–2. Portions of this text are obscure. Clearly, however, Elihu frames a confession he considers appropriate for Job. Such a confession would be evidence that Job was willing to seek God rather than his own ingenuity as his *guide* and 'teacher' in learning true wisdom.

33. Elihu seems to be demanding that Job, who has previously refused to confess his guilt and therefore rejected God's forgiveness, must now decide whether he will seek any future mercy from God's hands. The translation of this verse, however, remains uncertain.

34. *intelligent hearer* is literally 'man of wisdom'. Elihu's comment is a sarcastic remark implying that Job is an idiot. Wise men have only one verdict for Job: he is a godless fool.

35. Job lacks the normal intelligence of others despite his claims of human wisdom equal to that of his opponents (12: 2–3).

36–7. These verses are perhaps the cruellest lines of all Job's friends. Job's refusal to confess his wickedness classifies him as an obdurate sinner who compounds his guilt with *endless ranting against God*. Elihu therefore proposes that the tormented Job should be put to the acid test for his blasphemous replies. Elihu's attitude matches that of Satan; hit a man hard enough and he will break (1: 11). *once and for all* (verse 36a) can be rendered 'to the very limit'.   ✶

Elihu's Third Discourse

✶ This discourse is a brief consideration of the sovereignty of the Creator as it affects human life. He is a supreme God whose distance from man puts him beyond the reach of direct human influence. Human beings cannot manipulate or threaten him with good or evil. The actions of people on earth affect other people, not God. If the oppressed, like Job, would but acknowledge the grand wisdom and providence of the sovereign

overlord, they would be much happier. The wicked are fools
if they think God's remoteness means apathy. All must eventually humble themselves before the exalted monarch of
heaven. ✣

GOD IS UNIMPRESSED BY YOUR DEEDS

Then Elihu went on to say: 35

Do you think that this is a sound plea   2
or maintain that you are in the right against God? –
if you say, 'What would be the advantage to me?   3
how much should I gain from sinning?'
I will bring arguments myself against you,   4
you and your three[a] friends.
Look up at the sky and then consider,   5
observe the rain-clouds towering above you.
How does it touch him if you have sinned?   6
However many your misdeeds, what does it mean to
    him?
If you do right, what good do you bring him,   7
or what does he gain from you?
Your wickedness touches only men, such as you are;   8
the right that you do affects none but mortal man.

Men will cry out beneath the burdens of oppression   9
and call for help against the power of the great;
but none of them asks, 'Where is God my Maker   10
who gives protection by night,
who grants us more knowledge than the beasts of the 11
    earth
and makes us wiser than the birds of the air?'

[a] *So Sept.; Heb. om.*

12 So, when they cry out, he does not answer,
    because they are self-willed and proud.
13 All to no purpose! God does not listen,
    the Almighty does not see.

14 The worse for you when you say, 'He does*[a]* not see
      me'*[b]*!
    Humble yourself*[c]* in his presence and wait for his word.
15 But now, because God does not grow angry and punish
    and because he lets folly pass unheeded,
16 Job gives vent to windy nonsense
    and makes a parade of empty words.

* 3. Job had not actually said these words, nor had he admitted to committing any crime. Elihu had heard Job pronouncing the justice of God inoperative and therefore oblivious to whatever Job chose to do. His actions changed nothing in heaven (cp. 10: 3; 22: 2; 34: 9).

4–5. Elihu answers Job's assumed position, and that of the three friends who apparently reflected some sympathy with it, by appealing to the transcendence of God (cp. 9: 8–11; 11: 7–9). His infinite distance above man puts him beyond direct human influence. For Job the difference and distance of God from man enabled God to ignore injustice and prevent Job from forcing his case into court.

6–7. God is a detached sovereign, unmoved by human deeds or misdeeds, and Job need not think that any of his challenges will provoke God to act (cp. 22: 2–4). Job was aware of God's elusive presence but he refused to relinquish his efforts to drive God from hiding and compel him to handle Job's charges (13: 15–22; 23: 2–17; 31: 35–7).

8. The corollary of the preceding verses is that human conduct affects only human beings. This proposition is related to

[a] *So Vulg.; Heb.* You do.   [b] *So some MSS.; others* him.
[c] Humble yourself: *prob. rdg.; Heb.* Judge.

a biblical theme that good and evil deeds have the inherent power to bring their own reward and punishment without direct divine involvement (cp. Prov. 9: 12). Underlying Elihu's statement is a valid concern for maintaining God's absolute authority.

9-13. Job had complained bitterly about the prosperity of the wicked and the oppression of the unfortunate (21: 7-15; cp. 24: 2-12). Job considered himself unjustly oppressed by God. Elihu answers these contentions by impugning the motives of the oppressed; they are proud creatures who refuse to submit to God's will and meekly acknowledge him as their Maker. Job, it would seem, is the classic example of the oppressed from which Elihu is drawing his conclusions.

11. God the Creator instils in man the wisdom to know him as the great protector. Whether this knowledge is greater 'than' that of the animals or an insight to be learned 'from' them is debatable (cp. 12: 7-8). *than* can also be translated 'by' or 'from', making nature the medium of this wisdom.

14. The N.E.B. rendering of this verse suggests that Elihu is repeating a theme of Eliphaz about the self-delusion of the wicked about divine surveillance (22: 12-14). Hence the appeal for Job to *Humble* himself (but cp. footnote). More consistent with the text is the more literal rendering, 'Though you say you cannot see him, the case is before him; so wait for him.' Job's problem had been the hiddenness of God. Elihu counters by contending that Job will get his just deserts in due time.

15-16. The justice Elihu foresees for Job is a visitation of divine fury. Job should not be encouraged by the delay in God's advent to flaunt arrogant arguments. *

Elihu's Fourth Discourse

OPPRESSION IS GOOD DISCIPLINE

36 Then Elihu went on to say:

2   Be patient a little longer, and let me enlighten you;
     there is still something more to be said on God's side.

3   I will search far and wide to support my conclusions,
     as I defend the justice of my Maker.

4   There are no flaws in my reasoning;
     before you stands one whose conclusions are sound.

5   God,*a* I say, repudiates the high and*b* mighty

6   and does not let the wicked prosper,
     but allows the just claims of the poor and suffering;

7   he does not deprive the sufferer of his due.*c*
     Look at kings on their thrones:
     when God gives them sovereign power, they grow
        arrogant.

8   Next you may see them loaded with fetters,
     held fast in captives' chains:

9   he denounces their conduct to them,
     showing how insolence and tyranny was their offence;

10   his warnings sound in their ears
     and summon them to turn back from their evil courses.

11   If they listen to him, they spend*d* their days in prosperity
     and their years in comfort.

12   But, if they do not listen, they die, their lesson unlearnt,
     and cross the river of death.

[a] *Prob. rdg.; Heb. adds* a mighty one and not.
[b] and: *prob. rdg.; Heb. om.*
[c] deprive. . .due: *or* withdraw his gaze from the righteous.
[d] *Prob. rdg.; Heb. adds* they end.

Proud men rage against him   13
and do not cry to him for help when caught in his toils;
so they die in their prime,   14
like male prostitutes,[a] worn out.[b]

Those who suffer he rescues through suffering   15
and teaches them by the discipline of affliction.

Beware, if you are tempted to exchange hardship for   16
   comfort,[c]
for unlimited plenty spread before you,[d] and a generous
   table;
if you eat your fill of a rich man's fare   17
when you are occupied with the business of the law,
do not be led astray by lavish gifts of wine   18
and do not let bribery warp your judgement.
Will that wealth of yours, however great, avail you,   19
or all the resources of your high position?
Take care not to turn to mischief;   21[e]
for that is why you are tried by affliction.

✳ 2–4. Elihu opens his fourth discourse with an announce-
ment of his intention to defend his Maker's justice with perfect
reasoning and thereby refute Job's faulty arguments on the
subject.

   5. As the N.E.B. footnotes indicate, the original text of this
verse is uncertain. The focus of the passage is on the superior
might of God.

   6. Though God's advent may sometimes be delayed (35:
14–15), he will eventually execute justice for all: death for the
wicked and liberation for the oppressed.

[a] *Cp. Deut. 23: 17.*   [b] worn out: *prob. rdg.; Heb. unintelligible.*
[c] for comfort: *prob. rdg.; Heb. om.*
[d] *So one MS.; others* her.
[e] *Verses 20 and 21 transposed.*

7a. The N.E.B. footnote translates the present Hebrew text. Both renderings reflect the compassionate concern of God for the rights of the faithful.

7b–10. Job repudiated Zophar's contention that the wicked tyrant is executed with dispatch (20: 5–9; 21: 27–33). Elihu counters with the thesis that the Lord who makes *kings*, also breaks them when *they grow arrogant*. Their debacle, however, is intended as a divine message exposing their guilt and summoning them to repentance. God's punishment is to be understood as disciplinary (cp. on 5: 17), and not necessarily final (cp. 33: 15–22). Verse 10a can be rendered, 'He opens their ear for discipline.'

11–12. Those who respond to divine discipline are showered with good things; those who are obdurate die in their ignorance. On the *river of death* see at 33: 18.

13–14. The godless remain angry under his discipline and refuse to submit to his will. A premature death is their reward (cp. 20: 5). The precise rendering of verse 14b is uncertain. On *male prostitutes* or 'sodomites' see Deut. 23: 17; 1 Kings 14: 24; 2 Kings 23: 7.

15. This verse summarizes Elihu's argument about the function of disciplinary *affliction*. Suffering is God's tutor for the oppressed; it teaches the humility of submissive repentance.

16–19. The rendering of verses 16–17 remains uncertain. According to the N.E.B. translation Elihu exhorts Job to avoid the temptation to buy off hardships with the offer of personal wealth or favours, a temptation far removed from Job in his current plight.

21. This verse is transposed before verse 20 where it serves as an explanatory comment on verses 16–19. Devising evil schemes to avert *affliction* thwarts its very purpose, namely, the rehabilitation of the sinful schemer. ✱

THE MYSTERY OF GOD'S MIGHT

Have no fear if in the breathless terrors of the night   20
you see nations vanish where they stand.
God towers in majesty above us;   22
who wields such sovereign power as he?
Who has prescribed his course for him?   23
Who has said to him, 'Thou hast done wrong'?
Remember then to sing the praises of his work,   24
as men have always sung them.
All men stand back from*a* him;   25
the race of mortals look on from afar.
Consider; God is so great that we cannot know him;   26
the number of his years is beyond reckoning.
He draws up drops of water from the sea*b*   27
and distils rain from the mist he has made;
the rain-clouds pour down in torrents,*c*   28
they descend in showers on mankind;
thus he sustains the nations   31
and gives them food in plenty.
Can any man read the secret of the sailing clouds,   29
spread like a carpet under*d* his pavilion?
See how he unrolls the mist*e* across the waters,   30
and its streamers*f* cover the sea.
He charges the thunderbolts with flame   32*g*
and launches them straight*h* at the mark;

[*a*] *Or* gaze at.   [*b*] from the sea: *prob. rdg.; Heb. om.*
[*c*] in torrents: *prob. rdg.; Heb.* which.
[*d*] spread. . .under: *prob. rdg.; Heb.* crashing noises.
[*e*] *So Targ.; Heb.* light.
[*f*] its streamers: *prob. rdg.; Heb.* the roots of.
[*g*] *Verse 31 transposed to follow verse 28.*
[*h*] and. . .straight: *prob. rdg.; Heb.* and gives orders concerning it.

33   in his anger he calls up the tempest,
       and the thunder is the herald of its coming.[a]

37   This too makes my heart beat wildly
       and start from its place.

✻ 22. Elihu had previously emphasized the distant exalted supremacy of God (33: 12; 34: 13; 35: 5). Verse 22*b* is literally, 'What teacher is like him?' God, the sublime teacher, exhibits his prowess by leading men to the truth through the paths of punishment and agony (verses 16–21).

23. God is not only sovereign in power, but also in wisdom and justice (cp. 12: 13). His *course* is literally his 'way' (*derek*), the cosmic principle of wisdom by which the universe is governed. According to one rendering of Prov. 8: 22, wisdom asserts that 'Yahweh begat me first, his way before his works' (cp. 28: 23, 27). She was God's adviser in creation; she was the 'way' he followed. Elihu follows an alternative tradition which insists that the LORD had no counsellor to instruct him in the lessons of wisdom prior to creation (Isa. 40: 12–14). He is his own teacher (verse 22). See also on 26: 14 and the introduction to Bildad's third discourse (p. 132).

24–5. Man's response to the majestic cosmic deeds of God is one of wonder and praise.

26–33. Taking his cue from verses 24–5, Elihu breaks into a hymn of praise to God as the lord of rain and storm. This hymn serves to support his contention that God is in total control of the heavens, the symbol of sovereign rule (cp. 5: 8–10; 9: 5–10; 12: 13–15). The waters above and below the earth are at God's disposal to manipulate as he pleases (cp. Gen. 1: 6–8; 7: 10–12).

26. On the unfathomable mystery of God see 5: 9; 11: 6–9; 12: 22; 26: 14; 28: 23–7.

27. The Hebrew term for *mist* can be rendered 'flood' (as in Gen. 2: 6) and parallel the conjectured addition 'from the

[a] in his anger...coming: *prob. rdg.; Heb. obscure.*

194

sea' (as N.E.B. footnote indicates). The subterranean *sea* was
a source of moisture and waters for the earth.

31. This verse is transposed after verse 28 where it provides
the goal for God's dispensation of fertility from the heavens
(cp. Ps. 104: 13-15, 27· 8).

29. The heavens are God's *pavilion* where he rides his clouds
as he appears in glorious splendour (see on 26: 7; cp. Pss.
104: 2-3; 18: 9-12). *spread like a carpet under* can be translated
'thundering from' thereby emphasizing God's self-manifestation in the storm.

30. *mist* is literally 'light' meaning 'lightning' as in 37: 3.
streamers are literally 'roots' (as N.E.B. footnote). God covers
the roots of the sea, that is, the foundations of the earth (cp.
Ps. 104: 5-6). The advent of God in meteorological brilliance
penetrates the entire universe (cp. 26: 5-11).

32-3. As the N.E.B. footnotes indicate, there are uncertainties about the translation of these verses. The new element
underscored by Elihu is the correlation of God's anger with
the advent of *thunder* and lightning. God's spectacular appearance in the storm ought to move sinners like Job to retreat in
penitent fear. ✵

IN PRAISE OF THE STORM GOD

Listen, listen to the thunder of God's voice   2
  and the rumbling of his utterance.
Under the vault of heaven he lets it roll,   3
  and his lightning reaches the ends of the earth;
there follows a sound of roaring   4
  as he thunders with the voice of majesty.[a]
God's voice is marvellous in its working;[b]   5
  he does great deeds that pass our knowledge.
For he says to the snow, 'Fall to earth',   6

[a] *See note on verse 6.*
[b] *Prob. rdg.; Heb.* thundering.

and to the rainstorms, 'Be fierce.'
And when his voice is heard,
the floods of rain pour down unchecked.[a]

7   He shuts every man fast indoors,[b]
and all men whom he has made must stand idle;

8   the beasts withdraw into their lairs
and take refuge in their dens.

9   The hurricane bursts from its prison,
and the rain-winds bring bitter cold;

10   at the breath of God the ice-sheet is formed,
and the wide waters are frozen hard as iron.

11   He gives the dense clouds their load of moisture,
and the clouds spread his mist[c] abroad,

12   as they travel round in their courses,
steered by his guiding hand
to do his bidding
all over the habitable world.[d]

14   Listen, Job, to this argument;
stand still, and consider God's wonderful works.

15   Do you know how God assigns them their tasks,
how he sends light flashing from his clouds?

16   Do you know why the clouds hang poised overhead,
a wonderful work of his consummate skill,

17   sweating there in your stifling clothes,
when the earth lies sultry under the south wind?

18   Can you beat out the vault of the skies, as he does,
hard as a mirror of cast metal?

[a] And when...unchecked: *prob. rdg.; some words in these lines transposed from verse 4.*
[b] indoors: *prob. rdg.; Heb. obscure.*   [c] *So Targ.; Heb.* light.
[d] *Prob. rdg.; Heb. adds* (13) whether he makes him attain the rod, or his earth, or constant love.

Teach us then what to say to him;   19
for all is dark, and we cannot marshal our thoughts.
Can any man dictate to God when he is*a* to speak?   20
or command him to make proclamation?
At one moment the light is not seen,   21
it is overcast with clouds and rain;
then the wind passes by and clears them away,
and a golden glow comes from the north.*b*   22
But the Almighty we cannot find; his power is beyond 23
    our ken,
and his righteousness not slow to do justice.
Therefore mortal men pay him reverence,   24
and all who are wise look to him.*c*

✴ 2–5. Elihu dwells on the thunder and lightning of God's
advent in the storm. Thunder was understood as the *voice* of
God (Ps. 18: 13; Exod. 20: 18–20). Thunderstorms struck fear
into the heart of ancient peoples who viewed them as expressions of divine majesty and anger (see Ps. 29; 104: 7).

4. As the N.E.B. footnote indicates a portion of this verse
seems to fit better as part of verse 6.

6. The voice of God's thunder is a command which directs
the distribution of rain and snow from the storehouses of
heaven (cp. 38: 22, 25–6).

7–8. When God manifests his presence in the storm all his
creatures, including human beings, run for shelter from his
terrifying display of power. *indoors*: the text is slightly emen-
ded to produce a phrase similar to that of Gen. 7: 16, where
God 'closed the door' on Noah.

9–10. *prison* can be rendered 'chamber'. The harsh winter
blizzard bursts from the heavenly chambers where wind, ice

[a] *Prob. rdg.; Heb.* I am.
[b] *Prob. rdg.; Heb. adds* this refers to God, terrible in majesty.
[c] to him: *so Sept.; Heb.* not.

and hail are stored (38: 22; Ps. 135: 7). The cold winter wind is here described as *the breath of God*.

11–12. *mist* is literally 'light' (as in verse 15). *load of moisture* may also be rendered 'lightning'. The allusion, then, is to God scattering his lightning wherever he directs it across the earth. Verse 13 (see N.E.B. footnote), which the N.E.B. editors found too uncertain to include in the text, refers to the purposes for God's advent in light and lightning, namely, as a rod of judgement, for the fertility of earth and even for the expression of his love.

14. Elihu closes his discourses with an appeal for Job to heed his arguments about the wondrous works of the Creator. The questions he poses anticipate, to some extent, the probing challenges of God himself in the next chapter. Elihu implies that Job's ignorance about the great mysteries of the universe disqualifies him from claiming the right to challenge God's justice in his management of the universe and his handling of Job's life.

15–17. Elihu challenges Job's knowledge of how God manipulates and controls heavy summer clouds that float overhead charged with lightning. Job cannot match the ingenuity of God in determining the weather.

18. Nor does Job have the power to create the sky as God has done. The heavens were thought by Israelites to be a solid vault or firmament stretched across the sky like a huge shield or mirror (cp. Gen. 1: 6). In the ancient world mirrors were made out of polished metal. The sky is here described as being made in a similar manner.

19–20. The rendering of these verses is uncertain. The implication of Elihu's comment seems to be that human beings lack the mental capacity to address God directly about his mysteries. If Job's wisdom is comparable to God's, taunts Elihu, he ought to illumine his fellows on the subject (cp. 15: 7–9).

21–2. The sudden appearance of the sun when the wind clears away the clouds is comparable to the spectacular manifestation of God from the north. Verse 22b, which the N.E.B. editors unnecessarily relegate to the footnote, makes clear that the *golden glow* announces the coming of God, 'terrible in majesty'. *the north* is the abode of the gods in many ancient myths, including the myths of Canaan (cp. on 26: 7; Isa. 14: 13-14). God comes from the 'North' in much the same way that Baal leaves his golden palace in the northern mountains of the sky.

23-4. Despite his splendid self-disclosures in the sky, the Almighty remains inaccessible, his might incomprehensible and his righteous rule irreproachable. Job ought therefore to capitulate to God's will and respond in reverent fear. Then Job would exhibit wisdom instead of folly; for the fear of God is the beginning of wisdom (cp. 28: 28). ✻

God's answer and
Job's submission

✻ Now God answers the demand of Job to present his case against him (31: 35-7). Job had accused God of being an elusive enemy and an inhuman accuser who refused to vindicate Job and prove his innocence. God had robbed Job of all honour and left him wallowing in a chaos of meaningless disgrace. His experience contradicted the wisdom teachings on which he had been raised. Even God seemed to be a lie. Yet through it all Job maintains his integrity, vents his honest anger on God and demands an answer. That answer is rather unexpected; it is not the verdict of a judge at court or the pronouncement of a priest in the cult. Job is neither condemned nor cleared. Rather, God enters into the very dispute of the book about himself. He becomes involved in the struggle to grasp what the mystery of God is all about. He challenges Job as the first man of primordial times to grapple with God over the riddles of the universe. God's challenge takes the form of a long series of ironic and rhetorical questions which on the surface may appear to be little more than a cosmic sneer. Closer examination reveals how Job is led to experience afresh the primordial wisdom of God in designing creation, and the mysterious care of God in his governing of the universe. So Job's question about God's justice is placed in a broader context. Symbols of cosmic justice lie scattered throughout God's speeches even though they do not become the centre of the discussion. The foundations of earth, the control of chaos and the laws of heaven are typical of these symbols. Just as the question of divine justice and human suffering is only answered in passing, so also many of the earlier cries and accusations of Job are only broached indirectly by the topics of God's speech. More important, however, than any intellectual answer to the dilemma of life and the apparent injustice of God, is Job's personal experience of God. That experience is not confined to his confrontation with a whirlwind or tempest. For through God's challenges to Job as the first man, God leads his opponent back through the arena of his primordial labours and conquests where Job can vicariously experience anew the struggle and joy of the creator at work. For Job the possibility of a new beginning grows out of his deep experience of the beginning of all things. Job is not pampered with easy answers, but is challenged to be born again from chaos. Job's answer indicates that he is aware of just that truth. For through the theophany speeches, his understanding of God goes beyond hearsay; he has seen God in the harshness and potential of reality. Job can be created again from nothing and rise from the dust and ashes. The N.E.B. arranges the final speeches of Yahweh and Job as follows:

> Yahweh's first speech 38–9; 41: 1–6 and 40: 1–2
> Job's first response 40: 3–5
> Yahweh's second speech 40: 6–24 and 41: 7–34
> Job's second response 42: 1–6

This N.E.B. arrangement, placing 41: 1–6 in the first speech, introduces an interpretation of ch. 41 which appears to be very doubtful. For a fuller discussion of the problem, see p. 225.

Yahweh's First Speech

THE THEOPHANY OF YAHWEH

Then the LORD answered Job out of the tempest: **38**

Who is this whose ignorant words   2
cloud my design in darkness?
Brace yourself and stand up like a man;   3
I will ask questions, and you shall answer.

✱ Yahweh does not address Job in the still small voice of his conscience, but through the turmoil of a tempest. Job had previously insisted that if God ever bothered to confront him, which he doubted, God would hit him with a whirlwind and give him no chance to catch his breath (see the comment on 9: 17).

1. Elihu's words portended the advent of this storm theophany (37: 2–5). Storms are a common mode of divine self-manifestation in the Old Testament, the *tempest* or 'whirlwind' being a severe form of storm relatively rare in Palestine (Ps. 50: 3; Nahum 1: 3; Zech. 9: 14). Throughout the Old Testament theophanies are usually public appearances of God for the sake of the community (e.g. Exod. 3: 1–12; 19: 9–20). Job is privileged to experience a private theophany. The *tempest* symbolizes the dramatic way in which he encounters God directly. God is no longer an obscure teaching with which Job grapples in mental combat; he confronts God totally. The questions which follow are the poet's groping for words to express and interpret the nature of this confrontation.

2. God does not answer Job with an indictment or an approbation. He enters the dispute as the final spokesman. Like

his human predecessors, he begins his response with a retort challenging his opponent's insights. He asks the identity of this figure who is obscuring his cosmic *design*. God's 'design' or 'counsel' in ordering the universe is from 'ancient times' (Isa. 46: 10). Here, as in what follows, Job is led by God back into the primal scenes of creation. In creation, wisdom was the counsellor attendant upon God (Prov. 8: 22–31). Marduk, the Babylonian creator god, also had a counsellor for his creative deeds. Thus the LORD poses the question: Who is this man obscuring God's cosmic counsel instead of being his 'man of counsel'? Isa. 40: 13f. argues that God is such that he needs no counsellor at all.

3. Job is given a chance to redeem himself by being a *man*. Such a challenge does not destroy Job; it honours him. Job as man is not humiliated as a worthless worm, but confronted as one invited to dispute with God about cosmic mysteries. Job is a potential primal counsellor.   ✳

MYSTERIES IN THE STRUCTURE OF THE UNIVERSE

4   Where were you when I laid the earth's foundations?
     Tell me, if you know and understand.

5   Who settled its dimensions? Surely you should know.
     Who stretched his measuring-line over it?

6   On what do its supporting pillars rest?
     Who set its corner-stone in place,

7   when the morning stars sang together
     and all the sons of God shouted aloud?

8   Who watched over the birth of the sea,[a]
     when it burst in flood from the womb? –

9   when I wrapped it in a blanket of cloud
     and cradled[b] it in fog,

[a] Who...sea: *prob. rdg.*; *Heb.* And he held back the sea with two doors.
[b] *Lit.* swaddled.

when I established its bounds,   10
fixing its doors and bars in place,
and said, 'Thus far shall you come and no farther,   11
and here your surging waves shall halt.'*a*
In all your life have you ever called up the dawn   12
or shown the morning its place?
                                                                     13
Have you taught it to grasp the fringes of the earth
and shake the Dog-star from its place;*b*
to bring up the horizon in relief as clay under a seal,   14
until all things stand out like the folds of a cloak,
when the light of the Dog-star is dimmed   15
and the stars of the Navigator's Line go out one by
    one*c*?

✲ In his opening queries God challenges Job's comprehension
of the original governing structure of the universe. In so doing
he leads Job back into the primordial scene to experience
afresh the original mysteries of the cosmos. If Job is the first
man endowed with ancient wisdom (cp. verse 21), where was
he when the rest of the heavenly council was celebrating the
founding of earth? Was he absent that day? Did he see the sea
emerge from its cosmic womb like some baby monster? Does
he know how it was controlled by the Creator? Can he summon the dawn to shed light on the mysteries of earth?

4. The LORD laid the *foundations* of earth by wisdom (Prov.
3: 19; Jer. 10: 12). The foundations are more than a physical
basis for the world; they establish the very possibility for an
ordered and meaningful existence on earth (Ps. 93: 1-5; 1 Sam.
2: 8). Job should have known that. Isa. 40: 21-3 declares that
the nature of the LORD's total rule has been 'told' since the
foundation of the earth.

[a] *Prob. rdg.; Heb.* here one shall set on your surging waves.
[b] *Lit.* the Dog-stars from it.
[c] *Lit.* and the high arm breaks up.

5-6. The work of founding the earth is described in terms of constructing a building according to set plans. It is possible that there was an early tradition about God using various members of his heavenly council in the several tasks of creation. 2 Esdras 6: 41 mentions an 'angel of the firmament' responsible for its establishment (cp. Gen. 1: 6). The *pillars* of earth remained a mystery for Israel. If God founded the earth on the chaos waters, on what were its pillars resting? (Ps. 24: 2).

7. Creation happens in the context, and perhaps with the help, of the heavenly council. Like wisdom (Prov. 8: 30-1), its members celebrate the making of the universe. The presence of astral figures, like *the morning stars*, in the heavenly council is probably derived from Canaanite mythology. Job's friends maintained that these astral figures were impure before God (25: 5).

8-11. Job had accused God of watching him relentlessly as if he were the sea or a great sea dragon (7: 12). Now God challenges Job to grasp the import of his control over the chaos waters. Through them the world could revert to chaos. God is not only the architect who orders the earth, but the overseer who keeps the forces of chaos in check.

8. Verse 8*b*, like the proposed N.E.B. rendering of verse 8*a*, alludes to an ancient tradition about *the birth of the sea* found nowhere else in the Old Testament. In ancient mythology birth was a common mode for representing the origin of phenomena in the universe. Ps. 90: 2 speaks of the birth of the mountains and the earth.

9. Like a baby in its shawl, the monster sea is wrapped in *cloud* and *fog*. The metaphor of a child suggests the ease with which God masters the sea. Any hint of a cosmic battle between God and the sea has receded far into the background (cp. 26: 12-13).

10. The *bounds* for the sea are more specifically the ordinances which govern the limits and allotted territories for the components of creation (cp. Prov. 8: 27, 29; Job 28: 26). In a

Babylonian creation myth the god Marduk slays the chaos monster and fixes the boundaries of the primal sea by setting up bars to keep the waters at bay. The *doors and bars* symbolize the confinement of the sea within its destined realm.

11. The sea, born clothed and confined to its cosmic playpen, is now given the paternal command never to cross the appointed boundaries (cp. Ps. 104: 6–9). Chaos is kept in check by a primordial decree, not by natural laws. It is this Lord over chaos whom Job confronts in his own personal chaos.

12–15. Job had invoked a curse on the night of his birth to prevent it from seeing the dawn, but to no effect (3: 4–8). Job complained that man should not even behold the light of day; birth only means a life of torment. God's response is that with the dawn the earth itself comes into existence and evil is kept in check.

12. Each *dawn* is apparently seen as a repetition of the first primordial dawn *called up* by the creator's word. The primal word governs the heavens (cp. Isa. 40: 26). The dawn, like every other phenomenon of creation, has its divinely ordained *place*. (See the comment on 'place' in ch. 28, p. 144.)

13–15. The *Dog-Star* in verses 13 and 15 translates a Hebrew word that is normally rendered 'the wicked'. Verse 15*b* is regularly translated 'the uplifted arm is broken'. The N.E.B. proposes a consistent set of celestial imagery throughout these verses (cp. verses 31–2). The Dog-Star is Sirius, the brightest star of the heavens; the *Navigator's Line* refers to several stars, which, when lined up with a major star, provide directional bearing for travellers. Other scholars maintain, however, that the Hebrew text makes good sense as it stands. With the dawn everything on earth is revealed. The contours of the earth stand in bold relief and 'the wicked', who use the night as a cloak for their evil deeds (24: 13–17), are exposed to the light. Job had complained bitterly about the prosperity of the wicked, but now he lacks the ability to invoke the dawn and *shake* the wicked off the earth like dust from a rug (verse 13).

15. Verse 15*a* reads in Hebrew, 'the wicked are deprived of their light'. The dawn, therefore, seems to be a symbol of potential justice for the wicked and of new life for the earth. ✻

RIDDLES IN HIDDEN REALMS OF THE COSMOS

16 Have you descended to the springs of the sea
or walked in the unfathomable deep?

17 Have the gates of death been revealed to you?
Have you ever seen the door-keepers of the place of darkness?

18 Have you comprehended the vast expanse of the world?
Come, tell me all this, if you know.

19 Which is the way to the home of light
and where does darkness dwell?

20 And can you then take each to its appointed bound
and escort it on its homeward path?

21 Doubtless you know all this; for you were born already,
so long is the span of your life!

22 Have you visited the storehouse of the snow
or seen the arsenal where hail is stored,

23 which I have kept ready for the day of calamity,
for war and for the hour of battle?

24 By what paths is the heat spread abroad
or the east wind carried far and wide over the earth?

25 Who has cut channels for the downpour
and cleared a passage for the thunderstorm,

26 for rain to fall on land where no man lives
and on the deserted wilderness,

27 clothing lands waste and derelict with green

and making grass grow on thirsty ground[a]?
Has the rain a father?   28
Who sired the drops of dew?
Whose womb gave birth to the ice,   29
and who was the mother of the frost from heaven,
which lays a stony cover over the waters   30
and freezes the expanse of ocean?

* Job is here confronted with another limit to his knowledge
of the universe, namely, the hidden realms above and below
the earth. The primal first man who observed the formation
of these places may be expected to remember their nature and
locations. Job is summoned, as if he were the first man, to give
a report of his journeys into the nether world and of his
knowledge about meteorological realms beyond the experience of ordinary men.

16. The *deep* is the watery chaos from which the world was
made (Gen. 1: 2), but which continues to exist as the waters
beneath the earth and the sea which surrounds it. The *unfathomable deep* refers to the extremity of the subterranean sea.
The *springs of the sea* probably designate the same region. In
Canaanite mythology the creator-God El was said to dwell
at the confluence of the cosmic deeps and the springs of the
subterranean rivers (see the comment on 28: 11). Job has never
penetrated these mythological realms.

17. In spite of the number of ancient Near Eastern myths
about the descent of heroic figures into the underworld and
their subsequent return, the Old Testament views the realm
of death as a land of no return (7: 9; 10: 21). In many Near
Eastern myths the nether world is the abode of the god Death.
The successive doorways to his subterranean dwelling were
sometimes guarded by *door-keepers* or monsters. If Job had
probed these realms he would have had to master death and
his attendants before returning to earth with his story.

[a] thirsty ground: *prob. rdg.; Heb.* source.

19–20. Another mystery evoked by ancient cosmology was the abode to which *light* travels. *light* and *darkness* are like two lesser deities who at God's direction return to their respective abodes beyond the horizon. They too have an ordained limit and course which prevent them from violating the cosmic order established by God. In his earliest cry Job had longed for this darkness to erase his origins (3: 4–6).

21. The ordering of chaos and the separation of light from darkness belong to the first works of creation (Gen. 1: 3–4). If Job were the heavenly first man in the divine council, he would have observed these primal events and grasped their nature. The concept of the first man in Job is not that of a human being made of clay at the completion of creation, but of a heavenly figure originating from God before the ordering of the physical universe (see on 15: 7-8). Even if the comment of verse 21 is ironic, God nevertheless leads Job through the primal course of events as this first man, thereby enabling him to experience anew the cosmic design of the universe where the great primordial realities are ordered into a purposeful superstructure.

22-30. In the ancient world the weather was regularly viewed as the manifestation of a specific storm god or related deity from mythology. Here, however, the elements of the weather are viewed in terms of hidden patterns or created structures which lie outside the realm of human investigation.

22. Some ancients thought *hail* and *snow* were kept in heavenly 'storehouses' (cp. Deut. 28: 12). Verse 23 suggests that they have been viewed as a kind of armoury.

23. The day of *battle* recalls the holy wars of Israel when God repeatedly intervened with meteorological phenomena (Josh. 10: 11; Judg. 5: 20-1). The purposes of the weather, therefore, are not confined to its seasonal roles; it is also available for the execution of divine justice.

24. N.E.B. renders the word 'light' as *heat*. Some emend the word 'light' to a similar word 'flood' (see the note on 36: 27). The word 'light' may be understood in terms of

'lightning' (see the note on 37: 11); this verse then belongs with the thunderstorm motif of the following verse.

25. In the flood narrative the waters above the heavens pour down through windows or sluice gates (Gen. 7: 11). *channels* or trenches cut through the firmament offer an alternative picture of how torrential rains reach earth from the waters above. Even thunderstorms have an appointed *passage* in the total weather pattern.

26–7. God's purpose in planning the weather is greater than the welfare of those regions inhabited by man. Previously Job had cited the wild animals as creatures who also knew the injustice of God's ways (12: 7–9).

28–30. If many of the questions to Job are more than rhetorical then these verses may refer to a myth about the origin of certain natural phenomena similar to the myth about the birth of the sea alluded to in verse 9. When Baal, the Canaanite storm God, appears in all his splendour, he is attended by several of his daughters, one of whom is the goddess *dew*. Whatever the precise mythological allusion, the challenge of God again forces Job back to the mystery of primordial origins where the ultimate riddle of life must be faced. ✳

WISDOM IN THE LAWS OF HEAVEN

Can you bind the cluster of the Pleiades   31
or loose Orion's belt?
Can you bring out the signs of the zodiac in their season   32
or guide Aldebaran and its train?
Did you proclaim the rules that govern the heavens,   33
or determine the laws of nature on earth?
Can you command the dense clouds   34
to cover you with their weight of waters?
If you bid lightning speed on its way,   35
will it say to you, 'I am ready'?

36 Who put wisdom in depths of darkness
     and veiled understanding in secrecy[a]?
37 Who is wise enough to marshal the rain-clouds
     and empty the cisterns[b] of heaven,
38 when the dusty soil sets hard as iron,
     and the clods of earth cling together?

✳ The destiny of men was thought by many ancient peoples to be related to the movement of the stars. Job is challenged to demonstrate his authority by directing the constellations. If Job has the power to determine destinies then he must have been the one who first established the laws of heaven by which the universe is governed. The implication for Job is that the laws of heaven correspond to the true principles of wisdom, a position Job had previously challenged.

31–2. Job has no power to determine the movements of the constellations or establish the laws of astrology (cp. verses 13–15). The precise identification of the stars remains uncertain (cp. 9: 9).

33. The *rules* of heaven and the corresponding laws for earth refer to the eternal ordinances as part of the design of the universe. The term translated *rules* appears as 'bounds' in verse 10; this term connotes cosmic limits fixed by these laws. These ordinances determine not only the course of the stars but also the government of the world from the heavens. Thus in verse 33b Job is questioned about his ability to make the eternal *laws* of heaven effective on earth. The Hebrew for *laws* is literally 'his writing', suggesting that the laws of heaven were viewed as celestial inscriptions similar to the Babylonian tablets of destiny.

34–5. The issue is whether Job has the capability of producing a storm. A similar question about the efficacy of Job's words in the cosmic realm was posed in verse 12. The

[a] secrecy: *prob. rdg.; Heb. word unknown.*
[b] *Lit.* and tip up the water-skins. . .

response '*I am ready*' is identical with Isaiah's reply 'Here am I'
when he is addressed in the heavenly council (Isa. 6: 9). These
meteorological phenomena are therefore apparently considered messengers from the heavenly council (cp. Ps. 104: 3–4).

36–7. These questions return to the identity of the figure
who implanted wisdom in the world and employed wisdom
in aspects of its government (cp. verses 5–6). The role of wisdom at creation is enunciated in Prov. 8: 22–31; the hiddenness of wisdom is presented in Job 28. The translation
difficulties of verse 36 can perhaps be resolved by recognizing
an allusion to two Egyptian deities. The text would then read,
'Who put wisdom in Thoth? Who gave Sekwi insight?' Thus
the sequence of questions from the first half of Yahweh's
speech, which pertains to the creation and governance of the
universe, closes with references to the involvement of wisdom.
In the last analysis, all these questions return to the ultimate
riddle about the wisdom of God operative in the cosmos.   ✶

STRANGE CREATURES OF THE WILD

Do you hunt her prey for the lioness   39
and satisfy the hunger of young lions,
as they crouch in the lair   40
or lie in wait in the covert?
Who provides the raven with its quarry   41
when its fledglings croak[a] for lack of food?
Do you know when the mountain-goats are born   **39**
or attend the wild doe when she is in labour?
Do you count the months that they carry their young 2
or know the time of their delivery,
when they crouch down to open their wombs   3
and bring their offspring to the birth,
when the fawns grow and thrive in the open forest,   4

[a] *Prob. rdg.; Heb. adds* they cry to God.

and go forth and do not return?

5 Who has let the wild ass of Syria range at will
and given the wild ass of Arabia its freedom? –

6 whose home I have made in the wilderness
and its lair in the saltings;

7 it disdains the noise of the city
and is deaf to the driver's shouting;

8 it roams the hills as its pasture
and searches for anything green.

9 Does the wild ox consent to serve you,
does it spend the night in your stall?

10 Can you harness its strength[a] with ropes,
or will it harrow the furrows[a] after you?

11 Can you depend on it, strong as it is,
or leave your labour to it?

12 Do you trust it to come back
and bring home your grain to[b] the threshing-floor?

✵ The second half of Yahweh's first response to Job (38:
39 – 39: 30 and 41: 1–6) turns from the origin and operation of
the cosmos to the mysteries of nature. The ways and nature
of domestic animals were well known to ancient man, but
wild creatures held a special fascination for the wisdom student. The listing of animals and birds incorporated in this
speech may have been derived from an early zoological
classification of wisdom teachers, comparable to those found
in Egypt. The first man, who named and ruled the animals
according to the traditions of Genesis (1: 28; 2: 18- 20), could
be expected to know the answers to many of these questions.
Divine concern for these creatures highlights a goodness in
the ordering of the world that extends beyond the care of
what man might consider his immediate needs.

[a] *Prob. rdg.; Heb. transposes* strength *and* furrows.
[b] *So Sept.; Heb. adds* and.

39-40. Even the ferocious lion needs food. Does Job have either the goodness or the ability to care for that kind of creature? In Ps. 104: 21 the *young lions* are said to get their food directly from God, who is there designated by the ancient title of the creator god El.

41. Here the *raven* also cries to El for help in time of crisis (see the N.E.B. footnote). Even birds and animals which might be spurned by human beings as creatures of prey are God's immediate concern.

39: 1–4. These animals represent the shy elusive creatures of the mountains whose ways are hidden from civilized man. The gestation period and birth processes of the ibex and the *doe* remain a mystery. They need no human help to give birth; God tends their needs at the time of their delivery. The recurring motif of birth and birthpangs suggests another subtle hint of what Job is experiencing as he returns to the origin of things.

5–8. The *wild ass* is the symbol of a liberated animal. In contrast to the domestic ass, it can *range at will* with total *freedom*, or, as the literal meaning of the text indicates, it is 'sent free' and 'liberated from its bonds'. The same language is used of freeing a slave (Deut. 15: 12–13). In the *saltings* or 'salt flats', where men do not normally pasture animals, the wild ass need no longer fear its *driver*, literally 'its taskmaster' (cp. Exod. 3: 7). In the barren wilderness the wild ass finds sufficient food to survive (cp. 24: 5). The implication is that God liberates and nourishes his animals just as he does his people.

9–12. Unlike the wild ass the *wild ox* represents an animal who has never been enslaved and rebels against domestication. The wild ox is here said to possess an irrepressible inner drive to be free of human control; it can therefore never be a reliable servant of man for agricultural pursuits (but cp. Prov. 14: 4). The wild ox is the wild buffalo once hunted by gods and kings, especially in ancient Syria. In the Old Testament, as in the ancient Near East, the wild buffalo was a symbol of fierce strength (cp. Num. 23: 22; 24: 8; Ps. 22: 21). ✳

BIZARRE AND BEAUTIFUL CREATURES

13 The wings of the ostrich[a] are stunted;[b]
[c]her pinions and plumage are so scanty[d]

14 that she abandons her eggs to the ground,
letting them be kept warm by the sand.

15 She forgets that a foot may crush them,
or a wild beast trample on them;

16 she treats her chicks heartlessly as if they[e] were not hers,
not caring if her labour is wasted

17 (for God has denied her wisdom
and left her without sense),

18 while like a cock she struts[f] over the uplands,
scorning both horse and rider.

19 Did you give the horse his strength?
Did you clothe his neck with a mane?

20 Do you make him quiver like a locust's wings,
when his shrill neighing strikes terror?

21 He shows his mettle as he[g] paws and prances;
he charges the armoured line with all his might.

22 He scorns alarms and knows no dismay;
he does not flinch before the sword.

23 The quiver rattles at his side,
the spear and sabre flash.

24 Trembling with eagerness, he devours the ground
and cannot be held in when he hears the horn;

[a] Heb. *word of uncertain mng.*
[b] are stunted: *prob. rdg.; Heb. unintelligible.*
[c] *Prob. rdg.; Heb. prefixes* if.
[d] *Prob. rdg.; Heb.* godly *or* stork.
[e] as if they: *so Vulg.; Heb.* those that.
[f] *Lit.* while she plays the male.
[g] *So Sept.; Heb.* they.

at the blast of the horn he cries 'Aha!'　　　　25
and from afar he scents the battle.[a]
Does your skill teach the hawk to use its pinions　　26
and spread its wings towards the south?
Do you instruct the vulture to fly high　　　27
and build its nest aloft?
It dwells among the rocks and there it lodges;　　28
its station is a crevice in the rock;
from there it searches for food,　　　29
keenly scanning the distance,
that its brood may be gorged with blood;　　30
and where the slain are, there the vulture is.

✵ 13–18. The ostrich is the symbol of the bizarre in nature. Her appearance is odd and her ways unlike those of other birds. It is a testimony to the miraculous intervention of God in nature that a bird apparently devoid of any natural wisdom and protective instinct should survive in the desert.

13. The text is uncertain. *stunted* can be rendered 'flap'. The *ostrich*, whose *pinions* lack the necessary proportion for flight, still flaps them, but to no apparent end.

14. *abandons* may be translated 'lay'. Students of natural history indicate that the ostrich may divide her eggs into several groups and hatch but one of these. While absent from the nest she may cover her eggs with a little sand.

16. The tradition that the ostrich is heartless to her young is also reflected in Lam. 4: 3. The testimony of natural historians does not substantiate this tradition.

17. The stupidity of the ostrich is proverbial also in the ancient world. Implied in this passage, however, is the idea that all creatures of the wild have implanted in them a measure of wisdom which enables them to survive and play their

[a] *Prob. rdg.; Heb. adds* the thunder of the captains and the shouting.

role in the design of creation. The ostrich who lacks this gift would appear to need special attention from God.

18. Despite her stupidity and inability to fly, the ostrich can match the speed of a horse.

19-25. The war *horse* represents a spirited beast unafraid of the sights and sounds of warfare that normally terrify men. In ancient Israel the ass and the ox rather than the horse were used for agricultural purposes. The horse, once condemned in Israel as a pagan symbol (Deut. 17: 16; Josh. 11: 6), was especially suited for war chariots and cavalry. The mystery of the war horse is not only his great strength, but his joyous spirit of participation in the terror of battle. He relishes danger and cries his exultant '*Aha!*' at the sound of the trumpet blast for attack. The horse's lust for the battle is even more vivid in the colourful line which the N.E.B. editors have dropped unnecessarily from the text (see footnote to verse 25).

26-30. The *hawk* and the *vulture* or 'eagle' symbolize those creatures who can soar to great heights with grace and ease. According to Prov. 30: 19 the 'way of a vulture in the sky' is one of the great mysteries of the natural world. Comparable to mysteries mentioned here are its ability to nest on mountain cliffs and to discover food on the ground while flying at great heights.

26-7. The term *skill* renders a Hebrew word that was translated 'understand' in 38: 4. This term, which can also be rendered 'insight' or 'understanding', is often parallel to wisdom, as in 38: 36. Thus Job's wisdom, which had been challenged at the beginning of God's speech (38: 4) and at several points during its delivery (38: 21, 36, 37), becomes the focus of God's final remarks concerning Job's relationship to these remarkable birds and animals of creation. Job, unlike the first man, does not have a close bond with the wild animals.

27. The inadequacy of Job's wisdom is balanced by the inefficacy of his word for directing the course of God's creation (cp. 38: 12, 35).

30*b*. A proverbial statement (cp. Matt. 24: 28).   ✻

THE WHALE

Can you pull out the whale[a] with a gaff   41[b]
or can you slip a noose round its tongue?

Can you pass a cord through its nose   2
or put a hook through its jaw?

Will it plead with you for mercy   3
or beg its life with soft words?

Will it enter into an agreement with you   4
to become your slave for life?

Will you toy with it as with a bird   5
or keep it on a string like a song-bird[c] for your
   maidens?

Do trading-partners haggle over it   6
or merchants share it out?

* The passage 41: 1-11, as it appears in the original text,
describes in consummate detail the character of Leviathan, a
sea-monster known also from Canaanite mythology (cp. also
Isa. 27: 1). The N.E.B. identifies this figure with the 'whale'
and transposes verses 1-6 to the end of ch. 39. It then forms a
climax to the catalogue of beasts whose mysterious ways are
beyond human comprehension. The mythological understanding of Leviathan in Canaan and the Old Testament,
however, militates against the N.E.B. interpretation. Cp.
further on p. 225 for comment on 41: 1-6 in relation to its
sequel in 41: 7-34.

1-2. The known techniques for capturing huge beasts are
ineffective against a monster of Leviathan's proportions. No
hook, noose or harpoon can snare him: he is invincible.

3-6. The thought of relating to this fearsome monster in

[a] Or Leviathan.
[b] 41: 1-6 (in Heb. 40: 25-30) transposed to this point.
[c] like a song-bird: so Sept.; Heb. om.

any traditional way is ludicrous. He cannot be made the pet of human beings. God alone can control his terror and transform him into a plaything of the ocean (Ps. 104: 25-6). ✻

JOB'S FIRST RESPONSE TO GOD

40 Then the LORD said to Job:

2　Is it for a man who disputes with the Almighty to be stubborn?
　　Should he that argues with God answer back?

3　And Job answered the LORD:

4　What reply can I give thee, I who carry no weight?
　　I put my finger to my lips.
5　I have spoken once and now will not answer again;
　　twice have I spoken, and I will do so no more.

✻ 2. This summary comment of God can be taken as a rebuke (following the N.E.B. translation) or as a challenge in line with the mood of verse 7. In the latter case *be stubborn* is rendered 'yield', and verse *2b* 'Let the disputer with God answer him!' God had entered the dispute with Job and posed a host of questions. It is now Job's turn to answer God (38: 3; cp. 38: 18, 21).

4-5. Instead of accepting God's challenge Job capitulates. He has no answer to God's questions about the origins and structures of the universe. Before the tremendous majesty of God's cosmic mysteries Job confesses his smallness (cp. Amos 7: 2); in this debate his word carries no weight. The angry Job has been humbled; his response, however, is not a confession of guilt, but an acute awareness of his insignificance as a finite creature. ✻

God's Second Speech

GOD CHALLENGES JOB'S MIGHT

Then the LORD answered Job out of the tempest: 6

Brace yourself and stand up like a man;   7
I will ask questions, and you shall answer.
Dare you deny that I am just   8
or put me in the wrong that you may be right?
Have you an arm like God's arm,   9
can you thunder with a voice like his?
Deck yourself out, if you can, in pride and dignity,   10
array yourself in pomp and splendour;
unleash the fury of your wrath,   11
look upon the proud man and humble him;
look upon every proud man and bring him low,   12
throw down the wicked where they stand;
hide them in the dust together,   13
and shroud them in an unknown grave.
Then I in my turn will acknowledge   14
that your own right hand can save you.

* 6. The introduction to a second set of divine speeches (see 38: 1).

7. By repeating 38: 3 at the beginning of this new speech, God renews the challenge for Job to be a worthy rival and answer God's great riddles (see on 38: 3).

8. God's justice is given scant attention in his own speeches and Job's accusations of divine oblivion to evil are all but ignored (cp. 9: 19–24). Finally, God addresses the problem directly. He does not accuse Job of lying about his own innocence but of violating God's integrity. Job had assumed that

if he were *just* God had to be unjust. God challenges this assumption by asserting that Job went beyond affirming his own righteousness. He made God guilty in order to justify his own human integrity. Is it necessary to condemn God to affirm one's own integrity? asks God.

9. If Job seeks to establish his own standards of justice superior to God's, he must demonstrate his right by a show of celestial power. The *arm* of the deity is the symbol of his divine might and just rule (see Exod. 15: 16; Pss. 89: 13; 98: 1).

10-13. Job's demonstration of power is not to be a mere display of meteorological fireworks. He is to use his might to execute judgement on the wicked, an administrative function which Job had accused God of neglecting. Job's keen sense of justice must be backed by his divine might if he is to play God.

10. Job is to assume the divine attributes associated with the office of judge and king (cp. Pss. 21: 5; 45: 4; 104: 1).

11. *unleash* suggests the image of Job striking the wicked with lightning bolts (see on 37: 11; Ps. 18: 14).

12. Job is to demonstrate his full power and authority by sending *the wicked* to the oblivion of the underworld.

14. If Job can execute total justice on the wicked, then God will *acknowledge*, that is, literally, 'praise' Job as a god-like hero, and a worthy rival. Job, who had lamented the absence of any mediator to vindicate or save him (9: 33; 10: 7; 16: 21), could save himself if he exhibited the power God delineated. ✳

THE GREAT BEAST BEHEMOTH

15 Consider the chief of the beasts, the crocodile,[a]
    who devours cattle as if they were grass:[b]
16 what strength is in his loins!
    what power in the muscles of his belly!

[a] chief. . .crocodile: *prob. rdg.; Heb.* beasts (behemoth) which I have made with you.
[b] cattle. . .grass: *prob. rdg.; Heb.* grass like cattle.

220

His tail is rigid as^a a cedar,   17
the sinews of his flanks are closely knit,
his bones are tubes of bronze,   18
and his limbs like bars of iron.
He is the chief of God's works,^b   19
made to be a tyrant over his peers;^c
for he takes^d the cattle of the hills for his prey   20
and in his jaws he crunches all wild beasts.
There under the thorny lotus he lies,   21
hidden in the reeds and the marsh;
the lotus conceals him in its shadow,   22
the poplars of the stream surround him.
If the river is in spate, he is not scared,   23
he sprawls at his ease though the stream^e is in flood.
Can a man blind^f his eyes and take him   24
or pierce his nose with the teeth of a trap?

* These verses deal with a strange primordial figure whose
Hebrew name is 'Behemoth', literally, The Beast. The
N.E.B. rendering 'crocodile' reflects a common effort to
identify this figure with a specific historical animal (see N.E.B.
footnote to verse 15). Some scholars suggest an identification
with the hippopotamus. The characterization of this beast,
however, seems to be more mythological than it is zoological.
Why is this figure introduced at this point? Is comic relief the
answer to the enigma of Job's plight and meaningless human
existence? Does God parade a clumsy hippopotamus across
the stage for all human beings to laugh their troubles away?

[a] *Or* He bends his tail like. . .
[b] *Lit.* ways.
[c] *Prob. rdg.; Heb.* his sword.
[d] *Prob. rdg.; Heb.* they take.
[e] *Lit.* Jordan.
[f] Can a man blind: *prob. rdg.; Heb. obscure.*

Hardly! Behemoth, like Leviathan (see on 41: 1, p. 217), is a symbol of primordial chaos, that first great rival power which God overcame by his might (cp. Enoch 60: 7–8). Thus Job, whom God had challenged to demonstrate his wisdom as the great first man (38: 3, 18, 21) and his might as a god-like hero capable of obliterating the wicked (40: 7–14), is now confronted with the great primordial power which God himself overcame to establish order in the universe. Once again, Job relives the primordial as he experiences God's conquering and creative power. Comparable mythological figures may be the bovine monsters fought by Baal in a Canaanite myth and the Bull of Heaven killed by Gilgamesh in the Gilgamesh Epic (cp. *The Making of the Old Testament*, in this series, p. 7).

15. Literally,

> Behold Behemoth which I made with you;
> He eats grass like the cattle.

The expression 'which I made' is absent from the Greek version and may indicate an early effort by Hebrew scribes to modify the mythological and assert the creatureliness of this monster. The idiom 'with you' reflects the previous situation where Job is addressed as the first man present with God as his counsellor at creation (38: 3, 18, 21). The N.E.B. conjecture that this beast *devours cattle* is consistent with a mythological interpretation.

16–18. The strength of this monster is described in vivid terms that exceed the attributes of any known creature. His arched tail is described as being like a *cedar*, a rather inappropriate image to describe an erect hippopotamus or crocodile tail. In the Canaanite myths Baal's cedar is his spear. Perhaps the 'cedar' of Behemoth is one of his destructive 'weapons'. Other parts of his body offer protective armour and enduring power.

19. Literally,

> He is the first of the ways of God,
> Made to draw near with his sword.

'First' or 'beginning' is preferable to *chief* (see 8: 7). In contrast to Prov. 8: 22 where a similar idiom is used, Behemoth rather than wisdom is the first 'way' or design of God. (On 'way' see the notes on the Third Discourse of Bildad, p. 132.) The universe began with chaos, personified as a monster overcome by God. Although a mythological figure could be depicted with a sword, the N.E.B. emendation of verse 19*b* offers a plausible alternative.

20. The meaning of the text remains obscure.

21–3. This monster, like Leviathan, is associated with waters and raging rivers, the visible manifestation of chaos. The *lotus* mentioned here is not a water lily but a thorny shrub.

24. Behemoth cannot be captured by normal hunting techniques. God alone can overpower this primordial monster. The minor emendation *blind* (in N.E.B. footnote) clarifies an obscure text. ✳

THE INVINCIBLE MONSTER

Can you fill his skin with harpoons   **41**7*ᵃ ᵇ*
or his head with fish-hooks?

If ever you lift your hand against him,   8
think of the struggle that awaits you, and let be.

No, such a man is in desperate case,   9*ᶜ*
hurled headlong at the very sight of him.

How fierce he is when he is roused!   10
Who is there to stand up to him*ᵈ*?

Who has ever attacked him*ᵉ* unscathed*ᶠ*?   11
Not a man*ᵍ* under the wide heaven.

[*a*] *40: 31 in Heb.*
[*b*] *Verses 1–6 transposed to follow 39: 30.*
[*c*] *41: 1 in Heb.*
[*d*] *So some MSS.; others* me.
[*e*] *Prob. rdg.; Heb.* me.
[*f*] *So Sept.; Heb.* and I am safe.
[*g*] *Prob. rdg.; Heb.* He is mine.

12 I will not pass over in silence his limbs,
      his prowess and the grace of his proportions.
13 Who has ever undone his outer garment
      or penetrated his doublet of hide?
14 Who has ever opened the portals of his face?
      for there is terror in his arching teeth.
15 His back*a* is row upon row of shields,
      enclosed in a wall*b* of flints;
16 one presses so close on the other
      that air cannot pass between them,
17 each so firmly clamped to its neighbour
      that they hold and cannot spring apart.
18 His sneezing sends out sprays of light,
      and his eyes gleam like the shimmer of dawn.*c*
19 Firebrands shoot from his mouth,
      and sparks come streaming out;
20 his nostrils pour forth smoke
      like a cauldron on a fire blown to full heat.*d*
21 His breath sets burning coals ablaze,
      and flames flash from his mouth.
22 Strength is lodged in his neck,
      and untiring energy dances ahead of him.
23 Close knit is his underbelly,
      no pressure will make it yield.
24 His heart is firm as a rock,
      firm as the nether millstone.
25 When he raises himself, strong men*e* take fright,

[a] *Prob. rdg.; Heb.* pride.
[b] *Prob. rdg.; Heb.* seal.
[c] *Lit.* eyelids of the morning.
[d] full heat: *so Pesh.; Heb.* rushes.
[e] strong men: *or* leaders *or* gods.

　　bewildered at the lashings of his tail.
　　Sword or spear, dagger or javelin,　　　　　　　26
　　if they touch him, they have no effect.
　　Iron he counts as straw,　　　　　　　　　　　27
　　and bronze as rotting wood.
　　No arrow can pierce him,　　　　　　　　　　28
　　and for him sling-stones are turned into chaff;
　　to him a club is a mere reed,*a*　　　　　　　　29
　　and he laughs at the swish of the sabre.
　　Armoured beneath with jagged sherds,　　　　30
　　he sprawls on the mud like a threshing-sledge.
　　He makes the deep water boil like a cauldron,　　31
　　he whips up the lake like ointment in a mixing-bowl.
　　He leaves a shining trail behind him,　　　　　32
　　and the great river is like white hair in his wake.
　　He has no equal on earth;　　　　　　　　　　33
　　for he is made quite without fear.
　　He looks down on all creatures, even the highest;　34
　　he is king over all proud beasts.

✶ For notes on 41: 1-6, see p. 217. As a result of moving these
verses to the end of ch. 39, N.E.B. treats 41: 7-34 as the
continuation of the description of Behemoth, identified as the
crocodile (see p. 221). But if the text is read in its normal order,
41: 1-34, the whole passage presents the mythological creature Leviathan. In Canaanite myths Leviathan is described as
a great and tortuous serpent with seven heads whom Baal and
Anat his consort slay in battle. Leviathan is described in almost
identical terms in Isa. 27: 1. Yahweh is said to have slain this
many-headed sea monster in primordial times (Ps. 74: 12-13).
Leviathan is one of several symbols for the primordial chaos
(cp. Gen. 1: 2) which Yahweh overcame in the ordering of the

[a] a mere reed: *so Symm. and Theod.; Heb.* chaff.

world. Leviathan and Behemoth (40: 15–24) are complementary symbols for the same threatening reality with which God confronts Job in his tour of primordial regions.

We may observe that in describing both these mythological beasts, the poet makes use of some terms which derive from real creatures, but others which have no natural counterpart.

7–8. Anyone who plans to capture 'Leviathan' with fishing gear had better think again, for it means a *struggle*, or literally 'war'. Like Baal and Yahweh, the person who takes on this sea monster must fight an epic battle.

9. This battle can have cosmic ramifications. In Babylonian and Canaanite myths the appearance of a chaos monster terrified the gods of heaven. This tradition suggests an alternative rendering of 9*b*, 'were not the gods cowed by the sight of him?'

10–11. No human being beneath the fearful heavens can expect to attack Leviathan and survive.

12. The text of verse 12 is obscure.

13–17. Leviathan is described as a monster with impenetrable natural armour. From his teeth there emanates a terror which petrifies his foes. Job was overwhelmed with the same terror from God (9: 34; 13: 21).

18–21. The terror of Leviathan is evident from his fire-breathing fury. *light* or 'lightning' is emitted when he sneezes, his eyes are burning red, flaming torches flash from his mouth and smoke billows from his nostrils so that his insides appear to be a huge flaming cauldron. This imagery belongs to the language of myth rather than metaphor; Leviathan is a supernatural mythic monster whom Job confronts in all its terror, a terror God alone has overcome.

22–4. This monster possesses abnormal strength and courage. Before him dances an *energy*, or 'terror', similar to that described in the previous verses (cp. Exod. 23: 27). He annihilates his foes with dread before they can approach him.

25. As the N.E.B. footnote indicates, the Hebrew '*ēlîm*, literally 'gods', can be rendered *strong men* or leaders. The

mythic language of the context favours retaining the literal meaning. The gods, too, are overwhelmed with fear by the terrifying appearance of Leviathan (see also on verse 9).

26–9. Gods and men are mesmerized by Leviathan's terror; he laughs at the weapons they use to attack him. They may as well tickle him with straw and reeds.

30–4. Leviathan is at home in the waters of chaos which he represents. The *mud* or mire, the *deep*, the *lake* (literally 'sea'), and the *great river* (literally 'the deep') are terms associated with the subterranean forces of death and chaos (see on 7: 12; cp. Jonah 2: 3–5; Ps. 89: 9–10; Hab. 3: 15). When Leviathan surges through his abode there is a violent upheaval and a boiling of the deep. Then chaos is roused once again and Leviathan is exposed as king of all proud rebellious beasts. He is the symbol of cosmic disruption whom God overcame in primordial times (Ps. 74: 12–15; cp. Job 26: 12–13). In the face of this feat, Job's challenge of God's righteous might trifles into insignificance. ✵

JOB'S LAST WORDS

Then Job answered the Lord: **42**

I know that thou canst do all things 2
and that no purpose is beyond thee.

*a*But I have spoken of great*b* things which I have not 3
understood,

things too wonderful for me to know.*c*

I knew of thee then only by report, 5
but now I see thee with my own eyes.

Therefore I melt away;*d* 6
I repent in dust and ashes.

[a] *So one form of Sept.; Heb. prefixes* Whoever conceals counsel without knowledge, *cp. 38: 2.* [b] *So Sept.; Heb. om.*
[c] *Prob. rdg.; Heb. adds* (4) O listen, and let me speak; I will ask questions, and you shall answer. [d] *Or* despise myself.

✲ Job's closing comments are terse and cryptic. How does Job 'see' God? In what sense does he repent? Apparently Job experienced the full impact of God's mysterious otherness as he confronted the majestic power and wisdom of the Creator. He 'saw' God by returning to the primordial world with his Maker and there reliving God's dramatic creative labours. God had honoured Job by entering into dialogue with him about these ancient wonders. He had left most of Job's questions un-answered but he had arranged a face-to-face encounter in his sovereign presence. Job, addressed as first man, had been led back to the beginnings, the archetypal realities governing the universe. Before the ultimate mastermind of all things Job is acutely aware of his own finitude. He is an ignorant creature whose end is to return to dust and ashes. To that lot he resigns himself, humble and penitent, but with his integrity as a human being affirmed by the very coming of the Creator. He is the God of all beginnings. With him a new birth, a new creation from the dust, is a real possibility. By affirming he is nothing, Job is in a condition to be re-created out of nothing.

2. Job acknowledges that God's power and purposes are limitless. What Job had confessed verbally (12: 13), he now knows through personal experience. On 2*b* cp. Gen. 11: 6.

3. The N.E.B. (see footnote) omits 3*a* which reads, 'Who is this that darkens counsel without knowledge?' In reflecting on his traumatic meeting with God, Job may be quoting God's earlier questions addressed to him as first man (38: 2). Job admits that he was trying to solve mysteries far beyond his human capacities.

4. Like verse 2*b*, verse 4 seems to be a quotation from God's speeches to Job as first man (cp. 38: 3). The N.E.B. editors consider this verse a misplaced addition (see footnote).

5. As in 40: 4–5, Job admits his inability to accept the challenge of Yahweh and answer his riddles. Why? Because all his prior information, like that of his three friends, was based on the hearsay of tradition. Now he has experienced God in an ultimate way. His earlier wish to see God (19: 26)

has been fulfilled in an unexpected manner. God had invaded the bleak night of Job's life and exposed his living presence, not in words of damnation or forgiveness, but in the grandeur and mystery of his primordial activities as the benevolent architect of the universe and righteous king over chaos.

6. 'despise myself' (N.E.B. footnote) expresses Job's total self-abasement before God's overwhelming majesty. The same term expressed Job's former despair beneath the oppressive hand of God as his enemy. The expression *repent* is ambiguous in the original. A change of attitude, however, rather than remorse over guilt, seems to be the primary meaning. Job accepts his own finitude and God's sovereign rule as inevitable realities of life. Job is one with the dust from which he came and his life is in God's creative hands. ✳

Epilogue

When the LORD had finished speaking to Job, he said to Eliphaz the Temanite, 'I am angry with you and your two friends, because you have not spoken as you ought about me, as my servant Job has done.[a] So now take seven bulls and seven rams, go to my servant Job and offer a whole-offering for yourselves, and he will intercede for you; I will surely show him favour by not being harsh with you because you have not spoken as you ought about me, as he has done.'[b] Then Eliphaz the Temanite and Bildad the Shuhite and[c] Zophar the Naamathite went and carried out the LORD's command, and the LORD showed favour to Job when he had interceded for his

[a] about...done: *so some MSS.; others* to me about my servant Job.
[b] about...done: *so some MSS.; others* to me about him.
[c] *So many MSS.; others om.*

10 friends. So the LORD restored Job's fortunes and doubled all his possessions.

11 Then all Job's brothers and sisters and his former acquaintance came and feasted with him in his home, and they consoled and comforted him for all the misfortunes which the LORD had brought on him; and each of them 12 gave him a sheep[a] and a gold ring. Furthermore, the LORD blessed the end of Job's life more than the beginning; and he had fourteen thousand head of small cattle and six thousand camels, a thousand yoke of oxen and as 13 many she-asses. He had seven[b] sons and three daughters; 14 and he named his eldest daughter Jemimah, the second 15 Keziah and the third Keren-happuch. There were no women in all the world so beautiful as Job's daughters; and their father gave them an inheritance with their brothers.

16 Thereafter Job lived another hundred and forty years, 17 he saw his sons and his grandsons to four generations, and died at a very great age.

* The Job of the prose epilogue is the same perfect and pious hero of the prologue. This closing account seems to reflect at least two stages in its composition, the first belonging to the ancient legend of the patient Job whose fortunes are restored after his ordeal (verses 10–17) and the second providing a correlation between this legend and the poetic dialogue of Job with his friends (verses 7–9; cp. on 2: 11–13). Job's integrity is vindicated publicly by God and the three friends exposed as hypocrites. Through his intercessions Job restores the friends to favour with God who, in turn, restores Job's fortunes twofold.

[a] *Or* piece of money.
[b] *Or* fourteen.

7. God addresses Eliphaz, the chief spokesman of the three friends, and censures him. Direct communication of this kind is typical of patriarchal prose legends; for Eliphaz there is no overwhelming whirlwind. Unlike Job, Eliphaz and his friends have not spoken as they *ought* about God. The implication of the original is that Job's angry speeches were 'correct', while those of the friends lacked genuine integrity. Ironically, Job's forthright accusations are closer to the truth than the orthodox teachings of the wise (cp. 13: 6–12).

8–9. Job, who is here designated God's *servant*, assumes his former role as the mediator, high priest and intercessor whose prayers and sacrifices avert any *harsh* (or literally, 'rash') affliction being imposed on the friends (cp. 1: 4–5). As the perfect sufferer his religious acts are reckoned as vicarious; he is like the suffering servant depicted in Isa. 53.

10. The restoration of Job's fortunes, according to the piety of the legend, appears to be a reward for his patient suffering. In the context of the poem and of Job's self-abasement before God, his twofold blessing stems from the Creator's grace alone.

11. This verse seems to be a fragment from an older version of the Job legend where Job's relatives rather than his three friends play the role of comforters. In the current version the concern of the relatives seems anticlimactic and unnecessary.

12–17. Job's restored possessions double his former wealth in the same ratio of perfect numbers (see on 1: 2–3). In addition, Job's daughters know world renown for their beauty – *Jemimah*: perhaps 'dove'; *Keziah*: 'cassia', noted for its fragrance; *Keren-happuch*: 'horn of antimony', which was used for darkening the eyelids – and receive *an inheritance* (for daughters as heirs, cp. Num. 27: 1–11). Job enjoys a long life like other great patriarchs (cp. Gen. 25: 8). The N.E.B. footnote mentions a secondary reading which also doubles the number of sons in accordance with the principle of verse 10. Later legend (partly to be found in the Septuagint) saw Job as the ancestor of the royal line in Edom.   ✲

✲   ✲   ✲   ✲   ✲   ✲   ✲   ✲   ✲   ✲   ✲   ✲   ✲

THE MESSAGE OF JOB

The book of Job deals with a deep-seated conflict between the integrity of God and the integrity of man. The stage is set for this conflict by the telling of a legend about Job, the pious patriarch whose ways and will are in complete accord with those of his Lord. In spite of the un-godlike way in which God makes a deal with Satan to test the limit of Job's faithfulness, Job's trust remains unshaken. He refuses to impute ulterior motives to the God who has stripped him of all but his life. The legend contends that heroes of faith can praise God with integrity even if all they possess is a slender thread of life. The poem of Job catapults the reader from the piety of legend into the harsh world of reality. A man like Job, who has suffered undeserved evils at the hand of his Creator, will vent his anger as an honest expression of his faith. He will explode with indignation and demand a hearing before the tribunal of heaven. Job does precisely that. During God's lengthy silence, Job's fury intensifies until the depths of his human fear and despair are put into words. Job becomes very human, an example of suffering victims everywhere. Through this example an underlying enmity between God and human beings is made explicit. Their wills are in conflict. The integrity of both is challenged in the face of inexplicable disasters. Job accuses God of being an almighty enemy who delights in spying on his human prey to detect their weaknesses and hunt them down like monsters. Before this enemy, man is robbed of his integrity. He is dehumanized. As a human being he has no meaningful reason for living.

Meaningless suffering is intensified when the victim suffers alone. The traditional advice of Job's companions offered no comfort. They showed no sympathy or understanding. Even Job's efforts to evoke God's compassion seemed futile. God remained silent through all of Job's tirades. In spite of these overwhelming odds, Job kept demanding an honest encounter with God. Job's integrity prevented him from committing suicide or pursuing a plea for God to put him out of his misery by taking his life. Such an act, according to Job, would be murder. God would be guilty of killing an innocent man. Job viewed all the catastrophes he experienced as crimes committed by God. Yet his community considered them just punishments for unconfessed sins of Job. This dilemma leads to an understanding of life as a court trial before God as the Judge. For Job God is really the guilty party. Yet he continues as judge and accuser. Job, however, refuses to plead guilty, even though his case seems hopeless. He is convinced of his own innocence and continues to challenge God's justice to the end. He dreams of a mediator or redeemer who can enter the court, control the judge and vindicate Job. His hope anticipates the Christ of the New Testament. But during his lifetime no such figure materializes. Job must face God alone. And face him he will, asserting his integrity to the very end.

God does not answer the enigma of life by putting Job on trial before a heavenly court or by offering standard replies comparable to those of Job's friends. Rather, God enters the dispute of the book about the meaning and order of life by posing a new set of questions. He places the human dilemma about the mystery of life in a broader context where Job experiences God in his overwhelming majesty as the Creator. Job becomes acutely aware that he is finite, small and human. He is led back to the original mystery of all things. He is addressed by the Creator as if he were God's counsellor, born before creation and present to discuss the mysteries of the universe as they came into being. There in the primordial world, Job, like other human beings seeking for ultimate meaning, confronts God as the Lord over chaos and the architect whose wisdom invested the world with a just order. Job is humbled before this God but not condemned. He is nothing before this Creator, but he is not rejected. He has probed to another level of meaning in an apparently meaningless world, yet he leaves with no glib answer. He is face to face with his own death, yet keenly aware of new birth and new creation as part of God's cosmic plan. Job experienced God in a new way by returning to the beginnings of all things. In those beginnings there is the potential for all human beings to find new meaning in life.

A NOTE ON FURTHER READING

For the main themes of the book of Job the reader is directed to S. Terrien, *Job, Poet of Existence* (Bobbs Merrill, Indianapolis 1957). The general subject of wisdom literature is treated by R. B. Y. Scott in *The Way of Wisdom* (Macmillan, New York and London 1971, 1972) and by G. von Rad in *Wisdom in Israel* (S.C.M. 1972). R. Gordis in *The Book of God and Man* (University of Chicago Press 1965) and N. H. Snaith, *The Book of Job: its origin and purpose* (S.C.M. 1968) offer an alternative analysis to many of the problems of the book.

M. H. Pope's commentary on Job (Anchor Bible, 2nd ed., 1973) offers extensive information on the Near Eastern background to Job, and the Canaanite connections in particular. The brief commentary by R. A. F. McKenzie in the *Jerome Biblical Commentary* (Chapman, London 1969; Prentice-Hall, Englewood Cliffs 1968) provides another brief but helpful guide to the book. General introductions to Job may be found in B. W. Anderson, *The Living World of the Old Testament* (Longmans, 2nd ed., 1967) or N. Gottwald, *A Light to the Nations* (Harper, New York 1959).

For the Near Eastern literature pertinent to Job the reader is directed to *Ancient Near Eastern Texts Relating to the Old Testament, with Supplement* edited by J. B. Pritchard (Princeton University Press, 3rd ed., 1969). Within the biblical context works like Ecclesiastes or Lament Psalms (e.g. Pss. 17, 69, 88) address themselves to many of the same problems as those of Job.

INDEX